A Clinical Guide to Organisational Health

A Clinical Guide to Organisational Health

Diagnosing and Managing the Condition of an Enterprise

By

C. M. Dean

**Cambridge
Scholars**
Publishing

A Clinical Guide to Organisational Health:
Diagnosing and Managing the Condition of an Enterprise

By C. M. Dean

This book first published 2015

Cambridge Scholars Publishing

Lady Stephenson Library, Newcastle upon Tyne, NE6 2PA, UK

British Library Cataloguing in Publication Data
A catalogue record for this book is available from the British Library

Copyright © 2015 by Dean & Associates Limited

ISBN (10): 1-4438-7075-7
ISBN (13): 978-1-4438-7075-7

TABLE OF CONTENTS

Part III: The Value of Health and Fitness

LIST OF TABLES AND FIGURES

ACKNOWLEDGEMENTS

Special thanks to Dave, Jennifer and William, not only for their support and encouragement, but also their practical input in all aspects of the book. Special thanks also to the owners of The Corner Shop for their approval to use their business as the case study in the book.

For specialist knowledge input and support I would like to thank the following persons in addition to the others who kindly assisted and advised me on various aspects of the book. For medical input: Will Dean, Jenny Dean, Kathryn Garnham and Natasha Whitehead. For business and academic input: Martin Parker, Adriaan Vorster, David Dean, Emmanuel Carraut, Helen Gilroy and Jenny Dean.

INTRODUCTION

If organisations have been compared to living organisms for centuries, why do business schools and organisational theorists mainly focus on competitiveness and how to succeed in the market? Even the popular health checks for organisations predominantly address their financial status, market position, goals and the determination of management to achieve success. In the human body, as an example of a complex living organism, acceptable healthy functioning of the organs comes before competitive fitness since the chances of winning can be seriously impaired by physical health concerns. This should also apply to organisations.

The focus on competitiveness dates back to the early twentieth century. Early functionalists accepted that there is a similarity in the functioning of organisations and living organisms, but this generalisation developed into two streams during the twentieth century[1]. One school of thought focused on the outward view of organisational functioning required by competitive participation. The second stream followed the humanistic inward-looking view that organisations consist of individuals and focusing on them is enough to ensure organisational success. While these two schools of thought are valuable, they tend to offer an either-or view instead of supporting managers in their tasks to manage all the functions performed by the organisation.

Research into management theories, and similarities of the functioning and competitiveness of organisations versus living entities[2], highlighted the need to revert back to a holistic view of organisational functioning. In this book the holistic approach enabled the development of a general health check, as used by medical practitioners, before committing to fitness regimes. The approach is offered in three sections, covering the general check and initial impression, followed by detailed functional checks, and concluding with the combination of health and fitness.

In Part I it is necessary to explore the similarity between organisations and living entities. Not every organisation can be defined as an independent living entity and the prerequisites of functional self-determination and maintenance as well as independence from its environment are explored[3]. This allows strategic business units to be accepted as independent members of a conglomerate family, while entrepreneurs are acknowledged as young developing entities.

The concept of self-maintenance resulted in the introduction of a model in which the main functions necessary for survival and persistence of the organisation have been identified as the functional categories of survival, protection, operations, information, language and strategy (SPOILS). Furthermore, Chapter Two introduces a broad set of action steps used by medical practitioners that can also be used to diagnose the health of organisations.

Part II extends the SPOILS model checklist to include specific in-depth health diagnostic questions for each of the different functional categories:

Survival functions (Chapter Three) are the essential functions without which no organisation can survive, namely: finance and accounting, analogous to the respiratory system; logistics, analogous to the digestive and cardio-vascular distribution systems; and workplace maintenance, analogous to the maintenance of the fluid and chemical balance by the kidneys, liver and colon. Cells require oxygen, nutrients and an ambient cellular environment, similar to the needs of employees in organisations.

Protection functions (Chapter Four) are defensive and preventative functions without which an organisation can find itself unprepared for, and unable to recover from, damaging events. This category includes access control functions, analogous to the skin or exoskeleton; security systems, analogous to the immune system; and health, safety and wellbeing functions, analogous to cell healing processes. The functions operate independently and may not have a significant impact on daily operational performance, but the impact of their absence or the consequences of poor functioning can be devastating.

Operations functions (Chapter Five) allow an organisation to be agile and mobile and therefore able to participate, defend or compete in its environment, analogous to the skeletal muscle units in the limbs, back and face. They identify the sector of operation of the organisation and receive attention from management through the initiation of products and services, as well as the measurement of performance. Sales, marketing, customer services and customer distribution are also classified as operations functions.

Information functions (Chapter Six) are the sensory functions of an organisation, allowing it to observe and obtain external and internal information. External information gathering, analogous to the effective use of sight, hearing and taste, offers the organisation the ability to detect trends, threats or opportunities in its environment. Similarly, internal information, analogous to the somatosensory perception of pain, pressure or temperature, can inform management about morale, the work environment or performance changes and issues within the organisation.

In all cases the importance of receiving and using this information for management decisions cannot be underestimated.

Language and communications functions (Chapter Seven), analogous to the use of language, emotions and body language for external communication and the hormonal system for internal communication, enable an organisation to negotiate, adapt and change in its external environment, or develop and change its internal processes and culture. Without the ability to use language and to communicate, organisations may find it difficult to adapt to changing circumstances.

Strategy and guidance functions (Chapter Eight), analogous to the cognitive brain, are the functions performed by the executive team to plan for and guide the organisation in its attempt to survive, strive and compete in its external and market environments. Like the operations functions, the executive functions are receiving attention from various theorists in the form of advice and implementation models for effective competition.

A single case study demonstrates the usage of the diagnostic model throughout the book and forms the link for bringing the functions together in Chapter Nine. The case study applies the information dashboard display method which offers a holistic perspective of diagnostic findings and supporting evidence for an organisation.

Part III identifies the differences between health diagnostics and fitness programmes. Health diagnostics do not distinguish between types of organisation, but fitness programmes tend to be unique by sector of operation. It concludes with the observation that health AND competitive fitness are important, with the need to address health before fitness.

Notes

1. The different classical management theories are summarised and discussed in the first three chapters of: Morgan, G. (2006) *Images of Organization*. Sage Publications Inc., Thousand Oaks.
2. A comparison between the physiology of living entities and organisations was researched and presented in: Dean, C.M. (2012). *Physiology of Organisations: An Integrated Functional Perspective*. Cambridge Scholars Publishing, Newcastle upon Tyne.
3. Prerequisites to the identification of living entities are discussed and presented by: Maturana, H.R. and Varela, F.J. (1980) *Autopoiesis and Cognition: The Realization of the Living*. D. Reidel Publishing Company, Dordrecht.

PART I:

IS YOUR ORGANISATION HEALTHY?

The objective of PART I is to address the following questions:

- Is it possible to identify an organisation as a living entity?
- If possible, how can the health of the organisation be determined and health issues addressed?

Chapter One compares organisations to living organisms in order to address the first question. The conclusions resulted in the requirements for an organisation to be self-responsible for its own structure and functioning, and clearly distinguishable as a separate entity by external parties based on its name, image, and/or offer to the market.

Following this conclusion, Chapter Two introduces a health checklist broadly recommended to medical practitioners for diagnosing the health status of their patients. Furthermore, it addresses initial impressions based on patient opinion, general observations and the collection and analysis of historical health records.

Chapter Two also introduces a case study which will be developed throughout the book to demonstrate the practical application of the various diagnostic checks discussed in Parts I and II.

CHAPTER ONE

WHY ANOTHER HEALTH CHECK?

Managers in organisations – at all stages of organisational development – are given advice on how to run their businesses not only to achieve the best returns on investments for their shareholders, but also to compete in their market sector in order to excel. However, the question that needs to be asked is whether this advice is comprehensive enough to prepare organisations for the potential concerns related to performance, damage or failures? And is this advice more interested in competitiveness and winning, thereby ignoring the need to detect early warning signals of deteriorating functions within the organisation?

Advice offered to management can be divided into two types: advice to new and young organisations offered by various business and financial institutes; and advice offered to managers in established and competitive organisations:

- Entrepreneurs are advised to develop business plans to attract the necessary funding for the business, including: business goal; product or service offering; action plans; and commitments towards implementation, i.e. to focus on financial support and competitive viability[1].
- Advice to management of established organisations focuses on the market economy; customer and supplier relationships; innovation; and management of people and processes to increase profitability. Again, the advice tends to focus on competitiveness in the market[2].

The advice is aimed at enabling organisations to get established and compete in a growing global and competitive market, and is mainly concerned with the product/service, customer and competitor market of the organisation. However, if we consider the reasons for serious failures or the demise of organisations within the two categories, the emerging picture is different:

- For organisations that are young or just starting up, the most common reasons for failure have been identified as a mismanagement or lack of funds, and the inexperience of the entrepreneur and/or management team in the running of a business. Various reasons summarised under the heading of inexperience include: inattentiveness to essential regulatory requirements; absence of supporting functions such as an adequate supply chain or damage protection and limitation procedures; or the overambitious goals set by the entrepreneur[3].

- In the case of established organisations the reasons for demise, serious downsizing or take-overs are more complex and usually have multiple causes. However, considering the reasons behind some of the headline failures of well-known organisations, certain patterns can also be detected. Examples include: an inability to plan for, or cope with serious disaster or damaging incidents to the survival of the organisation or the satisfaction of the market; a reluctance to heed and respond to early warning signals of serious internal fraudulent activities; or pressure from external parties about unethical practices[4].

Advice on how to target the right market and obtain external funding may not comprehensively address the inexperience of entrepreneurs and managers in the effective running of a business. Similarly, advice on how to become a winner in a competitive market does not necessarily prepare established organisations on how to cope during and after damaging events.

The objective of this book is to enhance the advice to organisations by revisiting the functionalist view of organisations as living organisms. By using this approach it is possible to introduce a total business health check based on clinical health checks for other living beings – a proven approach used by veterinary surgeons and medical practitioners. However, before it is feasible to develop an analogy of integrated functioning between organisations and living organisms, it is necessary to clarify what is meant by organisations as living entities.

Organisations as Living Entities

The concept of an organisation as a living entity is not new and can be traced back to the proponents of functionalism, as well as scientific and classical management theories in organisations. These theorists compared organisational functions to those of living organisms and not only used them to promote the concept of job separation and specialisation as part of scientific management, but also as the underlying framework for organisational structuring, which is still popular today[5]. However, functions are not directly comparable to structure, for the same reason that the physiology or functioning of a human body is not a direct reflection of its anatomical structure. Functions are often performed by more than one organ in the body, or the same organ performs multiple functions.

There have been various ways in which functionalists defined independent organisations for study. The main prerequisites are that it must be possible to[6]:

- Identify organisations which are responsible for their own decisions on how to maintain their functioning and structure.
- Distinguish the organisation from its environment and how it relates to this environment.
- Determine an acceptable boundary.

This is different from the commonly used method of viewing an organisation as a legally established business operating within its commercial environment, which applies to single businesses and conglomerates while entrepreneurs and small subsistence businesses may be ignored.

Self-Determination and Maintenance

A global organisation or conglomerate with a holding company is not always responsible for the detailed functional structuring and maintenance of its independent business units, only for the functional structuring of the holding company and broad guidance to members of the group. The conglomerate operates more like a family of businesses in which the overall group strategy and objectives are set by the holding company while the business units have freedom to self-activate and self-maintain their functions in the pursuit of their own and the group's objectives. Each member has its own identity within the group and therefore the potential to function independently. However, if the conglomerate or global company regards its business units as branches, directly controlled by the head office, the conglomerate as such must be regarded as the entity[7].

On the other end of the spectrum it is also necessary to apply the same rules of validation to sole traders and entrepreneurs. During the initial stages of setting up a business, the entrepreneur mainly operates alone. Although not recognisable or legally accepted as a separate entity, he/she is personally responsible for all the functions required by the business, analogous to a single cell amoeba. Essential functions could include the effective management of finances and supplies, analogous to the intake of oxygen and nutrients, and its operation in the market place, analogous to the mobility of the organism in its environment.

Since one of the main prerequisites is the ability of the entity to take sole responsibility for its functioning towards survival instead of concentrating on profit realisation, charitable organisations and independently operating government departments can also be recognised as living entities. Apart from a zero-profit objective, they rely on the same functions to that of a business organisation.

It is, however, unlikely that informal groups such as social gatherings, protestors or informal clubs operate as independent living entities. Similar to conglomerates, a group may have a central formal administrative unit which meets the requirements of self-structuring and self-maintenance, but the group or club members are not permanent parts of this self-maintenance and operate more like shareholders, customers or family members, able to join or leave at will. When the leader or head of the group leaves, the members are likely to disperse. Only after a conscious decision to structure for survival can the group operate as a living entity.

- An organisation as an independent living entity has sole responsibility for its internal functioning, processing and structuring, in order to survive and meet its own goals or goals set by sponsors.

Identifiable in Operating Environment

An organisation, as a living entity, must be recognisable as separate and unique by its external and market environments, and be able to distinguish itself from this environment. Living organisms are observable through their external appearance. This approach is problematic in identifying organisations since it is not always possible to visualise an organisation through the external appearance of its buildings, legal name or brand, all of which only offer a part image or a possible misrepresentation of the organisation.

Buildings can be used to distinguish smaller business enterprises from their peers and competitors, but this can be misleading for larger organisations spread over multiple locations or even countries. Buildings do, however, offer an image of the type of business and how the organisation would like it to be perceived by the external environment, even though it could be misleading.

A better indication of the separate identification of an organisation as a living entity in its environment would be through a recognisable name and/or brand, and its unique offering of service and culture as perceived by the market. This identification by external observers is not only more objective, but offers a closer link to the distinction of strategic business units as the living entities within a conglomerate family of businesses. As a result of mergers, take-overs and the marketing of product brand names, the strategic business unit with the unique offer of the service or brand product to the market should be identified as the independent living entity within the family.

- An organisation as an independent living entity can be identified by its name, its product/service brand image and its perceived culture and supporting value set.

Determinable Boundary

We could query whether everyone within an organisation is included and which employees are covered, namely full-time, part-time, local, remote, voluntary and contract workers. A criterion for boundary delimitation which may enhance the understanding comes from the perspective of 'self' and 'non-self' used in the study of immunology of living organisms[8]. Based on this analogy, an organisational boundary should include organisational assets and those that are contributing to the realisation and self-maintenance of the organisation on a contractual or committed basis, i.e. all of the above mentioned contributors. On the other hand, shareholders and customers would be 'non-self'. Although they contribute financially to the organisation, they are not involved in the day-to-day running or management and can easily withdraw. However, the acquisition of resources including staff, or a take-over of another organisation, could lead to the assimilation of the acquired resources, assets and employees from outside or from the acquired organisation to become 'self'.

There is one type of 'self' component that requires further clarification, namely the role performed by capital investments in buildings and equipment such as manufacturing machinery, or electronic equipment and systems. Although equipment has to be operated and managed by individual employees, their role is observable in the consequences of their absence and the benefits arising from their use[9]. This concept of machines and electronic equipment playing a role within the organisation can be regarded as analogous to the study of the physiology of living organisms in the roles of skeletal bones and joints, acting as structural support and levers in conjunction with muscle cells and tendons to perform tasks of mobility. It can be regarded as a stepwise change in the evolutionary development of organisations, initiated by the Industrial Revolution and more recently by the vast increase in the use of technology.

- An organisation as an independent living entity can easily identify its own assets, including staff, and be able to distinguish between 'self' and 'non-self' as being part of the organisation.

Mergers can be regarded as the establishment of positional relationships, analogous to marriages and families, in which each unit is still independent, although in a close relationship with its partner or holding organisation. Successful mergers are usually based on the independent existence of the merged business units within a successful union of a family with a common set of values under a single holding company as the parent. Not all mergers are successful and could fail due to cultural differences and incompatible values which could be unacceptable at various levels in the organisation or family of businesses.

On the other hand, acquisitions or hostile take-overs (e.g. for asset stripping) can potentially be compared to cannibalism or killing in the food chain by living organisms; or as a transplant of selected organs into the bidding organisation. The organisation taken over during acquisition loses its identity and is assimilated as an integral part of the bidder (i.e. 'non-self' becoming 'self'). The acquiring organisation, however, benefits from the acquisition by absorbing the functional strengths of the acquired organisation as part of an assimilation process, such as the vertical integration of expertise or supplies in the manufacturing of products. Nowadays the distinction between mergers and acquisitions are more blurred – mergers may result in a completely new organisation while acquisitions could develop into a family relationship instead of the destruction of the acquired organisation.

A reversal of this process also applies to the acts of decentralisation, devolution and outsourcing. The concept of spin-off or radical decentralisation addresses the construction of a separate business unit within the conglomerate family of businesses. The new business will gain control over all its functions, including the essential survival and self-maintenance functions, similar to the birth of a child. In the case of outsourcing the comparison depends on the function being outsourced. If it is one of the internal functions, important to the self-maintenance of the organisation, the equivalent in living organisms could be the removal of a life supporting organ, causing a reliance on machines such as kidney dialysis equipment to perform its essential function. It ties the organisation to the outsourced service 'machine' as an alternative to improve a non-functioning activity in the organisation, or to acquire a working function through acquisitions, analogous to a transplant. Organisations can, therefore, be defined and identified as independent living entities, responsible for their own self-maintenance within their environments.

An organisation can be defined as an independent living entity if it:

- Has sole responsibility for its internal functioning and structuring.

- Operates with clearly identifiable image, products or services.

- Can identify a boundary around its own assets, whether operating as a single business or as a member of a family of businesses.

The Functionality of Living Entities

By accepting the concept of organisations as independent living entities, responsible for the self-maintenance of their functioning towards survival, it becomes possible to learn from living organisms. Scientists link the functions of organisms to roles that need to be performed as the prerequisites for life. Whereas many functions and roles have been identified, the main accepted prerequisites are the essential need to "take in a source of energy to maintain the organism's integrity, the ability to reproduce, (and) the ability to respond to stimuli"[10]. The definition supports the fact that an organisation may have a goal to pursue, but its initial purpose is to stay alive within itself and its environment by responding to stimuli, and only then to consider expansion and goal achievement.

This perspective on organisational functioning differs from traditional approaches, in that the main focus is on the integrated functioning of all parts of the organisation in the attempt to keep it alive for the benefit of all members. Integrated functioning does not imply operational harmony, but rather the need for each function to ensure that it does not disadvantage other functions or members by being ineffective in its own operations. In living organisms, cells are accepted as the building blocks or base members of the organism. A cell also contains[11]:

- An active strand of the DNA with the allocated task list for the cell.
- The necessary tools in the format of small components to assist in the operations.
- Adequate provision of the necessary oxygen and nutrients to generate energy in order to fulfil the tasks.
- A permeable membrane which allows the nutrients and chemical messages to be transferred while still allowing personal space.
- The space being kept at acceptable levels of temperature and chemical balance.

In other words, the focus is not only on the combined effective operation of a function, but starts with the wellbeing and support of each individual cell or member.

This need to cater for individual cells and to react to external stimuli in order to ensure overall survival and healthy functioning of an organism is observable in the functions performed by it. It is possible to map the functions of organisms to organisations, as attempted by functionalists and presented in Table 1.1. The functional categories identified have been summarised as survival, protection, operations, information, language and strategic functions.

An analysis of the functional categories presented in Table 1.1 identifies the survival functions, analogous to the respiratory, digestive and cardiovascular systems, and the protection functions, analogous to the immune system, as being focused on the wellbeing of the individual members of the organisation, and therefore the organisation as a whole. On the other hand, the operations functions, analogous to skeletal muscle units, allow movement and competitive participation of the entity within its environment as guided by the strategic management functions. These management functions, analogous to the cognitive brain, however, rely on information from both internal and external to the organisation – its perceptive senses – to guide decision-making. They also require a language and means of communicating both internally to all parts of the organisation as well as to parties in its external environment as can be linked to the hormonal, emotional and language systems.

Functional Categories	Organisational Functions	Analogous Functions of Organisms
Survival	Finance and accounting	Respiratory functions
	Logistics	Digestive and cardiovascular systems
	Workplace maintenance	Renal, liver and colonic functions
Protection	Access protection	Skin and exoskeleton
	Security and wellbeing	Immune systems
Operations	Operating units	Skeletal muscle units (limbs and facial muscle units)
Information	Internal and external information	Sensory functions
Language	Internal and external communications	Hormonal, emotional and language functions
Strategy	Decisions, planning and guidance	Cognitive functions

Table 1.1 Organisational versus organismic functioning [12]

The book is based on this comparison, not as a philosophical or scientific means of defining organisational functioning, but to use the comparison as a model to diagnose the health of an organisation in an attempt to offer a wider means of detecting potential serious concerns which can be treated before it's too late for the organisation. The model, abbreviated as SPOILS, is based on the functional categories in Table 1.1 and is presented in Figure 1.1. In this figure, not only have the categories been identified, but also the main integrated links to the other functions within the organisation. This categorisation does not only offer an integrated picture of the functionality of an organisation, but also a model similar to the checklist used by medical practitioners in diagnosing the health of an individual, in order to check the health of an organisation.

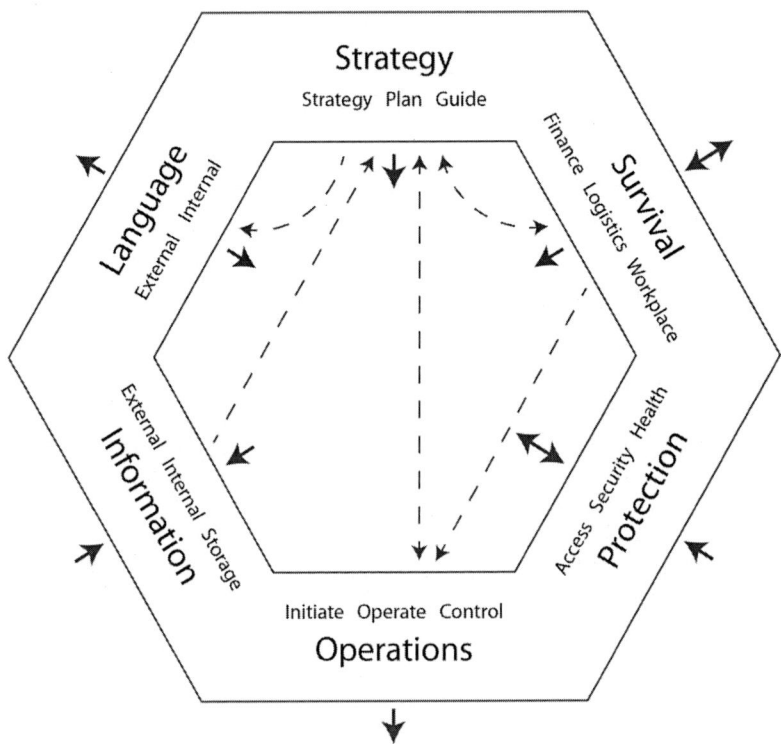

Figure 1.1   Functional interrelationships – the SPOILS model

The diagram presented in Figure 1.1 is a broad interpretation of the functional categories observable in organisations as living entities. It is therefore suitable to use as a model in order to diagnose the extent of healthy operation of all the functions within an organisation.

Survival functions, as implied in the name, are the essential functions without which the organisation cannot operate effectively, analogous to the respiration, digestion, cardiovascular and renal systems in a living organism. The functions offer essential support to all members in the organisation, and since they operate in a background mode, are often mistaken as non-core functions, not necessary for successful operational competition and therefore of lesser importance. For this reason, they are often the first functions to be outsourced, possibly to organisations with different values and standards. This could result in serious problems due to clashes in culture and standards. These are also the functions causing the most serious concerns, such as financial mismanagement, inadequate logistical support or staff dissatisfaction, all of which may result in organisational damage or even failures.

> Without oxygen a person can only live for a few minutes; without water for a few days and without food for a few weeks. Taking care of cell requirements is essential for survival.

The protection functions, including access controls, security compliance and staff wellbeing, are often not regarded as academic subjects to be covered in business schools. The specialist functions are entrusted to operate independently and their knowledge base therefore becomes restricted within the relevant disciplines. Again, this is a potential problem, sometimes of misdirected trust. If organisations are not: adequately prepared against potential external attacks on the organisation; concerned with adequate internal controls to ensure legal and regulatory compliance; do not have adequate means of early detection of fraudulent activities of their own staff, they expose themselves to damaging incidents without adequate means of recovery. This has been identified as a key potential reason for failure in established organisations.

> Without adequate innate immunity or immunisation a person is vulnerable to attacks from viruses and bacteria. Without adequate skin or membrane protection an organism is vulnerable to accidental damage.

Operations functions, analogous to the skeletal muscle unit operations in the limbs, back and face of individuals, enable organisations to be mobile and agile and therefore compete or defend themselves within their environment. Since these functions are used to compete, they are also the functions receiving the most attention and advice from consulting bodies. Organisations are continually advised on how to compete through being effective, efficient and innovative. However, as will be noticed in Chapter Five, there is a difference in the functioning of the units, analogous to the difference in the use of the legs, fingers or facial expressions of individuals. Not all of these units require continuous innovation, but all rely on people, equipment and supplies to fulfil their tasks. There is also a closer link between the action of the units and the strategic goals and plans for the organisation in order to persist and compete.

With damage to limbs and skeletal muscle units a person is less able to move or participate against aggressive physical competitors.

Information functions, analogous to the senses of a living organism, are essential in observing, interpreting and providing relevant information to the executive management in order to offer a basis for decision-making and planning for immediate action or future direction. This does not only cover external information, analogous to the use of sight, smell and hearing; but also internal information of morale and staff health, analogous to the detection of pain, temperature and pressure from internal organs or the skin of organisms. It is possible to decide on action by ignoring relevant information from these functions. However, decisions based on realistic evidence-based information are likely to have a better chance of successful execution.

Without senses a person can become isolated and unable to position him/herself within his/her environment.

The functions of language and communication usually react to decisions taken from the information received. Internal communications to all members in the organisation can be compared to the hormonal system, for instance in the case of 'fight or flight' decisions when motivation is necessary throughout the organisation to avert danger or respond to competitive pressure. It is also necessary for the public relations function of an organisation to communicate to the external environment in order to market itself, build a positive image, or protect its image in cases of incidents of poor performance or fraudulent activities committed by the organisation, or after major damaging events.

Without healthy functioning hormonal and emotional systems, a person can become unable to respond appropriately to danger or display social skills.

The functions receiving most attention with respect to advice and management training are the functions of strategy, planning and guidance, analogous to the cognitive functions of an individual. Although important for competitive operations, it should be realised that not all organisations want to be winners in their field of operation, and may be quite satisfied with their niche market and level of success. Strategies and plans are necessary to change and compete, but could be a hindrance or only paper statements if there is no need to change. It is, however, still important for the executive management to heed information received, and then to decide when it does become necessary to change for survival. Examples include the updating of equipment and systems when necessary, or adapting products and services to meet changing customer preferences.

> Without good cognitive and decision-making functions a person may be able to survive, but he/she is unlikely to be able to strive towards full achievement.

By being aware of the functions and their interrelationships within an organisation, it will be possible to gain a more holistic overview of its health status, and be able to address shortcomings and concerns at an earlier stage.

Conclusion

This book expands on the concept of organisations functioning along a similar pattern as living organisms, and explores how they can learn from the medical sciences to check and ensure that the organisation is operating healthily before concentrating only on competition. It follows a diagnostic plan and checklist to identify major symptoms, and a detailed checking of each functional category towards a concluding prognosis of the status and seriousness of health issues for the organisation.

Chapter One explored the characteristics to be applied to accept organisations as living entities and introduced the similarity of the functioning of living organisms to the functioning of organisations. The similarity of functioning in preference to structure or anatomy was found to be important. Whereas anatomical structures may be different for different species of living organisms, the essential functions to ensure survival and persistence were found to be common. The importance of this distinction in organisations can, for example, be found in organisational departments of human resource management (HR) or information technology (IT) in which case each department may have to address more than one function. Functional categories of survival, protection, operations, information, language and strategy were identified as analogous organisational functions, resulting in the introduction of the SPOILS model to guide the clinical health diagnosis for organisations.

Chapter Two discusses information requirements to enable an initial diagnosis of symptoms and what to focus on in the detailed diagnostic checks. This information includes: history, initial impression, lifestyle and ambition. It also addresses some means of how this information can effectively be gathered and presented to ensure maximum impact on interpretation and decision-making. The chapter introduces a case study that will be followed throughout the book to demonstrate the practical application and potential value of a health diagnosis for an organisation.

Chapters Three to Eight, in Part II, cover the functional diagnostics that could be followed, based on the SPOILS model. Each chapter covers one of the functional categories of survival, protection, operations, information, language and strategy, including a section of the diagnostic application to the case study.

In the final chapters the similarities and differences between health and fitness for competitiveness are compared and eventually integrated, concluding that health needs to precede fitness.

Notes

1. Various institutes offer preparatory checklists to entrepreneurs, for example www.smallbusiness.co.uk, www.newbusiness.co.uk, www.businessadvisers direct.co.uk, and various banks. Most of the time the advice is funding related.
2. Popular subjects offered for MBA studies at most UK business schools include: economics, finance, marketing, strategy and human resources management. Refer also to: Locke, R.R. and Spender, J-C. (2011). *Confronting Managerialism: How the Business Elite and Their Schools Threw Our Lives out of Balance*. Zed Books, London, p. 186.
3. Various studies are available around the reasons for start-up failures, such as studies conducted by Patricia Schaefer posted on www.businessknowhow.com/ in 2011; Jay Goltz posted on http://boss.blogs.nytimes.com on 5th January 2011; Michael Amis in his book *Small Business Management*, referred to in http://usgovinfo.about.com/od/smallbusiness/
4. Examples of reasons for failings in established companies can be linked to specific companies such as: Paté-Cornell, M.E. (1993). Learning from the Piper-Alpha Accident: A Postmortem Analysis of Technical and Organizational Factors. *Risk Analysis*. Vol. 13, No. 2; Pfarrer, M.D., Decelles, K.A., Smith. K.G. (2008). After the Fall: Reintegrating the Corrupt Organization. *Academy of Management Review*. Vol.33, No.3, pp. 730-749; Sigurjonsson, T.O. (2010). The Icelandic Bank Collapse: Challenges to Governance and Risk Management. *Corporate Governance*. Vol. 10, No. 1, pp. 33-45;
5. An interpretive description of different types of organisation is presented in Morgan, G. (2006). *Images of Organization*. Sage Publications Inc., London;

Smith, M. (2006). *Fundamentals of Management*. McGraw-Hill Education, Maidenhead, pp. 15-18.

6. Refer to Maturana, H.R. and Varela, F.J. (1980). *Autopoiesis and Cognition: The Realization of the Living*. D. Reidel Publishing Company, Dordrecht; Radcliffe-Brown, A.R. (1948). *A Natural Science of Society*. The Free Press, Glencoe, Illinois; and to von Bertalanffy, L. (1968). *General Systems Theory*. George Braziller, New York.

7. Multi-business companies and SBUs are presented in: Kaplan, R.S. and Norton, D.P. (1996). *The Balanced Scorecard: Translating Strategy into Action*. Harvard Business School Press, Boston pp. 36-37; Goold, M., Campbell, A. and Alexander, M (1994). *Corporate-Level Strategy: Creating Value in the Multibusiness Company*. John Wiley & Sons, New York.

8. The concept of 'self versus non-self' is addressed in Playfair, J.H.L. and Chain, B.M. (2005). *Immunology at a Glance*. Eighth Edition. Blackwell Publishing Ltd., Oxford.

9. Latour emphasises the fact that 'actors' in an organisation need not only be individuals, but can also be objects. Refer to Latour, B. (2005). *Reassembling the Social: An Introduction to Actor-Network-Theory*; Oxford University Press; pp. 70 – 82.

10. Scientific opinions on prerequisite factors for life are discussed in Silver, B.L. (1998). *The Ascent of Science*. Oxford University Press, p. 322. Also refer to more theoretical publications such as Capra, F. (1997). *The Web of Life: A New Synthesis of Mind and Matter*. HarperCollins London; pp. 154-164.

11. Cell structure and functionality is discussed and offered both at biological and more general levels in: Barrett, K.E., Barman, S.M., Boitano, S. Brooks, H.L. (2010). *Ganong's Review of Medical Physiology*, twenty-third edition, McGraw Hill Medical, New York; Capra, F. (1996). *The Web of Life: A New Synthesis of Mind and Matter*. HarperCollins Publishers, p. 158.

12. Based on research conducted and published by: Dean, C.M. (2012). *Physiology of Organisations: An Integrated Functional Perspective*. Cambridge Scholars Publishing, Newcastle upon Tyne.

CHAPTER TWO

FIRST IMPRESSION AND HISTORY

Winning is often interpreted in terms of the financial success or market penetration of an organisation based on the demand for its products or services. Clinical wellbeing of an organisation, on the other hand, is determined by the effective integration of its functioning, thus ensuring that an organisation is healthy in order to survive and compete. By accepting organisations as living entities – as argued in Chapter One – the following topics are covered in Chapter Two to gain an initial impression of the health of an organisation:

The Diagnostic Process

Status, Management Perspective and History

General Performance of Vital Survival Functions

This chapter introduces the process for a comprehensive health check in line with the standard checklists recommended to medical practitioners, and discusses the initial steps in the application of the process. The subsequent detailed health-check steps are covered in Chapters Three to Eight.

A standard layout is used in Chapters Two to Eight to assist in the practical application of the various checklists. Shaded insert blocks in subsections offer a reference to the analogous medical processes or physiological functions that will guide the checks. These inserts can be ignored by the reader since they offer additional and not essential information.

A single case study is followed throughout the book and presented at the end of each chapter. Background information about the case study is also offered as a shaded insert and repeated throughout, although the diagnosis of the relevant functional categories will be unique for each chapter. Findings are presented in the format of a dashboard display in which the high level summary information 'dials' are followed by additional detailed information in support of the overall findings. This method is already widely used within organisations and supported by various financial or marketing systems[1]. The focus of Chapter Two is on the method and development of a high level initial impression of the health of an organisation.

The Diagnostic Process

Recommended lists for organisational health checks are not new to businesses[2]. These checks are usually based on questionnaires to evaluate business plans and their financial viability in order to obtain financial or consultancy support. The accepted method to diagnose medical concerns is, however, based on a logical sequence of steps, presented in the shaded insert box.

Logical Approach to Medical Diagnosis[3]

Diagnostic checklists taught to medics broadly cover the following steps:

Phase 1: First impression and history:
- Obtain personal detail and changes in social status.
- Determine and record symptoms, history and previous treatments.
- Perform a general examination of vital functions.
- Prepare an initial list of concerns.

Phase 2: Detailed functional diagnostic tests:
- Conduct differential tests and investigations of all functions.
- Confirm or adapt diagnosis.
- Recommend treatment.

A similar logical sequence of steps for organisational health checks will commence with a holistic general impression of the organisation, its general health and concerns. Each subsequent step thereafter drills down into more detail until a conclusion can be reached based on sound supporting evidence. The process may be more cumbersome than using a tick-box questionnaire, but the results are likely to identify more relevant issues to address than current methods.

An analogous diagnostic process for organisations could therefore consist of the following steps:

Start with current and historic information about the age, size, sector and competitive position of the organisation in its market. This information may already give an indication of potential concerns common to similar organisations as well as an indication of recent changed events and their impact on the organisation.

The rest of the initial evaluation should be dedicated to management's view of the status of health and identified concerns within the organisation. It is important even at this stage to gather as much history and information as possible around the concerns in order to gain a broad picture of health as perceived by management.

A general examination of critical survival functions, such as finance, logistics and workplace suitability, add more detail to the diagnosis. These checks, ideally performed objectively by management, or by independent external parties, should focus on the performance of these survival functions and include general questions to expand on the already identified management concerns. Although the examination at this stage is still general and symptomatic, it should be possible to highlight functions requiring further attention.

The next phase will be to conduct specific health checks for each of the functional categories performed by the organisation, as presented and discussed in Chapters Three to Eight. These checks may be able to confirm the preliminary prognosis arrived at in the initial examination, but is more likely to identify other serious issues which are contributing to the situation or may become serious in the future.

Consolidating the findings in order to reach a concluding prognosis of the state of health of the organisation and deciding on corrective action is covered in Chapter Nine.

The collection and recording of history is essential at all stages of the examination. This will not only offer a better perspective on trends and incidents which could have triggered the concerns, but also prevent early conclusions and recommendations based on single event occurrences, thereby resulting in repetitive action without enduring improved results.

Logical Approach to Organisational Health Diagnosis:

Phase 1 – General background, history and concerns (Chapter Two):
- Positional perspective to identify the type, size, age and level of independence of the organisation.
- Key concerns as viewed by management.
- General performance of key survival functions.

Phase 2 – Detailed checks and examinations of functional categories (Chapters Three to Eight).

Phase 3 – Final prognosis and possible recommendations (Chapter Nine).

The next sections address the steps in phase 1, covering the background, history, concerns and the general performance of the organisation. This information is important, not only to determine management's view of organisational concerns, but to position the organisation amongst its peers.

Status, Management Perspective and History

The process of health diagnosis starts by developing a broad view of the organisation's status and current management concerns before progressing to a better understanding of the functional areas from detailed investigations.

The tasks in this process require the examiner to:

- Obtain and record the positional perspective of the organisation within its environment in order to gain an understanding of its age, size and sector of operation.
- Identify current concerns from the point of view of the management team, directors or owners of the organisation, together with a history of events which could have impacted upon, and resulted in the identified concerns.
- Evaluate the general external image of the organisation and recent changes in order to determine whether deviations from a norm could have been problematic.

The process can be compared to checklists offered by institutes and consultants to organisations and are discussed in more detail below.

Positional Perspective

The positioning of an organisation within its environment offers a perspective of what can be expected from similar normal healthy functioning organisations, or of the common concerns which may affect organisations within the same category as defined by:

- Size, sector and age of operation.
- The degree of independence of the organisation and historic changes to this status.

Identifying the size of the organisation is important as it has a direct impact on the way in which the common functions, required for maintaining the independence of the organisation as a living entity, are structured. Organisations can be small such as entrepreneurial start-ups; medium sized stand-alone organisations; business units as part of a conglomerate family of businesses; or a large global organisation operating as a single entity.

Small to medium sized organisations with fewer employees are likely to be more flexible by combining certain functions under a single individual or department, be more informal and therefore less bureaucratic but at the same time be potentially more owner-driven than larger organisations. It is likely that not all policies, procedures and job descriptions are formal and often rely on mutual agreements and personal interpretation by the individuals. Similarly, fewer employees to perform the essential functions may mean that the organisation is not in a position to operate to required industry standards and thus needs to rely on external sources to assist in functions such as accounting, training, research and development.

It is theoretically easier to gain an overview perspective of larger organisations because of their more established approach to formal job descriptions, structures, strategies, policies and procedures. From a holistic health diagnostic point of view, these organisations should be examined for their ability to operate functionally and culturally at a level comparable to their peers, whether the functions are performed internally or externally on a contractual basis. It is not acceptable only to check whether the organisations comply with regulatory paperwork.

The level of independence of the organisational entity could be affected by their link to parent organisations in the case of conglomerates, the group culture and inherited restrictions, and the goals and objectives set within the 'family' and imposed on the individual organisation. As a member of a conglomerate family, the organisation may find that the focus is more on its competitive position of fitness due to strict group commitments and goals rather than on its own overall health.

Management Concerns and General Appearance

Management will be aware of the broad status of health of the organisation, even though not necessarily clear on specifics and how to improve the situation. It is important at this stage of the diagnostic process to allow them to explore their concerns, backed up by recent change events, without being constrained by restrictive questionnaires. The focus of this step in the process should therefore be on:

- Management concerns about the healthy functioning of the organisation.
- Events or changes in direction or objectives which could have resulted in the concerns.
- Current and recent changes to acceptance of the image by external customers or peers within the sector of operation.

Concerns which may be raised are wide and could include financial performance concerns, staffing problems, competitive positioning concerns, or the identification of specific events – such as natural disasters – resulting in the occurrence of the concerns.

Whereas this initial part of the diagnostic process cannot be regarded as scientific, it will enable management to brainstorm and set a framework which could guide further examinations to focus on important elements in the functioning of the organisation, thus enhancing the process and outcome. It is, however, important during this identification of concerns that the exploration should be wider to include historical events impacting them.

The historical trend in the market image of the organisation is another point to consider at a holistic level before focusing on a more detailed diagnosis of organisational functioning. Positioning an individual in a relevant social environment and lifestyle assists the clinician in diagnosing and comparing the appearance and wellbeing of the patient to his or her peers in a similar environment. Similarly, the organisational diagnostic questioning generates a perspective on normal and changing performance of the organisation within its sector of operation and the possible impact of the change on the morale of the workforce. Using the list of concerns identified in the initial diagnosis, questions to clarify the history could focus on:

- Performance indicators related to the ability to generate and sustain revenue and profit from its operations.
- The image accepted by its target market and peers.

Diagnostics can reveal struggling organisations, satisfied niche organisations, or high performing start-up organisations without adequate structure and support functions to ensure longer term stability and persistency. Examples of the latter were common with internet organisations during the dot.com boom at the turn of the century[4]. It is necessary to determine whether these factors have changed over the years and if so, why and with what impact on the organisation.

Health Checks Related to Status, Management Perspective and History:

- Positional perspective to identify the type, size and level of independence of the organisation.

- Key concerns as viewed by management.

- Sector of operation and acceptance of image within the sector.

- History related to the events and changes affecting areas of concern or performance.

General Performance of Vital Survival Functions

The logical next diagnostic step recommended to medical practitioners is to follow the initial discussion of symptoms and history with objective health checks of the vital functions before deciding on further action. These functions could include: the respiratory system (lungs and breathing); cardiovascular distribution (blood pressure and pulse rate); diet and digestive system (bodymass and dietary concerns); and general concerns with respect to muscle or skeletal structures (joints, fractures). This approach can expand on the patient's health concerns, but at the same time offers an immediate indication of other serious life-threatening issues which may have to be addressed.

In Chapter One the key survival functions of organisations were identified as the functions necessary to ensure that all employees are able to perform their allocated tasks effectively and included finance and accounting, analogous to the respiratory system; logistics, analogous to the dietary and cardiovascular systems; and workplace maintenance, analogous to the renal and colon filtering systems.

Healthy functioning of survival functions could be determined by observing their direct operations, or their impact on individuals and other functional departments in the organisation. The importance is that the first impressions should be from objective independent sources enhanced with, and compared to, management's diagnostic symptoms and views. By focusing on the key functions to ensure organisational sustainability it is possible to diagnose their health by reviewing the:

- External image of the organisation based on its financial assets and market performance.
- Financial performance of sustainability, profitability and selected key performance ratios.
- Logistics and suitable supplies delivered to individual departments such as the operating units, including parts for manufacturing or stock to retail units, as observed by customers.
- Internal image of morale and wellbeing based on staff satisfaction surveys.

External Image

The external image offers an opportunity to determine the view that the external stakeholders have about the organisation, both historical and in the current environment.

What is the balance sheet image of the organisation: asset rich or highly indebted in which necessary assets have been funded by loans? This offers an insight in the 'weight' status of the organisation, and therefore an indication of a safety net against future financial downturns. However, an asset rich organisation may also be vulnerable. This may point towards an inability of management to effectively manage windfall or high profit income to cover or prepare for future downturns or invest in improvements. These two health concerns are often observed in young and start-up companies, either struggling to finance the assets and running of the business, or are doing very well during the first years and are mismanaging this revenue only to be caught by a later downturn in its market performance.

Stakeholders are also interested in the integrity and general performance of the organisation in the market: Is the organisation known as a trustworthy player with a good image consistent with its stated goals, objectives and cultural standards? How has this image changed recently – has it improved or declined compared to its immediate competitors? Objective views can be obtained from surveys or from its financial positioning in the market, based on share price evaluations. Although susceptible to short term changes in the share market, changes in share prices can be a good indicator when viewed as a general trend. It offers an indication of deteriorating or improving health, required for the final prognosis.

Financial Sustainability

Profitability and financial performance, analogous to the observation of potential breathing concerns in individuals, can effectively be obtained from the regulatory profit and loss accounts required for all registered companies as well as stock market performance for listed companies. The normal requirement is to show the performance over recent sequential years, but as in the case of all the other observations, a longer history and trend – seasonal if relevant – can highlight improvements or declines and events influencing the changes.

Support to Individuals and Units

One of the survival diagnostics which is often ignored by businesses is the integrated support which needs to be offered to all individuals and functions within the organisation, analogous to the supply of nutrients, oxygen and a balanced cell environment in living organisms. A standard method to diagnose healthy functioning of a patient is to check on the health of the extremities of the body, such as the hands and feet. Signs of a poor blood circulation function or inadequate diet can be detected in these extremities.

Similar diagnostics can be conducted in organisations by checking on the availability of necessary supplies, funding and workplace acceptability in the operating units and other departments assisting them, in performing their tasks successfully. A 'walk-through' to observe the state of cleanliness and supply satisfaction in the units can be used to develop an overview of the culture of the organisation. Some concerns could already have been identified during the image observations, reflecting reduction in customer satisfaction or an inability to perform due to a lack of supplies.

Internal Image of Wellbeing

An internal image of well-being can be based on staff surveys or selected interviews in order to determine staff satisfaction, morale and motivation, analogous to the identification of signs of infection or illness in individuals. However, similar to the external image, a history and trend of survey results can give an indication of deteriorating or improving morale, together with incidents which may have resulted in the changes. Reasons for dissatisfaction could be multiple, from dissatisfaction with remuneration, inadequate support in the execution of tasks, to the intervention of external parties such as trade unions.

This general examination of the survival functions will at least help to identify the severity of the health concerns and to compile the list of further functions to be investigated in detail. Should specific symptoms be identified by management during the initial history taking and discussion review, the relevant functions need to be objectively reviewed before moving to a detailed diagnostic process.

General Objective Examination of Key Functions:

- External image of the organisation by market and stakeholders.

- Financial performance of sustainability.

- Level of support to operating units and other departments.

- Internal culture, morale and motivation.

What is the difference in learning from the diagnostic process of medical practitioners as opposed to the widely-used health checks offered to organisations? During this preliminary examination it allows management to identify initial areas of concern which can guide further analyses by brainstorming and substantiating the performance instead of being guided by a prescriptive checklist. It is, however, in the next stages that the difference will become visible when the process moves towards objective and evidence-based observations and diagnostics.

Case Study

A single case study, broadly based on a real start-up business situation, will be used to demonstrate the examination and diagnostic procedures in the book. For legibility, an insert block presents the background to the case study business, referred to as The Corner Shop, and this block is repeated in each subsequent chapter in Part Two.

In the case study of The Corner Shop, a franchise grocery business, the owners identified serious financial and cash flow concerns as critical survival issues. They decided to undertake a full business health check in order to determine whether there is a chance to save the business and start a recovery process for the future.

CASE STUDY – THE CORNER SHOP

An independent retail franchise grocery store and bakery, referred to as The Corner Shop, is part of a larger chain. Although the franchisee has the freedom to structure and run the business independently, the holding company is expecting a regular fee from the store as a member of its chain and requires the store to maintain a minimum set of standards. In return, the store owners can use the preferential rates for stock purchases negotiated for the chain and receive advisory assistance from the holding company. The store is in a favourable location in the main street of the town, conveniently situated for a wide range of customers, and the owners have had previous experience and knowledge of retail, finance and accountancy.

The store has been operating for five years. During the first two years it delivered record turnover and profits to the extent that the business was nominated as the 'winning' store in the chain. The customer base was classified as predominantly upper middle-class and the overall image of the store was vibrant and welcoming. The owners went out of their way to satisfy customer needs, for instance, by offering a type of bread made from a special recipe, sought after by many of the local hotels and restaurants, and by ordering and stocking special items on request.

During the third year, the owners decided to expand and diversify by acquiring a butcher shop in the adjacent town. The butchery was at the point of closing and they managed to get it at a reasonable price, including commitments of rental agreements undertaken by the previous owners. They managed to extend their bank loan to finance the deal and one of the owners is spending most of his time running the butchery. The combination of the additional workload for the owners together with mounting repayment burdens of interest and earlier stock purchases are making it difficult to maintain the previous standards of operation. The image of the store and service to the customers has been dropping and resulted in a loss of customers and sales.

Presentation of the findings of each of the diagnostic steps utilise the dashboard information facility[1], widely used and available for financial and management information systems. Findings differ per chapter and only focus on the relevant functional category being addressed in that particular chapter. Chapter Two, for example, presents the positional perspective of The Corner Shop and a brief reference to key functional information which will be further developed in subsequent chapters. Chapter Nine, on the other hand, offers the full dashboard set of information dials which can be used to arrive at a final prognosis of the health of the case study business and possible recommendations towards action and a future direction.

Table 2.1 presents the basic health information and positional perspective of The Corner Shop. Most of the information is either factual organisational information, or based on management views. Concerns have been highlighted by a rating system explained in the narrative section of the table.

Positional Perspective of The Corner Shop		
Narrative of Rating Indicators: W = warning; S = Serious; blank = acceptable or general background		
Category	**Information and/or Trend**	**Rating**
Identification	The Corner Shop Limited Address in town Date of incorporation – Yr 0 of a 5 year period	
Positional perspective	- Sector: Retail service organisation - Prime location on town high street - Customer base regarded as upper middle-class - Franchisee in well-known retail chain with good reputation	
Management concerns	Financial cash flow concerns	S
Health history	Yr 05 - Serious cash flow problems	S
	Yr 04-05 - Reduction in sales and difficulty to restock to a satisfactory level	W
	Yr 03 - Acquire butcher shop funded by loan	S
	Yr 00-02 - Highly profitable and thriving	
	Yr 00 - Start-up funded by personal and bank loans	W

Table 2.1   Positional perspective of The Corner Shop

The section on history contains a chronological record of health incidents and resulting impacts. Initially, this list reflects management's view, but after further diagnostic processes and updates, it should be based on evidence and therefore present an objective picture of the general state of health of the organisation. Serious concerns were highlighted for year 3 – purchase of the butcher shop – resulting in year 5's cash flow problems.

The positional perspective presented in Table 2.1 is based on the views of the owners of the business since this was the first time that a serious examination was conducted by an objective party. Previous reviews were mainly with the bank in order to arrange for additional loans or increased overdraft facilities to fund investments or, recently, the running cost of the business.

At this stage the focus of the management concerns is dominated by financial cash flow problems. This is a serious situation and one of the main reasons for many start-up businesses to fail[5]. The impact is also visible in the deterioration of the logistics situation, while the additional acquisition of a butcher shop could be an indication of a poor management decision based on defects in other functions, such as information gathering and utilisation. A health check will need to determine whether, by rearranging the debt and financial commitments, the business can be saved or whether it will be better for the owners to sell out before being forced out of business by their creditors.

However, before jumping to conclusions and offering more loans to alleviate the dire financial position, it will be necessary to examine each of the functional categories in detail. This is covered in Part Two and will help to identify the areas which led to this critical position and could therefore either be addressed to resolve the problems, or prevent future similar situations.

Conclusion

Accepting organisations as living entities in Chapter One, responsible for their own self-maintenance towards sustainability, allowed Chapter Two to explore a logical process recommended to medical practitioners for conducting a health check on patients.

The recommended diagnostic checklist discussed in this chapter starts with management's view of the general performance of the organisation and the identification of specific concerns about its functioning. This subjective view is systematically expanded by progressively adding more objective and detailed evidence until it is possible to reach a realistic prognosis and recommend a plan of action to address health concerns.

The chapter also introduces a case study based on an actual business, referred to as The Corner Shop, not only to demonstrate the application of the health diagnostic process in practice, but to explore a method of recording and presenting information as clear summarised findings supported by objective evidence. This case study is used and developed throughout the book in order to reach a prognosis in Chapter Nine.

The objective of an initial general examination is to gather historic and trend information about the general health of the organisation and to highlight areas for further in-depth functional examinations. The detailed examinations are explored in Part Two based on the SPOILS model to cover the functional categories of survival, protection, operations, information, language and strategy. Each functional category is addressed in a separate chapter.

The book concludes in Part Three with a diagnostic checklist to assist managers in determining the health of the organisation, and the reasons why health is regarded as a prerequisite to effective competitiveness.

Notes

1. Many software or presentation tools to produce a dashboard approach to information presentation are readily available. A reference, based on practical applications in various organisations is: Eckerson, W.W. (2011). *Performance Dashboards: Measuring, Monitoring and Managing your Business.* Second Edition. John Wiley & Sons, Hoboken, NJ.

2. Checklists to businesses are abundant and offered by various institutes or consultancy companies as marketing tools. Examples of checklists include: www.business-survival-toolkit.co.uk; www.docstoc.com/docs/81915280/Business-Health-Check; www.probiz-excellence.com/expertise/consultancy/

3. Various checklists are offered to medical students such as by Turner, R. and Blackwood, R. (1998): *Clinical Skills*, Third Edition. Blackwell Science Ltd, Oxford.

4. Examples include dot.com companies without suitable logistic cover for exceptional growth. Internet entries of reasons for the crash include: www.guardian.co.uk/technology/2005/mar/10 in a report titled: *Looking back on the crash*; Jonathan Skillings, ZDNet.com.au on March 8th, 2002: Explaining the "dot.cons"; www.cnet.com/1990-11136_1-6278387-1.html *Top 10 dot-com flops*, by Kent German.

PART II:

FUNCTIONAL DIAGNOSTICS

The objective of PART II is to explore in-depth checklists of potential health questions that can be used to evaluate the health of the functional categories identified in the SPOILS functional model.

- **Survival** functions in Chapter Three address finance and accounting, logistics and workplace maintenance as the functions focusing on individual employees and their ability to operate effectively.

- **Protection** functions in Chapter Four cover the access, security, safety, health and wellbeing functions required to protect and prepare an organisation against incidents of damage.

- **Operations** functions in Chapter Five identify the various operating units in an organisation and their ability to operate on behalf of the organisation in its environment.

- **Information** functions in Chapter Six focus on the collection, interpretation, reporting and storage of external and internal information.

- **Language and communications** functions in Chapter Seven address the means by which the organisation can communicate or present itself to the external environment, as well as the internal communication.

- **Strategy and guidance** functions in Chapter Eight address the planning and guiding functions required from executive management towards goal achievement.

Organisations are unique and the listed diagnostic questions and measurement tools should be customised for effective application.

CHAPTER THREE

SURVIVAL FUNCTIONS

Without healthy survival functions an organisation can die.

The main objective of the survival functions of living organisms is to offer support towards the wellbeing of individual cells and organs in order to enable them to effectively contribute to the survival of the organism. The analogous functions in organisations are correspondingly inward-looking and include:

Finance and Accounting

Logistics

Workplace Maintenance

The survival functions in organisms can be identified as respiration, digestion, cardiovascular circulation, and the control of the chemical balance in the body through filtering and waste elimination. They enable organisms to stay alive and thrive by ensuring that sufficient oxygen and nutrients are received and distributed to all cells throughout the body. The analogous functions essential for the survival of an organisation include: finance and accounting, analogous to the respiratory system; logistics covering procurement, storage and distribution, analogous to the digestive and cardiovascular systems; and workplace maintenance, analogous to the renal, liver, bladder and colon filtering and waste excretion systems.

In this chapter we will consider each of the organisational survival functions from a clinical diagnostic perspective. We will determine their importance by comparing them to the physiological functioning of living organisms and identify early warning signs of dysfunction that could be detrimental to the organisation if left unchecked. The shaded inserts, referring to the physiological functions, may be ignored as background information only.

Finance and Accounting

The importance of the finance and accounting function, comparable to the breathing function in organisms, has already been acknowledged in organisations and is supported by well-established professional institutes. Its role in organisational survival is accepted, concepts and procedures taught, and restrictions imposed by regulatory bodies. Therefore, as one of the most important functions contributing to the survival of an organisation, it is important to ensure that this function is healthy.

Respiratory Function[1]

Oxygen is the most important requirement for survival, without which an individual can die within minutes regardless of his or her state of health.

Respiratory functions include inhalation of air and the packaging of oxygen in red blood cells for distribution in the bloodstream to all cells, where it is utilised in the chemical processes to generate energy. Carbon dioxide, created by this process, is eliminated in reverse. It is important for an organism to ensure it has sufficient oxygen available in the air it breathes.

Breathing is controlled by an automatic pacemaker in the medulla in the midbrain and can be augmented voluntarily in depth and rate by the cognitive brain. However, it is difficult, if not impossible, to consciously stop the breathing process.

Learning from the diagnostic procedure used by medical practitioners, the status of health of the respiratory system can be detected by: measuring the oxygen intake under routine and stress situations; listening for possible obstructions due to smoking or other medical concerns in the lungs; and observing the effect of inadequate oxygen distribution to extremities such as hands and feet, or muscle cramps.

Following this guideline, the finance and accounting function is about the routine execution and processing of financial transactions, the internal allocation and distribution of funds to individuals and departments and the external financial dealings to ensure the sustainable economic viability of the organisation.

Management accounting is generally used to describe the accounting transaction processing within the organisation, analogous to normal breathing activities. Financial accounting, on the other hand, can be compared to the cognitive manipulation of the breathing activities, thus representing responses to feedback reports and the external financial negotiations of the organisation's finances.

Management Accounting

Accounting is an essential function in organisations in which financial transactions are executed, reported and interpreted[2]. Analogous to the respiratory system, the transactions cover the processing of income, fund allocation and expenditure of the organisation.

Income Accounting

Processing of income transactions involve: the management of the sales and debtors ledgers; expediting payments of outstanding customer invoices; and the control of cash, donations and miscellaneous income such as loans or investment income received by the organisation.

Effectively managing and expediting the income of the organisation is essential in ensuring that the organisation can rely on the timely recovery of its anticipated income commitments. Especially in start-up, young and growing organisations, delayed income can lead to a cash flow concern in which the organisation is unable to meet its immediate financial commitments, even if it is solvent and the assets of the organisation can cover its debts.

Good diagnostic auditing procedures should rate this as a high priority, similar to the need to ensure that a patient does not suffer from serious breathing concerns. The control process should also ensure that the funds received are legitimate and not part of fraudulent or money laundering activities, which could result in a breach of regulations and high fines.

Cost Accounting

Cost accounting, analogous to the packaging of oxygen into the red blood cells before distribution throughout an organism, covers the allocation and internal distribution of funds for operational expenditure including: salaries and wages; purchase of supplies; and overhead expenditure. Today, most of the fund allocation is either performed according to pre-determined budget and payment commitments, or on request to fund special projects, purchases or activities.

Accounting principles require a separation of responsibilities, for example, the separation of requests for expenditure from the actual payment from the funds. However, this activity also has its areas of concern, such as misuse of funds by individuals via fraudulent requests for payments, the creation of hidden accounts in the system, or unequal distribution of available funds. An analogy is the diversion of blood-flow in the body to cancerous growths.

This need for unexpected expenses, including expenses due to damage or natural disasters for which normal funds are not available, can be compared to increased oxygen requirements by muscle units or the brain during times of high activity, such as sport, or stress. Whereas this shortage of funds can lead to an inability in financing the increased demand, it can also mean that funds normally used for internal operational functions may have to be diverted. This danger, arising from unexpected costs, could be an indication of a lack of foresight and planning, usually starting in budget preparations without adequate built-in flexibility to ensure that unforeseen events and expenses can be covered.

Debt/Payment Management

Analogous to the removal of carbon-dioxide as the spent oxygen from the organism, the accounting function needs to be involved in the execution and management of the organisation's debt. Similar to income management, payments to suppliers, loan institutions and other external creditors need to be executed and controlled effectively. The inability of an organisation to repay large amounts of debt to its creditors is one of the main reasons for liquidity impairments, which could impact any organisation and result in insolvency. An organisation may be able to raise some funds to repay the short term debts, but if a major creditor recalls the debt owed by the organisation, other lenders may back off and the organisation may have to face serious financial problems[3].

Accounting Feedback and Controls

The breathing process is under local control. Similarly, the accounting process is locally controlled according to prescribed rules, regulations and the separation of duties to ensure accuracy and reduce the possibility of fraud. It is a separate and independent function, essential for the survival of the organisation and not under the day-to-day control of non-financial senior management. Senior managers and managers from other functions are able to request support, funding and information but are, however, not in a position to ignore or change the basic processing principles without the danger of illegal or fraudulent action[4].

Because of the rule-based operations of accounting, it was one of the first functions to be computerised in firms since the 1950s and today most organisations rely on computer systems for the processing of the recorded transactions. While this simplifies the work, it adds an additional concern of relying on the accuracy of the system, and the possibility of hacking and misuse of the electronic system by computer experts.

The health of the management accounting function can therefore be evaluated and judged by raising questions about effective transaction processing, fund distribution and compliance to legal and regulatory procedures, as listed below. The effectiveness of this process, including during times of adverse circumstances, can be closely linked to the organisation's ability to operate in competitive environments.

Possible Health Questions for Management Accounting:

- Do the accounting procedures adhere to regulatory requirements and are they executed accurately and compliant?

- How timely and effective is the processing of cash, debtor and creditor commitments?

- Can the fund allocation to various individuals and functions be regarded fair and equitable during normal as well as unusual periods?

- Can and does the system detect and guard against fraudulent transactions?

Financial Accounting

Healthy individuals rely on healthy lungs and need to be able to adapt their oxygen intake and breathing to support their professional or sporting lifestyles and activities. Similarly, the internal financial health of an organisation requires a longer term planning process. Financial managers, analogous to breathing controls initiated by the cognitive brain, need to react to financial reports, influence the budget process and be responsible for ensuring external financial resourcing[5].

Operating Budget Planning and Controls

The objective of an operating budget is to predict and regulate the need for, and the control of, income and expenditure of the organisation, and can be compared to the need to plan for effective breathing exercises before a physical competition.

The income part of the operating budget specifies the source of income by product or service category as well as non-operational income such as investment interests and gains. Pitfalls include overestimating the income budget and/or understating the expenditure. This sometimes occurs after a period of reduced income by adjusting the anticipated income for the coming period, or can be due to the inability to 'read and interpret' potential trends in the future performance of the economic and/or customer markets. It may also occur if the budget forms part of a cost-benefit analysis, required by banks or investment institutions, before approving a loan or new investment capital.

The expenditure section of the operating budget is split into operating expenses to cover the costs directly related to the products and services identified in the income budget, analogous to the provision of oxygen to skeletal muscle units; and an overhead cost section to address costs required by the other functions, including salaries and wages. Budgeted expenditure is often adjusted if cost cutting is required due to lower expected or actual operational income, for example through redundancies in the sales, service and mid-management personnel. This holds the danger of dismissing staff just to employ them again in the roles of highly paid consultants in order to be able to execute the specialist tasks after losing the expert knowledge as part of the redundancy.

Capital Budgeting, Financing and Investments

An additional responsibility of senior finance managers lies in raising money from external sources when required, and in deciding how to invest surplus funds as an additional safeguard for future and secondary income. This can be compared to the cognitive decisions in ensuring that the oxygen supply in the air is acceptable for planned activities.

The capital budget, as the starting point, addresses the planning activity and control of capital investments in land, buildings, plant, equipment and income-generating investments to assist future growth and expansion. It is necessary for these planned investment projects to be fully cost-justified and regularly monitored for progress against the plans. One of the main concerns is the overspending, both in money and time, of capital projects and the detrimental effect this can have on the organisation.

A method to obtain funds for the initial set-up or the expansion of an organisation is to negotiate external financial support either as loans or equity financing.

Loan financing requires the organisation to repay the money as per agreement such as loans from financial institutions, parent companies or sponsoring organisations. In the case of funds for capital investments, the financing can also come from leasing or renting the asset from a third party, usually at an agreed rent and for a minimum period of time. In all the cases of loan financing, the ability of the organisation to repay the regular interests or rents, and eventually the full loan amount, is essential in maintaining a good credit rating for the future.

In equity financing, instead of being repaid the loan, the lenders receive a share of the ownership of the organisation, taking on part of the financial risk. They are offered shares and dividends commensurate with their proportion of ownership. Shareholders or sponsors are not directly involved in an organisation's day-to-day operations, but may exert pressure on the organisation to meet their expectations of return on their investments.

Although insufficient funds can be a threat to the survival of an organisation, an excess of funds may also result in organisational health hazards. It is necessary for finance managers to plan for suitable fund investment activities that will add future value to the operation of the organisation. Standard options include: investment in new plant and equipment; expansion of the business by diversification or opening new branches; improved systems, especially technology; investment in land or buildings; or additional remuneration, facilities and development of staff. Care should be taken to avoid the hazards of unprofitable external investments or excessive internal levels of spending which may not be in line with the actual effort required for income generation.

Financial Feedback and Controls

While the aim of management and financial accounting feedback is to keep management informed on a regular basis about the profitability, cash flow and cost position of the organisation, external financial reports have a prescribed format and list of contents required by the relevant interested parties, such as the Internal Revenue and the Companies House in the UK.

Annual regulatory reports represent the organisation's financial performance over the reporting period. A profit and loss account shows the profitability of the operations over the accounting period while the balance sheet presents a snapshot of its assets and liabilities at a point in time. A concern of financial reporting is the ability of organisations to 'window-dress' their financial status, sometimes through a process referred to as creative accounting. This is a legal process and a temptation especially with conglomerates producing separate and consolidated profit and loss and balance sheet reports for the individual subsidiaries and for the group. Income, expenses, assets and liabilities can be transferred among subsidiaries in order to improve the image of an individual subsidiary or the consolidated financial statements. While offering a clear consolidated picture of health for the group, it is possible that individual subsidiaries may have serious health concerns which should be addressed.

Health issues in financial accounting are therefore concerned with management's ability to plan for balanced income and expenditure by means of realistic budgets, to raise money to fund planned operating and capital expenditures, and to realistically invest excess funds. These factors underlie successful competitiveness, but more importantly, ensure longer term survival of the organisation and form part of a healthy lifestyle or the ability to modify and adjust current unacceptable financial situations.

Possible Health Questions for Financial Accounting:

- How realistic are the budget forecasts and the control process of actual versus budgeted expenditure?

- Is the organisation able to raise the necessary funds for operational and/or capital expenditure at acceptable rates?

- How realistic and effective are the asset and financial investments of the organisation to cater for, or guide against future events?

- Do external financial reports accurately reflect the internal financial position of the organisation?

Diagnosing Finance and Accounting – The Process

Various ratios and tools have been developed to assist in the interpretation of the financial status of organisations. Financial ratios like profitability and debt ratios are important, but if we want to learn from the diagnostics conducted by medical practitioners, wider and more encompassing sets of tests and observations are required to check all aspects of: the breathing process in the chest; the volume of oxygen and carbon dioxide absorption and emission; the impact of oxygen delivery to various parts of the body; and the suitability of the work and lifestyle environment of the individual. Analogous diagnostic steps for organisations can be split into checks concerned with its financial status; normal accounting procedures; realistic fund allocation through budgets;

and the effectiveness of external fund raising and investment activities, as represented in Figure 3.1.

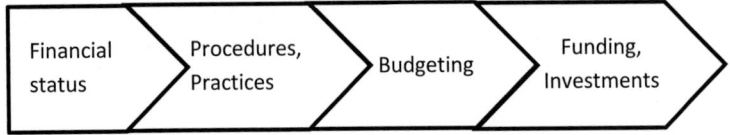

Figure 3.1   Diagnostic stages for finance and accounting functions

Financial Performance, Ratios and Trends

Analogous to the detection of breathing concerns in individuals, regular financial reports offer a view of the financial status of the organisation, can be interpreted by management and could highlight concerns in the current performance or trend over time.

Financial performance ratios are more specific and could be used to measure specific financial activities, analogous to the oxygen intake, effective distribution of oxygen and the elimination of carbon dioxide by the respiratory system of individuals. Selecting the best ratios for the organisation and a baseline of 'healthy' reading is likely to be influenced by the organisation's age and sector of operation, analogous to the age and lifestyle of a patient, and may require external expert assistance from auditors or financial advisors. These ratios include various revenue, profitability, operational performance and debt ratios[5].

- Profitability ratios measure the revenue stream and percentage of operating profit in order to determine whether the organisation can and will be able to survive on the income received. A trend analysis of monthly or year on year comparisons could reveal whether a drop in revenue income and/or a negative profitability ratio is temporary or is becoming persistent and serious.
- Operational performance ratios measure the effective utilisation of the organisation's assets and resources to ensure profitable sales, especially the effective use of inventory. This can highlight ineffective storage of slow moving inventory items.
- Debt ratios, on the other hand, measure the cost of additional funding from equity versus loan capital advances. Whereas the incursion of loans or additional share equity funding can be advantageous for stable organisations, it may cause problems for start-up companies.

Any concern arising from persistent and/or deteriorating performance according to these ratios should be taken seriously by the organisation and acted upon to prevent liquidity or insolvency problems.

Sound Accounting Procedures and Practices

Sound accounting procedures and practices, analogous to a healthy and non-smoking lifestyle, are essential for continued health and could be diagnosed by management as a tick-box list or as part of an audit review.

Young, start-up companies may have simplistic accounting and finance procedures due to the fact that there is no need at this stage for accounts to be independently audited. Employment of inexperienced bookkeepers and limited accounting systems may, however, not provide them with the information necessary to plan for future operations.

Established organisations could also be at risk of non-standard accounting practices and internal fraud which should be identified by independent auditors. Even if task separation and full audit controls are in place, another internal source could be invaluable, namely internal whistle-blowing which should be taken seriously as an indication of potentially detrimental issues that may exist in the organisation.

Budget Planning and Controls

Analogous to the detection of oxygen deprivation in parts of the body, one of the best diagnostic tools against unplanned expenditure is the availability of realistic budgets for income and cost distribution, and the ability of the managers to contain spending within their budget limitations.

Although the existence of a budget can be determined as a part of a managerial checklist, the diagnostics should not only be restricted to checking whether the organisation prepares and monitors operating budgets. It is important for an auditor or other independent parties to be able to determine whether the budgets are based on realistic income and cost distribution models, realistic cost benefit analyses of planned future capital projects or investments, and a feedback process and evaluation of actual expenditure versus previous budgets.

Financial Fund Raising and Investment Practices

It is important for individuals to live and work in an environment without unnecessary pollution or contaminants in the air supply. Both a potential lack of oxygen as well as excess could be detrimental to the health of the individual. Similarly, investment ratios can be used to offer information to external investors or sponsors about the health of the organisation, and at the same time obtain information on suitable external investments for surplus funds.

Similar to the financial ratios, the selection and baseline acceptance of a healthy ratio may require expert assistance to ensure that the correct ratios are used for the organisation. As an example, an important diagnostic tool for investors in the organisation, or by the organisation on its own investments, is the return on investments ratio. This ratio measures the investment income from dividends or other means, as a factor of the capital invested and should indicate a positive trend for investments.

In summary, some of the most telling signs of accounting and financial concerns in an organisation can be diagnosed. Uncontrolled over-expenditure and borrowing can lead to liquidity problems or insolvency; fraudulent activities can result in shortfalls; and unacceptable accounting procedures can cause damage to image together with fines. Possible health questions for each of the sub functions were discussed in previous sections and can help to determine 'what' to diagnose. However, a tick-box checklist is not the only or necessarily the best method to address the 'how' process of diagnostics – independent expert assistance can offer more in-depth perspectives to the finance and accounting functions.

Logistics

Similar to the importance of the finance and accounting functions, organisations cannot survive without effective management of the procurement, storage and flow of resources, including: supplies, material, people and information. In organisations the procurement and storage functions can be compared to the gastrointestinal or digestive system of living organisms, while the distribution function is analogous to the cardiovascular distribution system. In organisations these two functions are closely interrelated, often collectively referred to as logistics[6].

For an organisation to survive it is necessary to ensure that vacancies are filled by suitable individuals. In addition, job incumbents have to be provided with the funding, equipment, material, supplies and information required to perform their allocated tasks. The subsets of the logistics function, analogous to the digestion, absorption and distribution of nutrients, are discussed in the section as resource procurement and storage, and the internal distribution of people, supplies and materials.

Resource Procurement and Inventory Control

Resource procurement needs to be split into recruitment of people, analogous to protein essential for the formation of cells, the procurement of supplies/material, analogous to carbohydrates essential for the generation of energy, and minerals to enable the cells to perform their tasks. All types of procurement are relevant and suitable resources are essential for the survival of an organisation.

Gastrointestinal Functions[1]

The main gastrointestinal functions are to ingest, digest and absorb nutrients to be used for the creation of cells and the generation of energy within cells.

Structurally, the system consists of a continuous tract through the body, thus it is open to the external environment. It can be divided into different parts, each with specific dominant functions, such as the mouth and teeth for initial breakdown of food into manageable pieces; the stomach for the breakdown of proteins and fats; the small intestines for the breakdown of carbohydrates and absorption of nutrients into the bloodstream; and the colon in which waste material is collected for subsequent excretion.

The gastrointestinal system works in close cooperation with other organs, such as the taste and smell sensory receptors in the mouth, the liver to extract toxins, and the pancreas for the production of essential hormones to assist in the digestion of carbohydrates. The digestive system is also one of the systems in the body which tolerates and utilises the assistance of bacteria in the breakdown of food.

Examples of pathological conditions of the gastrointestinal system include blockage or problems with the breakdown and absorption of nutrients, such as lactose intolerance or the inability to effectively metabolise proteins, carbohydrates or sugars.

Recruitment of People

The recruitment and selection process is usually performed by a human resources function, although in smaller organisations this activity will be the responsibility of the manager requiring additional staff. The recruitment process acknowledges the fact that different jobs require different types of personalities, skills and experience. In the human body this can be compared to different types of protein to assist in the development of different types of cells such as red meat for the development of muscle.

Concerns with respect to recruitment and selection of the right person for the right position can arise from various sources, namely: imposed restrictions on the employment of additional or replacement staff required to perform the functions effectively; poor or vague job descriptions, making it difficult to attract the right type of person; employing the wrong person for the planned task; and the inability to find the right person in the market to match the job requirement or salary offer. During times of austerity a blanket freeze on recruitment is often used to cut cost, but can lead to understaffing in essential areas.

Procurement of Supplies, Tools and Material

Even if the organisation manages to recruit and select the right staff for the right positions, these personnel require relevant and adequate tools and operational supplies to perform their tasks effectively. This function of the procurement of equipment and supplies is analogous to the intake, digestion and absorption of nutrients such as carbohydrates for energy and minerals required by cells.

Purchasing of equipment and supplies originates as requests received from the relevant departments, or from senior management in case of changes in strategic direction within the organisation. A distinction is commonly made between supplies directly linked to the operating activities such as the supply of parts for manufacturing or stock for sale in shops, and tasks-related supplies of terminals, paper and pens to all functions. Appropriate supplies are essential for organisations in specialist areas such as parts for old or novel manufacturing equipment or specialist medical supplies.

Concerns in procurement are therefore linked to the inability in acquiring the right type of equipment or supplies at the right price and time, and the danger of poor quality or unwanted supplies being delivered to the stores and individuals.

Supply Storage / Inventory Control

Not all resources procured by the organisation are immediately utilised by the requesting functions. Analogous to the interim storage of fat in the body, resources can be stored either in warehouses or locally within the relevant departments until required.

Inventory control of supplies and material involves the classification and orderly storage of goods received to ensure easy retrieval for the distribution of individual items as and when required. The effectiveness of the inventory control system lies in the ability to manage the stock in the warehouse and danger signs can be associated with over/under supply of products, parts or equipment. Companies experiencing an unexpected surge in production may experience difficulties to ensure speedy delivery. It can also include the unnecessary storage of old stock or material which could take up space without contributing to the effective operation of the organisation. One method made popular during the second half of the twentieth century is the just-in-time (JIT) method of acquiring manufacturing supplies. This method cuts down on procurement and warehousing costs, but has the danger of stopping production if for some reason the supply chain fails as occurred after the Japan tsunami in 2011[7].

Possible Health Questions for Recruitment, Procurement and Storage:

- Are staffing levels adequate and of the right type and quality?

- How cost effective is the procurement process? Is it possible to obtain essential quality supplies and parts at affordable prices?

- How reliable and timely is the material and parts supply chain?

- How effective is the stock control system, including the recording and reviews of slow and fast moving items?

- Are there adequate safeguards built into the supply chain to prevent critical under-stocking during times of emergency?

Distribution

Procurement and storage of resources could be operating effectively but it is also necessary to be able to deliver the resources to the appropriate areas, efficiently and on time. Distribution, analogous to the functioning of the cardiovascular distribution system in organisms, forms an essential component of the logistics function.

Similar to the procurement function, the distribution function in organisations should cover people and material resources, but should also include the availability and functional support of the distribution of information. Each of the functions will be discussed separately in this section.

Cardiovascular Functions[1]

The main function of the cardiovascular system is to circulate blood around the body. The system consists of the heart as the central pumping station; the circulatory arteries, veins and capillaries as the pathways for the distribution; and the blood as the main carrier.

The heart has local pacemaker cells that regulate the pace and strength of the heartbeat. This pace and strength is further adjusted from the midbrain by means of chemical messages, especially if additional effort is required due to exercise or fright. Circulatory blood vessels consist of arteries to transport blood from the heart, veins to transport blood from the various organs and cells back to the heart, and minute capillaries in the tissue to ensure that all cells have access to oxygen and nutrients distributed by the blood.

Blood is the medium in which the various requirements for the cells are transported. The components include: dissolved nutrients; red blood cells transporting oxygen; white blood cells as part of the immune system; blood platelets to clot and stop blood loss; and hormones as chemical messengers. Intruder cells or organisms which have managed to bypass the initial immune filters in the skin or digestive and respiratory systems may also be transported around the body in the blood.

Heart failure occurs when the heart is unable to sufficiently pump blood around the circulatory system, leading to ineffective distribution to all parts of the body and could, within hours, be fatal to the organism due to the inability of the recipient organs to operate.

Distributing Equipment and Supplies

Common to all the distribution channels is the need for knowledge of the location of the various departments and individuals, and the need to keep these channels open and freely flowing. Blockage of supply channels, especially to outlying units, staff and departments, can lead to the inability of the personnel to perform their tasks effectively or can deter or endanger staff operating in remote locations.

The concept of distribution in organisations, however, does not only refer to internal distribution to the various departments, but also to external parties. This can include the distribution of the products purchased by the customers in the case of manufacturing, wholesale and retail organisations. Organisations specialising in third party distribution as their main operational service, such as courier services or airlines, will be covered in the operating unit section of Chapter Five. In all of these cases the closing of delivery channels has the same effect as internal distribution and can result in loss of business unless the blockages can be effectively resolved. It is also one of the areas in which the online ordering service of organisations may experience problems in their ability to deliver the products to clients at home. Health issues are therefore concerned with the blockage to delivery addresses or poor functioning of delivery times and volumes.

Distributing Information / Communication

An area mainly affecting the distribution channels and procedures rather than procurement, is the distribution of various types of communication and information. Within the body, communication messages are produced by the endocrine or hormonal systems, but the hormones thus produced are carried by the bloodstream to the cells responsive to the relevant chemical messages. Hormones can also be ingested from external sources and in some cases, such as with diabetics where the body is unable to produce a sufficient supply of insulin, an external source is essential. The analogy will be the ability of organisational members to communicate with each other, and with both management and relevant external parties as part of their work or as a means to motivate and expedite performance.

Different types of information and communication include: information required for the processing of tasks; communication as part of the innate culture of the organisation; and information used during times of change in order to motivate or inform. At this stage it is important to evaluate the effectiveness of how the messages are distributed throughout the organisation instead of evaluating the validity of their sources or contents – this will be covered in Chapter Seven.

Similar to receiving bays and warehouses, responsible for the initiation of the distribution of material and supplies, the hearts of information distribution are the control centres of these processes, namely the post room, the telephone exchange and the IT department for electronic information distribution. By the end of the twentieth century, a significant amount of paper post was replaced by electronic mail, both within and external to organisations, adding this channel as an essential flow of information. These centres have the responsibility to ensure that the messages reach their correct target audiences, timely, securely and effectively.

Health concerns with information distribution cover the degree to which the transfer of information is successful, the extent of misdirected messages, and the existence of blockages in the sending and receiving of messages and information. Today the IT department plays a major role in this distribution process and concerns are often linked to the reliance of the organisation on electronic processing which can be disrupted due to a

limitation in access and the loss of systems or information when no
backups are available.

Possible Health Questions for the Distribution of People, Supplies and
Information:

- Are all departments being supplied with necessary people, tools and
  materials?

- How applicable and effective are customer delivery services?

- How accurate and effective is the internal information distribution to
  all departments and individuals in the organisation?

- Are contingency arrangements in place to address blockages or
  recover from incidents disrupting the distribution flow of resources
  and information through the organisation?

Diagnosing Logistics – The Process

Management control of logistics or resource management functions is
at local level and the pace of these activities is usually volume related.
Close links exist among functions such as the operating units and other
organisational functions requesting supplies; warehousing to check and
house incoming stock; distribution to ensure that the supplies are delivered
to the necessary functional areas; and management's influence on the
volumes, types and quality of procured resources. Analogous to the
sequence of diagnostic steps followed by medical practitioners, the high
risk areas of blood pressure, pulse rate and body-mass checks precede the
check on a healthy dietary lifestyle. Organisational health checks, using
the questions developed in the previous section, can be used to check the
effectiveness of procurement, inventory control and distribution as
presented in Figure 3.2.

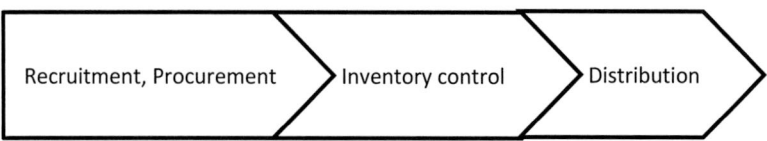

Figure 3.2   Diagnostic stages for logistics functions

Recruitment and Procurement

Diagnostic tools to ensure a healthy state of the recruitment and procurement functions within an organisation, analogous to a healthy diet, need to be able to determine whether the organisation's procurement is focusing on the resources essential for healthy operations.

Staffing levels need to reflect manpower resource plans and activities (overstaffing can be as inefficient as understaffing). It is especially necessary to be critical of under-staffing of key positions and functions versus possible over-staffing in the non-key areas, analogous to the inclusion of different types of protein in the diet to support the preferred lifestyle of an individual. It is therefore necessary to determine what is meant by key positions as part of the manpower plan by weighing the importance of positions and functions against each other both from the point of view of survival due to income generation, as well as survival based on the impact of not having the function available.

The provision of adequate resources can be detected by monitoring and analysing various staff productivity and staff satisfaction ratios, such as a staff retention rate or the analysis of reasons for staff dissatisfaction as observed in morale surveys. Senior management involvement usually lies in deciding about the staffing levels, types and quality of material to be obtained or, in the case of cost cutting, reductions in staffing or supplies.

Inventory Control

Diagnostics of healthy operations with respect to the inventory control of equipment, tools and supplies in organisations can be compared to the body-mass diagnosis to establish whether an individual is undernourished or overweight. This can be determined by checking the degree of overstocking or understocking of supplies, and measuring the stock turnaround to prevent ageing items from occupying valuable space.

The value of the stock can also be used as a measure of the importance of the relevant item to the organisation, although this may be biased to a measure about fitness and competitiveness rather than health. The stock turnaround can be refined by adding purchase dates to stock items. Measuring the effectiveness of the procurement and storage facilities in organisations offers the reassurance that purchases of essential material resources can be delivered to the relevant functions and departments.

Distribution

Diagnostics to ensure a healthy distribution function should focus on the existence of distribution channels for each type of resource, including up-to-date addresses of the recipient departments and individuals; speedy distribution of resources and information; and no observable blockages in the transfer of resources. Similar to the existence of an up-to-date staffing plan, networks need to be available for the distribution of electronic and manual information and post, as well as for the internal and external distribution of the supplies and resources.

The speed of distribution, both internal in the organisation as well as to the customers, can be measured by means of satisfaction surveys or more directly through selective time and material studies. Blockages in distribution channels can be detected from the productivity and satisfaction ratings at individual, departmental and customer levels.

Logistics, as one of the key survival functions focuses on the individual employee and department. It is essential to ensure that the manpower resources can meet operating requirements, and that each member of staff is provided with the necessary supplies, tools and funding to perform their allocated tasks. This affects the acquisition of suitable material and supplies, but also the assurance that internal distribution channels are operating effectively in order for the supplies to be delivered as and when required. It is, however, also necessary to address the actual workplace environment of the individual as will be discussed in the next section.

Workplace Maintenance

Analogous to the physiology of living organisms, the maintenance of the workplace environment of employees is another survival function within organisations. Unless the chemical and water balance in and around cells are maintained by eliminating excess water and harmful chemicals by the kidneys and waste products from the digestive system, there is a distinct danger of poisoning in the body which can become lethal.

The equivalent functions in organisations include the maintenance of an acceptable work environment such as utilities management including air quality, noise, lighting and temperature; cleaning and waste management within the organisation; and the maintenance of the buildings and equipment in the offices, field and plants. The need for workplace maintenance is essential for the health of office, operational and remote field-based workers.

Renal Chemical Filtering and Waste Systems[1]

The function of the renal system is to maintain the internal chemical balance (homeostasis) of intracellular, intercellular and blood plasma.

The renal system consists of the kidneys, the bladder and respective tubes. The kidneys filter the blood against excess water and chemicals to ensure that the correct water and chemical balance required by the plasma is maintained. The bladder acts as the receptacle of water and chemicals expelled by the kidney, which are stored until released externally as urine. The kidneys function in an automatic continuous process triggered by, and dependent on, the chemical composition of the blood it filters. The bladder is under voluntary control of the central nervous system to excrete urine.

The role of the colon, similar to the kidneys and bladder, is to accumulate waste from the digestive system, toxins from the liver and also to reabsorb some water and sodium.

Kidney failure can lead to an imbalance of the composition of blood and body fluids and could lead to death due to retained toxins or fluid overload. Poor performance or the inability to rid the body of the digestive waste could be improved by medical or surgical means, or by adopting a different life style, but if not treated can result in serious health concerns.

Healthy Workplace Environment

The functions of building/utility management, equipment maintenance, cleaning and waste management are good examples of what the French philosopher, Leriche, referred to in his statement that "health is life lived in the silence of the organs"[8].

Workplace maintenance, even more than the other survival functions, are usually performed in the background with very little attention to the effort involved. It is only when the functions are inadequate or not available that employees become disgruntled, succumb to illness or leave.

Building and Equipment Maintenance

The importance of building maintenance does not only lie in ensuring that the buildings of the organisation are safe for operation and habitation, but also that the image presented to the external environment is positive and healthy. From a diagnostic point of view, deterioration in the external and internal appearance and structural stability of a building is often an early health warning for organisations experiencing financial difficulty and therefore unable to retain expected or previous standards.

This function is also essential in the maintenance of equipment and tools required in service, manufacturing or production as well as office equipment such as photocopiers and computers. Equipment maintenance forms an essential part in the organisation's ability to offer a competitive service to its customers and breakdowns can result in a loss in revenue[9].

In order to be effective, health checks on building and equipment maintenance should not only identify and address problems and concerns, but must ensure that routine preventative maintenance is conducted according to regular schedules and checklists. This approach is widely used in organisations relying on safe and effectively operating equipment such as airlines and manufacturing companies, but is equally valid for all types of equipment and buildings. Health concerns of inadequate routine and problem solving maintenance can lead to serious safety issues within and external to the organisation, and therefore reduced revenue or image.

Utilities Management

Utilities management is part of the maintenance function which directly impacts employees in their daily work environment and covers the management of heating, ventilation, lighting and a healthy work environment. Inadequate functioning can lead to sickness and high levels of absenteeism in the workplace[10].

A healthy work environment is applicable to office personnel, but also to workers in factories and in remote and sometimes austere or hazardous environments. It is necessary for the organisation to acknowledge this and to compensate employees accordingly; attempt to improve the environmental conditions to acceptable levels; or to provide protective clothing and equipment. This is especially relevant for remote tasks to be performed such as prospecting in remote areas, charitable work or defence action in dangerous environments.

Issues with building, equipment and utilities maintenance directly affect the employees in the areas concerned and can lead to low morale, absenteeism, high turnover and at the most serious level, to injuries or fatalities. Common examples include: poorly maintained buildings and equipment resulting in accidents; inadequately maintained air conditioning systems increasing the sickness absenteeism; and hazardous work environments resulting in physical danger to employees. For the organisation the impact will be negative image, but more importantly, loss of staff or customers and potential claims for high compensation pay-outs.

Possible Health Questions for Workplace Maintenance:

- Are the buildings and essential equipment regularly maintained and checked according to set procedures?

- Are workplace environments, including utilities, regularly checked and improved to the standards required for the individual tasks?

- Are members of staff able to perform their tasks without undue stress or potential damage to their health and wellbeing?

Cleaning and Waste Management

Part of maintaining an acceptable work environment for employees lies in the removal and maintenance of waste material from offices, manufacturing plants, warehouses and other areas of operation. Again, it is one of the 'invisible' functions, often executed at times when no one is around, and not appreciated unless there are signs of deterioration in the workplace or external environments. The function consists of two parts analogous to the filtering function of the kidneys and digestive tract, and the waste storage and disposal functions of the bladder or colon; namely the internally focused function of cleaning and the external focus of waste management.

Cleaning

Cleaning is one of the functions which in today's competitive world is often regarded as 'non-core' and therefore given less attention, or is outsourced if funds are required for revenue generating functions of sales, service or manufacturing. While outsourcing to specialist cleaning organisations may offer better services at the outset, similar to the use of specialist accountancy firms for smaller companies, the end result may not be as positive as originally expected. The organisation becomes reliant on the quality and culture of the service provider, and subject to unconstrained increases in fees unless protected by initial service contracts. Whether the function is performed in-house, or outsourced, health checks need to include the effectiveness of the function from the point of view of the members in the various affected departments.

Activities involved in the cleaning function are, however, not only restricted to the tasks performed by cleaning staff, but also refer to a culture of a tidy and clean work environment as observed by all personnel. Lax and untidy practices can lead to health and safety issues detrimental to staff or customers of the organisation.

Waste Management

Waste management does not only affect the internal operation of the organisation, but directly impacts its external environment. The health of this function therefore also addresses ecological concerns.

Wastage of reusable material is not always cost effective for the organisation and may reduce the availability of these resources in the future, leading to higher costs. Examples of internal recycling of material can be detected in office supplies where old folders are discarded instead of being reused, but conversely also in warehouses where redundant stock is still retained instead of being recycled to specialist organisations.

Accidental or negligent disposal of waste material or excess resources can impact and endanger the environment. This is especially relevant to mining, chemical and other similar organisations where a lapse in waste management can contaminate the surrounding air, water or soil. With an ever increasing focus by pressure groups on environmental issues, this aspect of healthy operation is not only important for the organisation alone, but is contributing to a safer and sustainable environment for all.

Possible Health Questions for Cleaning and Waste Management:

- Is the level of cleanliness and order in the workplace meeting standards set for health and suitable for task performance?

- Is the organisation compliant with environmental health regulations applicable to organisational or industry waste?

Diagnosing the Workplace – The Process

Workplace maintenance functions, including cleaning and waste management, similar to the other internal survival functions, operate under local control and on a routine or incident-driven basis. Because of this local control, the functions are often outsourced to external specialist organisations. This may be acceptable but the performance of the outsourced organisation has to be monitored to the same extent as it is for internal operating personnel.

It is easier to diagnose the health of these functions by observing the outcome and effect of their activities on internal and external parties. This can be achieved by following the observation steps presented in Figure 3.3, analogous to the sequence of diagnostic steps followed by medical practitioners.

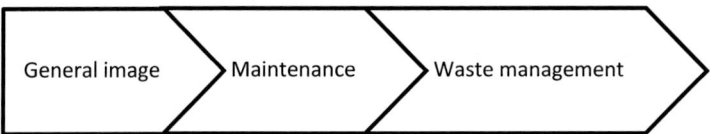

Figure 3.3   Diagnostic stages for workplace maintenance functions

Diagnostics based on image of the buildings, structures and operating environment to staff and customers would depend on the type of organisation and should be performed by objective third parties such as professional inspectors, internal walk-around or satisfaction surveys. Observers from the public or an internal member from a different part of the organisation are in a better position to pinpoint areas of concern for further attention or detect deteriorating trends. Measuring the morale, absenteeism and turnover of staff offers additional indicators of increased organisational health issues which could have been caused by poor utility management or unhealthy conditions of the workplace environment.

With respect to maintenance, the diagnosis should focus on the availability and execution of routine maintenance and management of the buildings, utilities, equipment and machinery; the scope and regularity thereof; recording and addressing of identified faults or problem areas; as well as the history and age of the equipment compared to the relevance of changing technologies. Since the results of poor maintenance and ineffective utility provision can be disastrous to the organisation, detection of preventative maintenance and lessons learnt from earlier concerns are important to guard against future incidents.

Diagnostic tools with respect to waste management compliance include the availability and monitoring of processes related to the recycling and disposal of production and operational waste material. It is essential for the organisation to meet regulatory requirements as well as concerns and complaints with respect to malpractices in waste management. These concerns and complaints voiced by external pressure groups or internal whistle-blowers must be monitored and acted upon. Recording of trends with respect to the image generated by workplace management can either be presented as a series of reports on findings, or a trend generated by ratios such as the number of relevant image complaints as a percentage of the total of complaints received from the source.

Workplace maintenance, as the third survival function directly aimed at supporting each of the members of the organisation, is the silent support function which is only noticed when not operating at acceptable levels. It includes the important maintenance of essential equipment and workplace utilities as well as cleaning and waste management. Identification of areas of concern or deterioration of the practices over time can impact the internal and external image, staff morale, and result in losses as well as fines or payment of claims to employees, customers or the public.

Case Study

A case study of a young retail business, as a franchisee member of a chain of stores, was selected to demonstrate the application of health checks, similar to clinical health checks performed by medical practitioners. Background to the case study is presented as shaded inserts in each chapter, and therefore repeated in this chapter. This is followed by additional diagnostic findings of the survival support functions of finance and accounting, logistics and workplace maintenance.

In the field of medicine the recommendation is to offer visibility of past concerns, history and trends to assist practitioners in guiding the prognosis of the state of health of the patient. For the case study, the information and diagnostic findings are similarly presented by using the 'dashboard' approach to display information at a summary level, supported by the drill-down evidence-based detail[11].

This is not an uncommon approach for management information presentations since it offers clear links to various sources of the information, and was therefore selected for the case study data analysis and presentation. At the top level, the summary information may, for instance, only present warnings of the severity of health diagnostic findings. This can be quickly interpreted and points to the functional areas requiring further in-depth investigations. The drill-down facility must contain the necessary detailed reports, performance ratios or survey results supporting the summary warning flags. The type and level of diagnostic information should be customised for each organisation using the simplistic views, as presented by the case study, as an example of possible dials.

CASE STUDY – THE CORNER SHOP

An independent retail franchise grocery store and bakery, referred to as The Corner Shop, is part of a larger chain. Although the franchisee has the freedom to structure and run the business independently, the holding company is expecting a regular fee from the store as a member of its chain and requires the store to maintain a minimum set of standards. In return, the store owners can use the preferential rates for stock purchases negotiated for the chain and receive advisory assistance from the holding company. The store is in a favourable location in the main street of the town, conveniently situated for a wide range of customers, and the owners have had previous experience and knowledge of retail, finance and accountancy.

The store has been operating for five years. During the first two years it delivered record turnover and profits to the extent that the business was nominated as the 'winning' store in the chain. The customer base was classified as predominantly upper middle-class and the overall image of the store was vibrant and welcoming. The owners went out of their way to satisfy customer needs, for instance, by offering a type of bread made from a special recipe, sought after by many of the local hotels and restaurants, and by ordering and stocking special items on request.

During the third year, the owners decided to expand and diversify by acquiring a butcher shop in the adjacent town. The butchery was at the point of closing and they managed to get it at a reasonable price, including commitments of rental agreements undertaken by the previous owners. They managed to extend their bank loan to finance the deal and one of the owners is spending most of his time running the butchery. The combination of the additional workload for the owners together with mounting repayment burdens of interest and earlier stock purchases are making it difficult to maintain the previous standards of operation. The image of the store and service to the customers has been dropping and resulted in a loss of customers and sales.

The health check for the business will be developed in Chapters Three to Eight and presented as it unfolds. The summary diagnosis for each functional category is presented as one of the 'dials' on the health information dashboard for the business as shown in Table 3.1 for the survival category of functions. Each function is rated in the middle column as explained in the narrative section of the table, followed by summary comments of the findings and diagnostic results.

Expanded tables are offered as drill-down options on the dashboard and presented in Tables 3.2 to 3.4. In reality, these drill-down information tables should be further expanded by supporting evidence of incidents, measures and reports.

Summary Dial of the Survival Functions of the Business		
Narrative of Rating Indicators: First indicator (findings): ○ = acceptable; ◉ = unacceptable; ● = serious Second indicator (trend): ↓ = deteriorating; ↑ = improving; no arrow = unchanged Third indicator (impact): W = warning; S = serious; blank = acceptable		
Survival Functions	**Rating**	**Comments**
Finance and Accounting	● ↓S	Acceptable procedures, but serious debt problems
Logistics	● ↓W	Problems in stock replenishment and distribution due to financial restrictions
Workplace Maintenance	◉ ↓W	Higher absenteeism rate and reduction in image of store to customers

Table 3.1   Survival functions summary diagnosis

The summary diagnosis of the health of the survival functions, presented in Table 3.1, confirms the serious concerns in the finance and accounting category, impacting the logistics and workplace maintenance functions. Table 3.2 expands on the finance and accounting functions.

Finance and Accounting Performance History			
Narrative of Flag: W = warning; S = serious; blank = acceptable			
Evidence of Events, Reports	**Date**	**Flag**	**Comments**
Financial Ratios -Financial ratios	Jun 05	S	Serious downwards trends
Accounting Practices -Regulatory compliant	Jun 05		Compliant
Reporting -Regulatory reports -Internal financial reports	Jun 05 Feb 03	W	Informal, mostly discussions
Budgeting -As part of initial plan	Apr 01	S	Initial budget only

Table 3.2   Finance and accounting functions

The most serious financial problem in Table 3.2 is the use of loans to finance the running and expansion of the business. This situation can be presented in a further drill-down to the five year trend of the financial ratios presented in Figure 3.4. The chart of the ratios indicates a slow deterioration in revenue and profitability from the third year, but then a serious downwards trend after the acquisition of the butcher shop in year four.

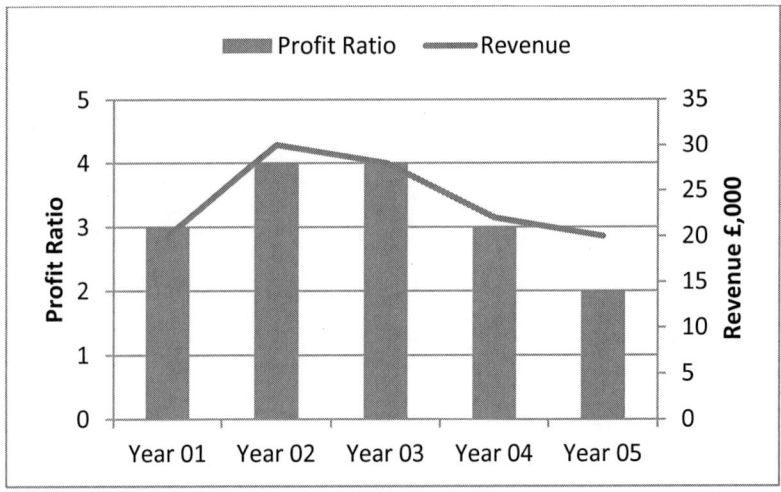

Figure 3.4   Trend analysis of the financial information

However, other deteriorating health indicators were also observed (although not presented here). The tight cash flow ratio pointed to the practice to pay yesterday's debt with today's reduced income and by increasing the loans based on tomorrow's over-optimistic sales forecasts. This was made worse by interpreting the planned product purchases and general mark-up percentage as future anticipated profit instead of calculating the actual profit from the sales per product type.

In the case study, the survival functions of logistics were also affected by the problems. Detailed diagnostic findings of these functions are presented in Table 3.3.

With respect to distribution, the service was generally acceptable except for a deteriorating personal delivery service to the affluent customers. Initial arrangements with some of the restaurants and hotels for personal delivery proved to be too expensive and had to be dropped, thus losing some of these customers.

Logistics Performance History			
Narrative of Flag: W = warning; S = serious; blank = acceptable			
Evidence of Events, Issues, Reports	**Date** Yr 0-5	**Flag**	**Comments**
Distribution Channels -Knowledge of addresses	Jul 05		Informal but acceptable
Distribution Blockages -Meeting staff needs -Meeting customer needs	Jul 05	W	Acceptable Deteriorating
Stock Levels -Old stock -Undersupplied	Jul 05	W S	Lack of product level restocking is becoming serious
Supplies and Material -Stock in shops -Supplies to workers	Sep 05	S	Unacceptably low Reasonable
Staffing Levels/Recruitment -Operator levels -Management/supervisors	Jul 05	W	Acceptable Low, burden on owners

Table 3.3 Logistics functions

The concerns of inadequate stock had a negative impact on the business image and staff morale. Initially, the store was well stocked and frequented by an affluent class of customer. They requested the stocking of certain high cost products. However, the stock control and sales systems did not gather, record and analyse purchases and sales at product level. It became difficult to identify fast-selling and profitable products which could offer a sustainable revenue stream and the best profit ratios. The result was that the monthly discount purchases through the franchise chain addressed the wrong type of product, thus replenishment was reduced and the shelves could not be fully stocked. This presented a poor image and the more affluent customers turned away.

Early expansion of the business, by adding an off-site butchery, resulted in unnecessary stretching of management time and effort. Some of the regular management functions had to be reduced, especially the monitoring of early warning signs of concern by staff and customers.

A detailed history and findings of concerns in the workplace are presented in Table 3.4.

Workplace Maintenance Performance History			
Narrative of Flag: W = warning; S = serious; blank = acceptable			
Evidence of Events, Issues, Reports	**Date** Yr 0-5	**Flag**	**Comments**
Image -Store image from customers	Jul 05	S	Deteriorating to serious
Morale and Health -Staff survey	Jul 05	W	Deteriorating
Workplace Maintenance - Building/equipment	Jul 05		Low priority
- Utility management	Yr 04	W	Bakery unacceptably hot – checked air conditioning

Table 3.4   Workplace maintenance functions

While the image of the building was still acceptable, the image inside the store and offices reflected a reduced focus on inventory control, cleaning and waste management. The impact on staff may not yet have been visible, but the initial target market of customers already moved their custom to competitors. The other area identified as a potential future concern is the irregular maintenance of the equipment in the bakery and butchery. Most of the equipment was still relatively new and the current status was therefore acceptable. However, this would not have lasted much longer.

The objective of the book is not to recommend cures for health concerns of organisations, but to offer means towards early diagnostics which can then be followed on with suitable advice on how to address or prevent serious consequences. In this case study the diagnostics of the survival functions in Table 3.1 showed that although the financial status of the business is still the most serious concern, early remedial steps could have been taken, or can be addressed, if the management:

- Implement and heed a meaningful budgeting and stock control system.

- Desisted from early expansion of the business and focus more on debt reduction.
- Pick up early warning signs of the loss of affluent customers and either woo them back or deliberately decide to refocus the target market.
- Pay more attention to the image of the store, both internally and externally to suit the target market and staff.

This case study focuses on a young start-up organisation, the type that generally has the most serious health problems. However, similar concerns can also affect mature organisations. These organisations could find that they become complacent and are expecting the current growth rate to continue indefinitely, or that their procedures and warning systems have become ineffective and insensitive to early warning signals of potential concerns.

Conclusion

In this chapter, the focus was on the survival functions within an organisation. Although often ignored in the struggle for competitive excellence, it showed how diagnostics can help to identify and address areas requiring correction, or change attention in order to prevent or delay future serious concerns for the organisation.

The survival functions were identified as inwardly-focused, therefore concerned with enabling individual members of staff to effectively execute their committed tasks. Organisational health problems in this category will affect staff directly, customers indirectly and could lead to operational malfunctioning as well as problems affecting the image and competitiveness of the organisation.

Chapter Four addresses the protection, safety and healing functions within organisations. In these cases the focus of the functions are on the protection of the organisation as a whole against unwanted interference from external influences.

Notes

1. Whole sections are dedicated to the physiology of the vital functions of respiration (Section VII), gastrointestinal systems (Section V), cardiovascular systems (Section VI) and renal functioning (Section VIII) in the standard handbook of: Barrett, K.E., Barman, S.M., Boitano, S. and Brooks, H.L.

(2010). *Ganong's Review of Medical Physiology*, 23rd ed. McGrawHill Medical, New York.

2. Various manuals and reference books exist on accounting concepts and practices. The concepts are also introduced in management literature. References used in this respect are: Drury, C. (2005). *Accounting for Business Decisions*, London: International Thompson Business Press; and Smith M. (2007). *Fundamentals of Management*, Maidenhead: McGraw-Hill Education.

3. Companies folding due to cash flow problems are often start-up companies, but could be any company finding itself in serious liquidity situation. See: Amis, M. *Small Business Management*, referenced in http://usgovinfo.about.com/od/smallbusiness/ accessed in 2011; Sigurjonsson, T.O. (2010). The Icelandic Bank Collapse: Challenges to Governance and Risk Management. *Corporate Governance*. Vol.10, No. 1, pp. 33-45.

4. Internal fraudulent transactions such as money laundering can have serious consequences. Examples include unauthorised speculative trading by individuals such as Leeson, resulting in the collapse of Barings Bank: Report of the Board of Banking Supervision Inquiry into the Circumstances of the Collapse of Barings, 18 July 1995, *The Bank of England Report*, accessed on www.numa.com

5. Finance and accounting textbooks, including financial ratios, include: Ryan, B. (2008). *Finance and Accounting for Business*, 2nd ed. Thomson Learning; Smith, M. (2007) *Fundamentals of Management*, Maidenhead, McGraw-Hill Education, pp. 189-194; Murphy, J.J. (1999). *Technical Analysis of Financial Markets*. New York Institute of Finance.

6. Various references can be provided on logistics, recruitment and procurement, including: Rushton, A., Croucher, P. and Baker, P. (2010). *The Handbook of Logistics and Distribution Management*, 4th ed. Kogan Page Limited, London; Smith, M. (2007). *Fundamentals of Management*, McGraw-Hill Education, Maidenhead, pp. 250-260; Gilliland, S.W. (1993) The Perceived Fairness of Selection Systems: An Organisational Justice Perspective. *Academy of Management Review*, Vol. 18, pp. 694-734; Batty, J. (1969). *Industrial Administration and Management*, MacDonald and Evans Ltd. London.

7. Inventory control forms an important part of warehousing and storage controls for both manufacturing as well as office supplies as identified in: Waters, D. (1992). *Inventory Control and Management*, John Wiley and Sons. The impact of disaster on supply chains was addressed in. http://www.forbes.com/sites/ciocentral/2012/03/13/japan-one-year-later-the-long-view-on-tech-supply-chains/

8. Leriche, a French philosopher as cited in Canguilhem, G. (2007). *The Normal and the Pathological*. Fifth Printing, Zone Books, New York, p.91.

9. Examples of damaging or disastrous incidents due to poor or inadequate maintenance include: McGingy, S. (2008). *Fire in the Night: The Piper Alpha Disaster*, MacMillan; Paté-Cornell, M.E. (1993). Learning from the Piper-Alpha Accident: A Postmortem Analysis of Technical and Organizational Factors. *Risk Analysis*, Vol.13, No. 2; Yu,T., Insead, M.S., Lester, R.H. (2008). Misery Loves Company: The Spread of Negative Impacts Resulting from an

Organizational Crisis. *Academy of Management Review*. Vol. 33, No. 2, pp. 452-472.

10. An example of work environment contributing to health problems of staff was examined by Taylor, P., Baldry, C., Bain, P., Ellis V. (2003). 'A Unique Working Environment': Health, Sickness and Absence Management in UK Call Centres. *Work Employment Society*. Vol. 17, pp. 435-458.

11. References to the use of dashboard displays for information are available from: Eckerson, W.W. (2011). *Performance Dashboards: Measuring, Monitoring and Managing your Business*. Second Edition. John Wiley & Sons, Hoboken, NJ.

CHAPTER FOUR

PROTECTION FUNCTIONS

Without healthy protection functions an organisation can be killed.

Protection functions, analogous to the skin or exoskeleton, as well as the immune systems of living organisms, protect the organisation from unwanted external intrusion and irregular internal practices; and include:

Access Control

Security, Regulatory and Ethical Compliance

Health, Safety and Wellbeing

In Chapter Three, the health diagnostics focused on the survival functions of finance, logistics and the workplace environment, concerned with processes to ensure that each member, and therefore the organisation as a whole, can operate effectively and survive. Organisations, however, also require protection against external intrusion as demonstrated by the presence of the exoskeleton, skin and membranes of organisms, and against unacceptable internal practices, analogous to the immune system of an organism. However, should damage occur, an element of damage control and attention to the healing process of individuals and functions is also important, analogous to the presence and action of blood platelets and white blood cells in organisms.

Chapter Four addresses how organisations can ensure that their protection functions are healthy. For each function a brief reference is provided to its analogous physiological system in the human body, followed by its functioning in organisations and a set of diagnostics to assist management in measuring the health of these functions. The references to physiology for each function are presented as shaded boxed inserts and may be ignored as they are not essential in clarifying the organisational diagnostics. The objective of this additional information is merely to enhance the arguments.

Access Control

Access security and control functions operate in the background and are invisible until a breach in the control causes concern or damage to the organisation. The main objective of this function is to operate as the first line of defence to prevent external people or material entering the organisation without approval or authorisation. The identification of external or 'non-self' influences was discussed in Chapter One as anyone or anything that does not belong to the organisation or is in a contractual arrangement to assist the organisation in its daily operations[1].

Skin and Membrane Barriers for Protection[1]

The skin and the membranes in the various systems, such as the gastrointestinal and respiratory systems, function as an initial protective shield against foreign material. The skin forms a non-permeable shield whereas more permeable membranes may allow foreign bodies to be filtered by the lymphatic nodes, such as the tonsils in the throat. The lymph nodes and cells in the throat and nose detect the presence of external harmful material.

Response to the identification of potentially harmful material is often automatic by means of coughing to remove material from the lungs and airways, or vomiting to remove dangerous detected or ingested material. However, overactive sensitivity can lead to allergies such as asthma, hayfever or intolerance to certain types of nutrient.

The analogy of access control in regards to living organisms is the existence of the skin, exoskeleton and membranes in blocking external entrances or guarding against damage to the organism, together with the lymphatic system in the nose, throat and intestine which reacts to unwanted material in air or food. Access control in organisations therefore refers to the physical protection and security of premises, equipment, people, supplies and information.

Physical Security and Protection

Most organisations require visible, physical security protection of their buildings, plant and equipment. This first line of protection is provided by security guards at the entrance of office buildings; boundary protection of premises containing accessible equipment or structures; or if serious protection is not required, access protection by means of locked premises and access cards to authorised personnel. Organisations that may not require visible premises protection in today's environment are the virtual organisations – operating mainly online – as marketing or software service providers. These organisations will still require protection of electronic equipment, but are likely to be more focused on the protection of information rather than equipment.

Physical security protects against manmade threats of theft, vandalism, strikes and riots; and natural threats such as fire, hurricanes and earthquakes which can cause damage to assets. Typical and frequent examples of theft and vandalism occur on building sites with damage and loss to supplies or equipment, or damage to premises and assets by extremist or pressure groups[2]. Protection against premises and people due to natural disasters was well demonstrated in the damage caused by the tsunami in Japan in 2011 where the protection plans of the nuclear plant did not expect the excessive water damage to the backup energy cooling system, causing the plant to close down.

Similar to survival functions, the function of physical security and protection operates locally and is often regarded as a necessary but specialised non-core function and therefore suitable to be outsourced. However, it is necessary to ensure that there is adequate compatibility between the organisational objectives and the services offered by the outsourced organisation.

To reduce the possibility of damage and loss of assets, the healthy operation of the physical security function should be checked for suitable protection and prevention processes against potential damage and the effective operation of the staff. Lessons from previous incidents should form part of future precautionary steps in the protection process.

Possible Health Questions for Physical Protection:

- How well are the physical assets, including people on remote sites, protected against wilful or accidental damage?

- Have the risks of natural disasters been evaluated with plans to protect or for damage limitation after the event?

- Have there been incidents of physical damage in the past, how were the incidents handled and what lessons were learnt?

People and Supplies

Analogous to the lymphatic protection in the nose and mouth, the protection function in organisations prevent the access of unauthorised people and supplies into the organisation by means of reception controls. Many office buildings have reception desks for visitors and locked access to inner offices, while trained security staff could be called to receiving bays of supplies, goods and mail in order to inspect suspicious individuals or articles.

Whereas the function of physical security is often outsourced, the access control of people and supplies may form part of the internal security function or even be allocated to administrative personnel, such as a receptionist. Most of the time this will not cause a problem as the probability of allowing dangerous or unwanted persons or supplies into the organisation is low. However, there are instances in which this is not true anymore. A key requirement of access security personnel has become the ability to identify danger signals in the attitude of individuals, or the appearance of material, in addition to the physical and background checks required before allowing them access to the organisation.

This level of access control is already visible in some vulnerable public places, including shopping centres, individual shops, gatherings or the screening of passengers before boarding their flights. However, overzealousness can also be crippling to organisations, analogous to the existence of allergies. Undue access restrictions can result in the isolation of the organisation or paranoia among staff.

Possible Health Questions for People and Supply Access Controls:

- How easy is it for an outsider to enter the operating premises of the organisation, especially when in possession of harmful material or with the intention to inflict damage?

- Are regular checks performed to ensure that the preventative procedures are effective and operating as required?

- How are incidents recorded, acted upon and analysed for future improvements?

Access to Information

The third area of access control, namely access to information, is becoming more relevant with the ever-increasing use of electronic means to process, access and distribute data and information, whether from internal databases or via the internet.

This method of access control directly addresses the availability of electronic firewalls to protect internal email networks, intranets and databases from unauthorised access. It also includes: the monitoring of the access of internal staff to unauthorised sources; the sending of unauthorised messages and information to external destinations; and backup of official databases to ensure adequate recovery in case of loss of data. The responsibility of the implementation and monitoring of this function usually falls to either the IT department or the technical personnel in the security department.

Examples of serious issues arising from the hacking of systems, even if firewall-protected, include fraudulent access to personal information on government and private databases such as banking records and access to voicemail, emails and electronic correspondence. An opposing action to hacking could also cause serious concerns and issues to organisations, such as the blocking of electronic access to organisational websites by numerous deliberate and often automatic access requests or spam.

Access to information also includes surface mail information and requires protective inspection of letters or other external information sources in addition to internet access. Information access security diagnostics should take into consideration the checking of correspondence; the level of firewall access controls; the reliability of the protective systems; and the balance between too much or too little controls.

Possible Health Questions for Data and Information Access Controls:

- How easy is it to access sensitive organisational data, information or messages?

- Is the organisation vulnerable to external blockage or interference with access to its websites or genuine correspondence with the organisation?

- Are backups produced of essential data, stored off-site or on alternative sites to cloud servers, and restoration practiced regularly?

Security, Regulatory and Ethical Compliance

Living organisms have immune systems to detect and deal with unwanted or damaging internal action that can cause harm to their existence. This immune system can be innate as part of a natural inborn defence mechanism; developed within the body as an adaptive defence after earlier attacks; or imposed by means of immunisation programmes initiated from external sources.

Over the past century awareness developed within organisations for the need to reinforce internal control and security systems. While some organisations have internal controls and ethical policies which developed as part of their normal culture, various government regulations were introduced to promote protection of individuals and processes within the organisations, and therefore the organisations themselves from harmful practices.

Immune System[1]

The immune system mainly acts against any foreign intervention by organisms already in the body. It includes lymph nodes, the spleen and free-floating lymphocytes in the blood. The lymphocytes, or white blood cells, in the bloodstream detect and react to foreign or 'non-self' material in the body often responsible for infection, or introduced after grafts or transplants. They respond to these foreign pathogens by attacking and destroying them and by building up antibodies as a memory of the intruding organism, in readiness for future attacks.

Although the control is local and independent from the central nervous controls, the immune reaction in the body can be enhanced by deliberate action of immunisation or desensitisation.

Adaptive immunity can, however, result in hypersensitivity and allergies or, in extreme cases result in the immune cells attacking the normal cells, such as in autoimmune diseases like rheumatoid arthritis.

This section explores the processes and diagnostic tools that can be used to determine the degree to which an organisation is protected by the imposed and innate controls and regulations, and to what extent the organisation is compliant with these controls. As indicated in the section heading, protection will be discussed as internal security; audit, legal and regulatory compliance imposed on the organisation; and ethical policies or other guidelines for morally acceptable processing.

Internal Security

Not everyone in the organisation can be trusted as loyal and ethical, and one of the roles of internal security is to monitor, control and police internal processes and the conduct of individuals within the organisation.

Analogous to the innate and adaptive immune systems in the body, internal security operates independently from senior management interference. They execute their monitoring and control tasks in line with the cultural and imposed operating restrictions for the organisation. This involves internal access controls to areas of operation such as: research laboratories for unauthorised personnel; restrictive access to information for personnel without a 'need to know'; and the identification of individuals with malicious intent to damage or defraud the organisation. Examples of internal security breaches or fraudulent activities by members of organisations include the theft or fraudulent handling of funds by individuals or the leaking of trade secret information by members of staff to external interested parties.

It is important to align the security controls with the culture, not to be overzealous in their application, and to be sensitive to internal whistle-blowers and staff complaining about individual activities or localised processes. These warning signals should be heeded rather than suppressed and can prevent external damage to the status and image of the organisation, for example, warnings about mistreatment of patients in care homes. In most of these cases the problems could be addressed internally before becoming serious industry concerns.

From a health point of view it is necessary to determine the underlying culture with respect to internal security, and the cover offered by internal security functions and processes in order to maintain and, if necessary, enhance the innate standard of security in the organisation.

Possible Health Questions for Internal Security:

- Are there sufficient access and process restrictions and protection in place for sensitive areas in the organisation?

- Does the organisation have an escalating process for security complaints and are the complaints taken seriously?

- Were lessons learnt and changes made from previous incidents?

Audit Controls

Auditors are trained as professionals, not only in the principles of accounting and finance, but also on how to identify irregular accounting practices and highlight warnings about areas of concern. Although the audit checks can be compared to other compliance controls, this function has been established and accepted as essential since the early part of the twentieth century. This endorses the importance of the accounting function, analogous to the respiratory system in living organisms, to the survival of the organisation. It furthermore highlights potential damage to parties internal and external to the organisation affected by unacceptable or illegal financial activities and became one of the early organisational functions to be legally regulated, analogous to the introduction of vaccination procedures against illnesses such as tuberculosis.

Small businesses usually do not have to present externally audited financial reports to the department of Inland Revenue or the Companies House in the UK. It is accepted that the revenue and profit may be too small to warrant expensive external audits and the acceptance of risk by the owners or directors of the company would suffice. While this enables small and young start-up companies some financial flexibility to grow, it can result in these organisations implementing only basic ineffective accounting practices[3], as discussed in Chapter Three. Help from accounting professionals or auditors to set up, operate, interpret and understand the financial status of the business can only benefit these organisations.

Unlike young, inexperienced organisations that may need protection against poor accounting practices, experienced and larger organisations could also be vulnerable to non-standard or fraudulent accounting practices. For these larger organisations audits are legal requirements, but the auditing firm may be one of the reasons for potential damage to the organisation. Court cases in which auditing firms have been accused of failing to meet the standards of professional interpretation of the accounting practices and the accurate presentation of the financial status of organisations are not totally uncommon[4].

The implementation of audit controls, adherence to the principles of accounting and regular checks by auditors and accountants, as well as the interpretation and attention of management to the warning signs in these reports, are important diagnostic tools for organisations to prevent potential pit-falls and serious financial and image concerns.

Possible Health Questions for Audit Controls:

- Does the organisation comply with the legal accounting principles and procedures required by the government of the country of operation?

- Are the accounting practices and results checked by external auditors, even if not required by law?

- Are concerns raised by audit reports heeded and improvements introduced?

Legal and Regulatory Compliance

Although audit control is one of the legal requirements for businesses above a set minimum revenue threshold, there are more legal and regulatory controls that have been introduced to protect organisations from internal 'malfunctioning' that can have a negative impact either on the business or on external parties. Laws affecting corporations date back to the sixteenth century, initially to protect owners and shareholders against losses but also to protect employees, consumers, suppliers and the public at large against exploitation by organisations. Countries have developed their own sets of business laws with some attempt towards standardisation, and larger organisations have internal legal departments to ensure that the organisation operates within the limits of the laws and global outreach of its country of registration. Smaller organisations either have access to legal advice and support from external institutions, or else have to ensure that they operate legally.

Examples include the regulations covering human rights, consumer protection, data protection and various employment regulations. While non-compliance to some of these regulations is not necessarily illegal, damage could be inflicted by pressure groups to the image of, for instance, companies outsourcing to organisations in countries who are not signatories to the various acts, or not compliant, and therefore not adhering to minimal standards.

Similar to the diagnosis of immune systems in living organisms, the methods to diagnose organisations on their legal and regulatory compliance will depend on the size, age and type of organisation. Smaller organisations have some flexibility and are offered concessions, such as exemption from value added tax, or unnecessary red-tape in filing audited accounts and company reports. Similarly, the regulations imposed by the

Human Rights or Data Protection regulatory bodies will differ depending on the type of business or country. Once a healthy set of legal and regulatory requirements have been established, it will be necessary to conduct regular checks on the degree of compliance by the organisation.

The same extent to which non-compliance can lead to high fines and damage to the image of the organisation, over-zealous internal policing of unnecessary regulations can limit the operational flexibility of the organisation. A healthy balance should be maintained.

Possible Health Questions to Consider for Regulatory Compliance:

- Is the organisation aware of the laws and regulations applicable to it, and the consequences of non-compliance?

- How compliant is the organisation to these regulations?

- Have there been inspections from regulatory bodies, and if so, what were their conclusions and the response to them?

Operating Ethically

Organisations have a legal standing and responsibility to comply with the imposed laws and regulations of the countries in which they operate. However, an accepted concept is that since organisations represent a community of individuals, it does not have a moral judgement as such and could therefore not be held responsible for acting immorally. This is being contradicted by opposing views that organisations have a responsibility to act morally towards all its stakeholders, including owners, employees, customers, suppliers, the community within which it operates and the environment affected by organisational processes. Only if an organisation can meet the needs of all of these parties can it be accepted as operating ethically as well as legally and commercially[5].

Ethics in business is based on the equal and fair treatment of internal members of the organisation. This includes employment equality based on the experience or suitability of individuals to perform their allocated tasks, regardless of their inborn characteristics of race and sex, or their age. This aspect of ethics is already incorporated in the Human Rights regulations of most developed countries and the organisations operating in the countries who signed up to these regulations therefore have to comply. Non-compliance may not yet mean illegal, but can induce fines and affect the image of the organisation.

Ethics in business is also based on the fair treatment of external stakeholders in business transactions such as shareholders, suppliers, customers and communities. Pressure groups, for instance, have been campaigning against the negative impact on local communities by major oil producers in parts of Africa or spills by chemical manufacturing companies. Today more organisations are moving towards ethical practices, including fair and free trade transactions with their suppliers and support for their local communities. Although ethical processing is still more of a lifestyle than an organisational health issue, organisations should ask themselves whether a move towards ethical functioning can improve their business operations and image.

Diagnostic measures should address the overall impact on the business of operating ethically from a legal, regulatory as well as an ethical point of view, and then determine the extent to which the organisation is actually living up to its own published policy statements on ethical behaviour.

Possible Health Questions for Operating Ethically:

- What is the organisation's publicly known position on the various ethical issues which could be applicable to it?

- Does the internal culture, value set and operating processes support the published ethical stance of the organisation, or present a 'words only' attitude?

Health, Safety and Wellbeing

While protection functions of access control, security and internal compliance will attempt to prevent unwanted access and deal with internal security and non-compliance incidents, it is as important to ensure that in the event of damage, the organisation can deal with the situation and ensure restoration of healthy operations. In living organisms these functions are achieved with the assistance of various white blood cells and the platelets in the bloodstream. Whereas the white blood cells or lymphocytes attack unwanted elements in the blood or body, they also assist in the healing process of inflamed and damaged tissue. The platelets on the other hand cause blood clotting to prevent unnecessary or excess blood loss after damage.

White Blood Cells and Platelets[1]

The immune system includes free-floating white blood cells or lymphocytes in the blood to assist with the healing process of damaged tissue. This is done by increasing the temperature around the area, secreting chemicals to assist cell healing and removing damaged cells in the tissue. The defence mechanisms also include blood platelets which will form a mesh to facilitate blood clotting in the case of damage leading to the loss of blood and its contents.

The lymphocytes and platelets are produced by the bone marrow and operate independently of the central nervous system. A lack of certain chemical elements in these cells can result in the body having a reduced ability to fight off damage to tissue or blood clotting. This can be observed in haemophiliacs and persons with low or slow healing ability such as diabetics.

Immunity can, however, also result in hypersensitivity or, in extreme cases result in the immune cells attacking the normal cells, such as in autoimmune diseases like rheumatoid arthritis.

Within organisations the equivalent functions will be health and safety as a preventative function, and the responsibility of a human resources department to address staff benefits and wellbeing both in general and during times of sickness or trauma. These functions are again preventative by protecting individuals in their workplace environment. At the same time, however, the organisation has to ensure that it has planned for, or implemented some means of damage control and limitation if damage has occurred to its people, physical assets or image, but more importantly to the morale and health of the staff.

Health and Safety

In most countries and organisations concern for the health and safety of the employees has become a regulatory requirement determined by bodies such as the Occupational Safety and Health Administration (OSHA) in the United States or the Health and Safety Executive (HSE) in the UK. Organisations are expected to implement and comply with the applicable regulations before receiving relevant certificates of safety. The focus is therefore on risk evaluation, the implementation of the regulations and preventative activities to address areas of risk and the reporting of incidents and accidents to the regulatory bodies.

However, being in possession of a certificate from the regulatory body does not necessarily mean that the organisation is operating safely and healthily with respect to its people, the work processes and the work environment. The danger of underreporting health and safety incidents and therefore presenting a false picture of the health situation in the organisation paints a picture of organisational non-commitment to the health and safety of its employees which could result in accidents within the workplace[6]. The opposite is also observable. An over-emphasis on health and safety regulations can, for instance, result in schools not wanting to take any risks with the result that the children miss out on school trips; playgrounds become more restrictive; and students have less chance of participating in contact sport.

From a diagnostic point of view the status of the health and safety function should be diagnosed by: identifying and evaluating the risks to be addressed; detecting the availability and implementation of processes and equipment to prevent the occurrence of high risk situations; measuring the effectiveness of the implementation of the processes; and checking the incident reports and action taken after events.

Possible Health Questions for Health and Safety:

- Is the organisation in possession of a health and safety certificate and/or has it implemented equivalent guidelines and procedures?

- Is the reporting of health and safety issues a true reflection of actual incidents and do these incidents receive the attention required by the relevant organisational functions?

- How restrictive are the health and safety guidelines as applied by the organisation and do they hinder normal acceptable processing?

Wellbeing

Analogous to the healing process of inflamed or damaged tissue, organisations have a responsibility to assist individuals and groups affected by hazardous operations in the organisation, or as a result of personal health and welfare issues.

In larger organisation this is addressed within a human resources function through the availability of private health insurance, pension support to employees; and in some instances by the employment (full-time or part-time) of medical, psychiatric and substance misuse support professionals. Employment laws in the UK already compel smaller organisations to assist their staff with benefits such as sick leave, maternity leave, pension savings and contributions, but further wellbeing assistance in smaller organisations is still linked to the prevailing culture.

It is possible to detect a close link of the wellbeing function to the survival function of workplace maintenance, discussed in Chapter Three. Workplace maintenance specifically addresses the availability of a safe and ambient work environment to meet the task related operating requirements. It is the task of the wellbeing function to ensure that these workplace maintenance activities have been addressed, especially for remote operating staff, but also for office personnel.

Wellbeing of staff is therefore closely linked to the employment protection laws and regulations already accepted by organisations, but in addition it relies on the current culture of support offered to employees within the organisation. The focus should still be on compliance with employment laws and regulations underpinned by observational evidence of support to individuals in the organisation.

Possible Health Questions for Staff Wellbeing:

- Do staff benefits offer health support and protection in accordance with, or even above, the legal requirements?

- Does the organisation have a health detection/complaints procedure for staff?

- What is the general state of health of the staff, compared to equivalent businesses, and how are exceptional conditions handled?

Damage Limitation

In situations where internal damage has already occurred, the organisation needs to be in a position to limit the damage and recover to an acceptable level of operation. This also applies to the impact the damage may have had on the external image of the organisation.

In the case of localised damage, for example internal theft, the organisation is usually allowed to address the damage by its own means without pressure from external sources. However, damage affecting the external image of the organisation or sector requires more targeted and diplomatic responses by management. Examples include the damage due to mismanagement of customer or public funds by organisational agents, analogous to damage caused by contagious elements in organisms which need to be addressed by means of immunisation or isolation, before affecting other organisms.

One approach to damage limitation after illegal or unethical behaviour of employees could be a quick acceptance of the events which caused the damage, followed by a transparency of planned and implemented action. This method is more likely to be accepted by the market than if the executive of the damaged organisation refuses to accept any responsibility for, or acknowledgement of, the damage[7].

As part of the process of damage control it is also necessary for the organisation in its own right, or the sector as a whole, to determine the actual causes of the damage and implement steps to prevent future recurrences within the company and the sector. This approach has been adopted in the airline industry where any aircraft disaster is submitted to independent investigations leading to improvements in the aircraft structure or personnel process improvements within the industry.

The role of damage limitation needs to address methods to learn from previous incidents that could be applied to prevent or limit recurrences.

Possible Health Questions for Damage Limitation:

- How are internal and/or external events leading to damage to the organisation reported?

- How effective is the internal damage limitations and corrective procedures of the organisation to guard against similar incidents?

- How effective is the organisation's external damage limitation communications and are they acceptable to relevant external parties?

- Does the organisation or sector have procedures in place to learn from events and how effective are the execution of these procedures?

Diagnosing for healthy protection functions in organisations is more than signing off documents to state that the organisation complies with the necessary risk, health and safety regulations. The questions identified for the different functions should not only form a checklist to be completed – responses must be supported by evidence. It is therefore as important to recognise the importance of the 'how' in conjunction with 'what' when diagnosing for healthy protection functions.

Diagnosing Protection – The Process

Protection functions are concerned with preventative and/or restorative action. Operating independently, the main objectives of these functions are to anticipate and where possible, prevent damage to the organisation, and in the cases of damage, to limit the impact and assist in restoring normal or acceptable operating practices.

Because of a relatively low risk of total failures due to damage or disasters[8], senior management may either ignore the need for adequate protection, or only afford it their token attention. Low protection may not matter over the lifetime of the organisation but, analogous to the protection offered by immune systems in the body, adequate preventative protection can limit damage when it does occur.

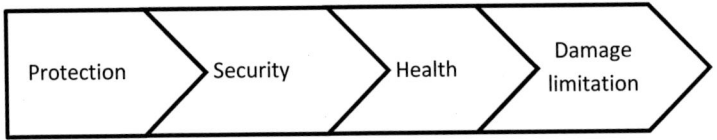

Figure 4.1   Diagnostic stages for protection functions

Figure 4.1 lists the protection functions that require diagnosis to ensure that the organisation is not only protected on paper, but in practice. The checks could be performed internally and should cover risk evaluations, preventative procedures, evidence of incidents and lessons learnt. Questions identified in this chapter, can help to identify what to check for.

Protection

Risk analysis exercises on how to effectively protect access and physical damage to organisations are, to a large extent, dependent on the sector within which the organisation is operating. Physical access control will be more important for organisations with exposed assets, while protection against cyber-attacks are more relevant for organisations with wide exposure to the internet either as a marketing or data storage tool. Similarly, the risk of theft or defrauding is likely to be higher in retail or financial organisations with easier access.

Assessment of preventative protection procedures and measures, and their continued checking and updating are important. Employing a night watchman on a building site can only be effective if he knows what steps to follow in case of attacks, and is effective in following the prescribed procedures when required. Independent and/or professional risk analyses or reviews of the existing risk and preventative plans will help to ensure that the plans and procedures address most of the potential risks of damage to the organisation.

Security

Being aware of the risk may be the first step, but complying with the preventative measures, analogous to relevant inoculations, is as important for internal protection and security. It is necessary to know whether employees in the relevant departments are aware of business laws, regulations and policies applicable to and accepted by the organisation. In addition, evidence of compliance to the laws and regulations and the submission of required incident reports to the regulatory bodies must be available. It is not enough to present certificates of membership, but regular checks should be made and recorded on compliance activities.

The diagnosis for security has an internal focus with respect to the secure and ethical execution of tasks by all members of staff. Regular security checks should be undertaken to ensure that, for instance, personnel responsible for maintaining essential manufacturing equipment, vehicles and other critical assets do not bypass essential steps in their work. It is also important that plans and procedures are regularly reviewed and updated to include more recent threats and risks.

Healing and damage limitation

If, in spite of good preventative action, the organisation experiences damage either from external sources or from within the organisation, it is necessary to ensure that the organisation has a plan to recover from and limit the damage. Initial damage limitation steps should form part of the risk analyses and action plans and address not only potential steps of internal support to affected functions, but also possible public relations stances that can limit damage to the image of the organisation. While these steps will usually be executed by other functions, such as the internal personnel, marketing or the executive public relations functions, it should still form part of the preventative protection plans and procedures, known to all relevant personnel.

In measuring the ability of the organisation to learn from its own past as well as from examples of other similar protection failures, regular checks on healthy protection functions may not result in immediate improvements in competitive operations, but can limit debilitating damage to the organisation when unexpected incidents do occur.

Case Study

A brief summary of the case study history is presented again followed by additional diagnostic findings of the protection functions of access control, security and regulatory compliance, and the health and wellbeing of the employees and the business.

CASE STUDY – THE CORNER SHOP

An independent retail franchise grocery store and bakery, referred to as The Corner Shop, is part of a larger chain. Although the franchisee has the freedom to structure and run the business independently, the holding company is expecting a regular fee from the store as a member of its chain and requires the store to maintain a minimum set of standards. In return, the store owners can use the preferential rates for stock purchases negotiated for the chain and receive advisory assistance from the holding company. The store is in a favourable location in the main street of the town, conveniently situated for a wide range of customers, and the owners have had previous experience and knowledge of retail, finance and accountancy.

The store has been operating for five years. During the first two years it delivered record turnover and profits to the extent that the business was nominated as the 'winning' store in the chain. The customer base was classified as predominantly upper middle-class and the overall image of the store was vibrant and welcoming. The owners went out of their way to satisfy customer needs, for instance, by offering a type of bread made from a special recipe, sought after by many of the local hotels and restaurants, and by ordering and stocking special items on request.

During the third year, the owners decided to expand and diversify by acquiring a butcher shop in the adjacent town. The butchery was at the point of closing and they managed to get it at a reasonable price, including commitments of rental agreements undertaken by the previous owners. They managed to extend their bank loan to finance the deal and one of the owners is spending most of his time running the butchery. The combination of the additional workload for the owners together with mounting repayment burdens of interest and earlier stock purchases are making it difficult to maintain the previous standards of operation. The image of the store and service to the customers has been dropping and resulted in a loss of customers and sales.

The 'dashboard' approach, used in management information systems to display information from summaries to the drill-down evidence-based details is followed in the case study analysis[9]. This approach offers the summary findings for each function in a dashboard dial style, which is linked to supporting further detailed or interrelated information sources at more detailed levels.

The summary diagnosis for the protection functions is presented in Table 4.1. The functions are rated in the middle column by three indicators as explained in the narrative section of the table. This is followed by expanded tables accessible as drill down options on the dashboard, as presented in Tables 4.2 to 4.4, and further expanded by evidence (incidents, measures, notes and reports) in support of the findings.

Summary Dial of the Protection Functions of the Business		
Narrative of Rating Indicators: First indicator (findings): ○ = acceptable; ◑ = unacceptable; ● = serious Second indicator (trend): ↓ = deteriorating; ↑ = improving; no arrow = unchanged Third indicator (impact): W = warning; S = serious; blank = acceptable		
Protection Functions	**Rating**	**Comments**
Access Control	◑ ↓S	Unguarded doors at receiving bay resulted in theft both in the store and butcher shop
Security, Regulatory and Ethical Compliance	○	Compliant with minimum accounting, legal and regulatory requirements
Health, Safety and Wellbeing	○ ↓W	Higher absenteeism rate recently, mainly due to stress

Table 4.1   Protection functions summary diagnosis

The summary diagnosis of the health of the protection functions in Table 4.1 indicates a general awareness of the importance of effective protection functions, especially for a retail business. Limited access control and wellbeing procedures were implemented and improved on as and when required, but without any concerted effort to conduct full risk analysis exercises.

The summary highlights deterioration in the access control as well as the health and wellbeing functions. The access control functions have reached a serious level of concern, especially with respect to the physical security and access control cover of the store and the butcher shop.

However, at summary level the ratings for security and regulatory compliance show acceptable performance and therefore a positive finding. Analogous to the cover against infectious diseases through immunisation, the diagnosis is that the business owners are aware of the required business laws and regulations and have been compliant in their application to the business.

With respect to the wellbeing of staff, an increase in absenteeism of staff is an indication of potential problems. This could be due to unforeseen personal issues, but on the other hand could be linked to an increased concern of stress among the staff.

It is therefore necessary to explore all three functions in more detail before reaching a conclusion. Evidence is presented in Tables 4.2 to 4.4. The flag indicates the level of concern as identified after the events or the performance measurement with respect to the health of the function. Most of the reviews and reports were prepared internally by the managers and as indicated by the dates, the reviews were either performed at the start of the business (year 01) or were event-driven after security incidents.

Access Protection Performance History			
Narrative of Flag: W = warning; S = serious; blank = acceptable			
Evidence of Events, Issues, Reports	**Date**	**Flag**	**Action**
Premises Risk/Security -Theft at delivery area -Theft at butchery -Risk and security as part of initial business plan	Jun 05 Apr 04 Jul 01	S S	-Still to address -Added security staff -Implemented basic precautions
Resources Risk/Security -Theft/pilfering in store	Feb 03	W	-Moved tills to exit
People Risk/Security -Staff security survey	Apr 04	W	-Arrange for staff transport
Data Risk/Security -Data and reports held by owners			-No serious concerns

Table 4.2 Access protection functions (resources, premises and people)

The main incidents identified in Table 4.2 were a recent burglary at the main premises in which the thieves gained access through unguarded back office doors in year 05; the detention of a shoplifter in year 03; and theft and damage to the butchery in an overnight raid in year 04. The store owners responded to each event individually instead of conducting realistic risk analysis reviews and plans for adequate protection based on the findings of the risk evaluation. This could have prevented significant financial loss due to theft and damage and improved the staff morale on the safety of the premises.

As a young and small business the access risk to data and information in the organisation is regarded as acceptable. Most of the information is either held on personal computers by the owners or as paper-based lists and reports. The supervisor office is on a raised platform overlooking the shop and is visible from the shop floor and therefore relatively secure against unwanted access. Backups of data on the laptops may be of concern, although in this case relatively low, since all important reports have been duplicated as paper copies.

Legal and Regulatory Performance History			
Narrative of Flag: W = warning; S = serious; blank = acceptable			
Evidence of Events, Issues, Reports	**Date**	**Flag**	**Action**
Licences and Registration -Licence as butcher -Licence as grocer -Registration as company	Apr 03 Mar 02 Nov 01		
Statutory and Financial Reports -Company & tax submissions -Earlier reports	Sep 05	W	-Late submission -On time
External Audit Reports			-Not required
Employment Regulations -Staff wages and benefits review -Health/safety certificate	Apr 05 Apr 02		Equality implied

Table 4.3 Legal and regulatory compliance

Analogous to compulsory immunisation, the diagnosis in Table 4.3 indicates a satisfactory status of health with respect to legal and regulatory compliance, including audit controls. The company has complied with all the legal registration licences and certifications and, except for one late submission, has been submitting its annual statutory and financial reports on time. It is adhering to employment regulatory standards and is in compliance with these ethical requirements. This is one protection function that is therefore showing healthy functioning.

The only potential warning is the fact that the compliance is with respect to the minimum laws and regulations required for small businesses, for example, the statutory reports are prepared internally without periodic external audit checks for accuracy and meaningful interpretation of information.

The diagnostics of the protection function of health and wellbeing of employees as well as the business is presented in Table 4.4, and shows a consistent deterioration.

Health and Wellbeing Performance History			
Narrative of Flag: W = warning; S = serious; blank = acceptable			
Evidence of Events, Issues, Reports	**Date**	**Flag**	**Action**
Illness/Absenteeism Statistics -year 05 15% absenteeism -year 04 10% absenteeism	Jul 05 Jul 04	S	-Improve bakery air conditioning
Morale -Survey year 04 – 60% satisfied -Survey year 03 – 80% satisfied	Jul 04 Jul 03	W	-Meeting with staff
Health and Safety -Disaster practice -Premises check	Jun 04 Jun 04		
Damage Limitation -News bulletin after theft	Jun 04	W	-Little effect

Table 4.4   Health and wellbeing performance

Absenteeism due to illness increased during the two most recent operating years. This was found to be mainly in the bakery where an ineffective air conditioning system resulted in very high temperatures for the workers. Although the temperature level was improved, it impacted on the morale of all the staff as reflected in the staff survey conducted in year 04, even before the increased absenteeism.

The survey results were discussed at a staff meeting and a few minor improvements were implemented as a result. However, the questions were general and did not highlight any real issues. Health and safety practices and checks were last conducted during the first half of year 04. Although no events occurred which required the implementation of additional procedures, it may develop into serious situations, for example in case of a fire on the premises.

Only one event of damage limitation was identified. This was the issuing of a news bulletin after the serious theft and damage to the butchery to inform clients that the company will operate as usual after the event. Customer surveys showed that it had limited impact. Internal damage limitation issues such as pilfering by members of staff or customers were handled on individual and event-driven bases.

While the diagnosis of the health and wellbeing functions were rated as acceptable but deteriorating, the indication is that without closer checks on the health and wellbeing of the staff and the prevention of potential damage through access control, health and safety practices, the business is exposing itself to losses in stock, staffing, illnesses and disasters.

This detailed diagnosis of health concerns in the protection functions of the business raises a few questions:

- Will it make a difference to the difficult position that the business finds itself in, if the functions receive adequate attention?
- Can attention to healthy operations of these functions help to prevent a serious financial breakdown?
- Is it practical and meaningful for a small start-up company with limited resources to spend time, money and effort to maintain effective risk prevention means and procedures?

The answer to the first question has to be yes. If good preventative measures are in place and regularly monitored, financial loss due to theft and damage to either the assets or stock can be prevented or reduced in the future. This also applies to any loss of image to the customers and the lowering of staff morale and wellbeing. Whether attention to the protection functions can make a difference to the financial situation of the business will depend on a full-cost risk evaluation exercise. If the cost involved in suitable protective measures can be made acceptable, it will help to prevent further loss of assets, resources, goodwill and morale.

With respect to the third question, the answer is that it is possible, financially feasible and advisable for start-up organisations to give serious attention to the health of their protection functions. The protection functions operate in the background and are therefore regarded as invisible and unimportant until after serious incidents of access violations or damage to the organisation. However, it is also a profession and many government institutes, including the police and security organisations, offer advice and assistance to organisations at all stages of their development for suitable and cost-effective solutions to their security and protection needs.

Conclusion

Healthy protection functions can prevent an organisation from being 'killed' either externally or internally by events or sources intent on damaging its staff, assets, information or other resources. In Chapter Four, the protection functions of access control, legal and regulatory compliance, and health and wellbeing were compared to the skin, exoskeleton and the immune systems of complex living organisms.

It is important for each organisation to base its protection procedures and measures on realistic risk analyses since the levels of risk differ for different sector organisations. However, once areas of risk have been identified, it is as important for the organisation to ensure that adequate protection is offered and to conduct regular checks on the effectiveness of the preventative procedures. Damage due to inadequate protection can be severe as demonstrated in the stated examples. Financial loss due to physical damage to property, assets and resources can be extensive and potentially unrecoverable. Loss of data and information due to hacking can lead to image or production concerns, while inadequate internal and external damage limitation procedures could lead to morale, image and turnover problems for the business.

Chapters Three and Four covered the internally focused functions of organisations in order to ensure that staff can operate effectively and safely in order to ensure that the organisation survives. In Chapter Five, the diagnostics move to the operations functions, i.e. the 'skeletal muscle units' of the organisation, responsible for allowing the organisation to be mobile and agile in order to compete and defend itself in its external environment. The chapter will follow a similar pattern in which each different type of operation is compared to its analogous physiological muscle units, how they operate and the best method of diagnosing concerns in their functioning.

Notes

1. The concept of immunology by identifying 'self' versus 'non-self' is used in the immune system of the body to separate the material that forms part of the body from the intrusive material as discussed by Playfair, J.H.L and Chain, B.M., (2005), *Immunology at a Glance*, Blackwell Publishing, Oxford, pp. 8-9. This method of identifying the members and assets of an organisation is also recognised in: Maturana, H.R. and Varela, F.J., (1980), *Autopoiesis and Cognition. The Realization of the Living*, D. Reidel Publishing Company, Dordrecht, pp. 8-11.

2. Unlike theft and vandalism, the attacks by fanatics, pressure groups or natural disasters are not for personal gain of the attacker, but for ethical reasons or natural events. Protection should be expanded to include transparency, and be wide enough to cover natural causes as identified by Regan, T., (2004), The Case for Animal Rights, 2nd ed. Berkeley, Calif.; and www.bbc.co.uk/news/world-asia, May 5 2012.

3. Various books and research papers highlight the importance of finance and how to use it for young and small businesses, including: Burns, P. (2010). *Entrepreneurship and Small Business*, 3rd ed. Palgrave MacMillan; Maskara, P.K., Mullineaux, D.J. (2011). Small Firm Capital Structure and the Syndicated Loan Market; *Journal of Financial Services Research*, Vol. 39, Issue 1, pp. 55-70; Lynn, Richard (ed.). (1974). *The Entrepreneur: Eight Case Studies*; Allen & Unwin: www.businessknowhow.com/startup/business-failure.htm.

4. References to corporate finance incidents are stated by Swartz, M. and Watkins, S. (2003) *Power Failure: The Inside Story of the Collapse of Enron*, New York, Doubleday; and "Starbucks pay corporation tax in UK for first time in five years": www.guardian.co.uk Jun 23 2013.

5. Key proponents in the stockholder versus stakeholder debates include Friedman, who maintained that a business is only responsible to its shareholders, and Freeman, who supported the stakeholder view: Friedman, M. (1970) "The Social Responsibility of Business is to Increase its Profits", *New York Times*, 14 September 1970; and Freeman, R. (1987) *Strategic Management: A Stakeholder Approach*, Ballinger, Boston MA.

6. Research was performed on the extent of underreporting of safety incidents by Probst, T.M., Brubaker, T.L. and Barsotti, A. (2008). Organizational Injury Rate Underreporting: The Moderating Effect of Organizational Safety Climate. *Journal of Applied Psychology*, Vol. 93, No. 5, p. 1147.

7. Organisational wellbeing and damage control research papers include: Yu, T., Insead, M.S., Lester, R.H. (2008). Misery Loves Company: The Spread of Negative Impacts Resulting from an Organizational Crisis. *Academy of Management Review*. Vol. 83, No. 4, pp. 1125-1146; and Pfarrer, M.D.,

Decelles, K.A. and Smith, K.G. (2008), After the Fall: Reintegrating the Corrupt Organization, *Academy of Management Review*. Vol. 33, No. 3, pp. 730-749.

8. An analysis of the main reasons for start-up business failures found that 46% failed due to the incompetence of the owners; 30% due to unbalanced experience or a lack of management experience of the owners; 11% due to a lack of experience in the relevant operating sector; and 1% due to neglect, fraud or disaster. http://www.statisticbrain.com/startup-failure-by-industry/ accessed 11/10/2013.

9. The use of dashboard displays has been widely accepted by organisations to allow a drill-down facility of information. A reference, based on practical application in various organisations is: Eckerson, Wayne W. (2011). *Performance Dashboards: Measuring, Monitoring and Managing your Business*. 2nd Ed. John Wiley & Sons, Hoboken NJ.

CHAPTER FIVE

OPERATIONS FUNCTIONS

Without healthy operations functions an organisation cannot compete.

The operations functions of an organisation can be compared to the skeletal muscle units in the human body, allowing the body to be mobile and agile within its environment. These functions are closely controlled and monitored, and the analogous organisational diagnostics should consider:

Different Types of Operating Units

Learning and Performance Control

Initiation, Research and Design

The functioning of the skeletal muscle units in living organisms differ significantly from the survival and protection functions. Whereas the survival and protection functions are stimulated and controlled at local level, independent from direct central nervous system interference or control, skeletal muscle unit activities have to be initiated from the brain and are closely controlled by the cerebellum to ensure a subconsciously smooth effective operation. The historically accepted hierarchical structure of: senior management – middle management – supervisors – operating unit workers, as a standard management structure for operating units[1] is analogous to the nerve structuring for skeletal muscle units in physiology and applicable to the three subsections of this chapter.

To clarify the similarity of health checks to the physiology of skeletal muscle units in the living body, shaded boxed inserts are provided. These offer additional information which is not essential for clarity and can therefore be ignored.

Different Types of Operating Units

Comparing operating units to skeletal muscle units in living organisms offers interesting and meaningful elements to be considered and questions some of the theories used to motivate organisations to pursue only productivity and efficiency as key to achieve a winning position.

Motor Functions[2]

The skeletal muscle groups are situated in the limbs, face, back and neck; and the main distinguishing features of functioning are the cooperation required by different types of cells to enable effective operation. Each group of muscle fibres and their controlling nerve cell is referred to as a muscle or motor unit and, based on "the duration of their twitch contraction, motor units are divided into S (slow), FR (fast, resistant to fatigue), and FF (fast, fatigable) units"[2].

The slow muscle unit fibres contract in the strong and sustained movement required for posture, standing, continuous movement and heavy lifting. The muscle fibres are attached by tendons to bones in the arms and legs, and operate over joints to enable required movements. Each nerve cell can stimulate up to 600 muscle fibres within one motor unit and the units have a longer continuous period of contraction. However, during excessive exertion, there is a possibility that the stored energy is exhausted and the cells compensate through a breakdown of the glucose to lactose. In these cases the muscle can develop an oxygen debt resulting in muscle cramp and the inability to operate.

Fast skeletal muscle fibres have a fast and short contracting period and are involved in fine, rapid, precise movement such as that executed in the fingers and hand movements. The feedback loop control is the same as for the slow muscle units, however, the feedback cycle initiated by the touch senses, especially in the skin of the finger tips, is much stronger than for the other motor units. Similar to the slow muscle units, the fast muscle fibres in the fingers are attached by tendons to the smaller bones in the hands and feet, and operate over joints to enable the precise movements required.

Fast muscle fibre units prone to fatigue have a fast and short contracting period, are involved in rapid and precise movement, and can tire easily, such as facial muscle units, the tongue in speech and the movements of the eye. Loss of the use of these muscle units result in the inability to vocalise or change facial expressions.

The body contains all the different types of skeletal muscle units. Individuals can, through training, develop one muscle type or group in preference to other types as demonstrated by athletes versus singers.

Skeletal muscle units in the body can be split into three types, namely units with a slow and enduring contraction period, units with a fast contraction period and units with a fast and short contraction period[2]. For an organisation to compete successfully, its main operating unit can normally be identified as one of the analogous types of skeletal muscle units. Diagnostically, the different types of the main operating units will be discussed as: endurance units competing in sectors such as heavy industry, analogous to the slow muscle units in the arms and legs; manufacturing and production units, analogous to the fast hand muscle units operating in conjunction with tools and machinery; service units such as health or care services, analogous to the fast hand muscle units connecting directly with customers; and the verbal units of education or media, analogous to the fast fatigable facial muscle units.

Skeletal muscle units in living organisms operate in conjunction with bones, joints and tendons to fulfil their allocated tasks, i.e. a diverse team effort, and not muscle fibre in isolation. The analogy in organisations is that of a team structure consisting of the operators in the units working in close cooperation with other diverse members of the team such as machines and machine operators, equipment maintenance teams and supporting administrators. In addition, the team members can only operate successfully if they are provided with the essential guidance, information and supplies from management and various associated support functions.

Another potential misconception is that the sector in which an organisation operates is the main determinant of the type of operating unit for the organisation. This will be analogous to athletes only concerned about the slow muscle units in their legs and ignoring other units such as the ability to communicate. In living organisms all the different types of muscle units are likely to occur, although the competitive unit may be better developed. As an example, retail organisations may rely on operating units that:

- Offer a personalised service to customers as their main operations function.
- Are involved in the precision tasks of product displays and customer service, analogous to fast precision muscle units.
- Communicate with customers through marketing, analogous to fast fatigable muscle units.
- Offer a transport delivery service to customers or operate heavy machinery, analogous to slow endurance muscle units.

The emphasis of cooperative support, however, differs for each type of unit as identified in research[3] and this should be recognised in the process.

Endurance Operating Units

The analogy of endurance operating units to the slow skeletal muscle units in the limbs, defines the units as working with heavy equipment according to clear instructions and processes, often with larger teams and longer shift durations. It therefore includes the operating functions of organisations in heavy industry, airlines, mining, energy, shipping and construction. It also includes the non-core units within other organisations that are, for instance, responsible for customer delivery transport.

In general, these operating units have a clear set of instructions and timetables to guide the operations and therefore do not need unnecessary or constant interference from senior management. Regular performance reports from supervisory or middle management will suffice. In order to achieve this level of reliable endurance operations, the teams, however, need to be fully trained, have all necessary supplies and rely on fully functional equipment.

While the training, funding and supplies are common to all types of operating units, the reliance of the endurance units on their equipment and the health and safety of their staff were found to be more important than in the other sectors. The equipment is expensive and essential for the execution of the tasks, and disasters as a result of faulty or poorly maintained equipment can be dangerous to the teams as well as the environment. This can be demonstrated in the seriousness with which aircraft accidents, drilling or mining disasters are being investigated to prevent future similar disasters due to faulty and poorly maintained equipment. Team members must be able to rely on safe equipment[4].

Healthy functioning can be detected by focusing on factors such as the effectiveness of training and teamwork, the reliability of the equipment, the consistency of reporting of damaging incidents, and the action taken based on lessons learnt.

Possible Health Questions for Endurance Operating Units:

- How reliant is the heavy duty equipment which forms an essential part of the operating unit?

- How effective is the training and mutual teamwork of the members of the operating unit?

- Have there been incidents of equipment malfunctioning or poor teamwork resulting in damage? How were the incidents handled and what lessons were learnt?

Manufacturing and Production Operating Units

Manufacturing and production operating units can be compared to the use of the hands and fingers by individuals such as craftsmen in order to make or assemble goods with the assistance of tools. The operations are concerned with precision, flexibility and quality and the tasks and schedules are likely to be shorter in duration. Operators need to be skilled but also flexible and adaptable. Machines and equipment still need to be reliable, but modifiable in order to adjust to changes in the products being manufactured or constructed. Products are usually sold to customers and therefore rely on good quality checks as part of the process.

Examples of organisations in this category include manufacturers of: parts to specific customers; utility and household appliances; chemicals or food production; and fashionable products, for instance clothes, mobile phone and electronic equipment. The competition is likely to be fierce and new products may have to be offered regularly in order to remain competitive in the market. The operating teams could be relatively small and subject to continuous monitoring and testing of the production performance and quality of the products[5].

In addition to manufacturing as a core revenue-producing part of the organisation, similar operating units could also be found in any organisation, such as: internal workshops for the servicing and repair of equipment and buildings; or the building of prototype products for future consideration.

Diagnostics should focus on the skill, flexibility and quality of the operating team. This flexibility and precision relies on speedy feedback, analogous to the increased number of touch sensors in the fingertips.

Possible Health Questions for Precision Operating Units:

- How effective is the operating team in adapting to flexible requests and schedules for product manufacturing?

- Are quality checks adequate and performed regularly?

- Are the operating units regularly supplied with the material, supplies and tools necessary for the manufacturing or production process?

- How reliable is the manufacturing equipment and their maintenance?

Service Operating Units

Service operating units are similar to the precision manufacturing units in that they operate analogous to the hand and finger movements of living beings. The main difference lies in the fact that tools and equipment used by operators form an integral part of their service and workplace environment, such as cash tills for shop cashiers, or medical equipment for surgeons and physicians. The service units operate directly with customers, either by selling products or through personal services directed to the customer. Organisations specialising in service operating units include care services, hospitals, tourism, retail, wholesale, and utility organisations. Customer service departments within most organisations may also meet the requirement for these organisational units.

Organisational health requirements are reliant on highly trained and skilled personnel. However, additional requirements were found to include an ability to be sensitive and flexible to the needs of the customer and be able to develop an awareness of, and empathy to, customer requirements. These units are also dependent on smooth internal distribution support functions to ensure that they have the appropriate, and sufficient, supplies and work equipment as and when required. Examples of unhealthy operations include shops with inadequate supplies available to customers, or hospitals and care homes that are unable to offer the appropriate service to patients[6].

Health diagnostics should focus on the sensitivity of the operators to customer needs, their ability to perform tasks based on the availability of adequate supplies and work related tools, and the skilled or trained performance of the staff.

Possible Health Questions for Service Operating Units:

- How flexible and effective are the operating teams in meeting specific customer demands with respect to the services offered?

- Are the operating teams equipped with all necessary equipment, tools and supplies to perform their tasks effectively?

- Are the teams customer-oriented, alert to customer requirements and sensitive in their customer approach?

Verbal Operating Units

Verbal operating units can be compared to the fast fatigable facial muscle units. The operations consist of the presentation of messages or images by individuals or very small teams, with relatively short sessions, but directly conforming to objectives and/or instructions from senior management. The contact with customers is not random, or direct as in the case of the service units, but targeted to specific categories of audience or customers.

Organisations specialising in this method of operation include educational institutions, professional advisers, media, performing arts, design and development services (e.g. software), public relations and advertising firms. It is, however, also a function which is relatively widespread in all organisations in the form of their public relations, customer call centres, marketing and sales departments. The message and the means of transmission, whether print, verbal or electronic, are important, but also the location if the contact with the audience is direct.

Most visible health concerns include the inability to communicate at all, or an inability to communicate the messages in line with organisational values. Examples of organisations not meeting these standards include media organisations misjudging the tone of their messages, or the public relations blunders of organisations unwilling to admit to errors in operation after disasters and thus losing face in the market[7].

Diagnostic tools for these operating units should focus on the messages and their consistency with organisational goals and values, and the image as observed by their external targeted market. The contents and initiation of the messages are discussed in more detail in Chapter Seven – Information Functions.

Possible Health Questions for Verbal Operating Units:

- Has the organisation developed a relevant target market for the messages it wants to specialise in or wishes to present?

- Are the messages offered to the target market of the quality acceptable to their audience?

- Are the messages consistent with organisational values and executive guidelines?

While the diagnostic process for operating units within an organisation can be diverse, it is important to identify and diagnose each type of operating unit separately, not only if they are core revenue-producing units, but also if they appear in supporting roles within the organisation.

Learning and Performance Control

Survival functions act in the background, are locally controlled and respond mainly to transaction volumes or incidents without direct interference from senior management. On the other hand, the operating units discussed in the previous section: need to be informed about which processes to follow and when; need the training in how to perform the processes; and are continuously monitored to ensure that the end products and services meet the targets and standards set by management and customers.

Middle management's role to plan, instruct and monitor operational activities date back to the concept of Scientific Management promoted by Taylor and Fayol during the early years of the twentieth century[1]. They proposed the separation of duties between planning and monitoring by managers versus the action of workers. This concept still forms part of today's structure in the operation functions, and an analogy can be found in the physiology of the body.

Motor Functions – Cerebellum Monitoring and Control[2]

Although the actual methods employed by the cerebellum part of the brain are not yet known, it is accepted as a key controlling centre of skeletal muscle units in the body.

The cerebellum acts by initiating and storing motor information as part of non-declarative memory in the brain and using this memory of action as a comparator or timing device in regulating smooth muscle action. The control loop for the stimulation of the muscle units is from the motor cortex area for voluntary control to the cerebellum for continuous subconscious control, to the skeletal motor units. The feedback part of the loop is from receptors within the motor units or other parts of the body to the cerebellum for reflexive response, or to the motor cortex.

The feedback loop of the fast muscle units is the same as for the slow muscle units, however, the feedback cycle initiated by the touch senses, especially in the the finger tips, face and tongue, is much stronger than for the other motor units.

The decision of which products or services to manufacture or develop may reside with senior management, but middle management takes over to ensure that the training is adequate and the targets and standards are met. This is analogous to the role played by the central nervous system in the control of skeletal muscle units in which the cognitive brain initiates action and the cerebellum monitors and controls the execution thereof.

From a health diagnostic point of view it is therefore necessary to determine the effectiveness of the functions of planning, training, target setting and performance monitoring, analogous to the role of the cerebellum. This is necessary to ensure that an organisation is competent, mobile and agile enough to enable it to compete in its environment.

Training and Planning

Training and planning are related to the subconscious functions in the cerebellum in which it 'learns' commonly used tasks which need to be performed by skeletal muscle units for activities such as walking, and uses this to stimulate and monitor the action subconsciously.

When a new or modified product or service is introduced by senior management, it is essential that the operators are aware of the changes and suitably trained to perform the new or changed task. Training has been identified by all types of operating units as one of the essential pre-requisites to successful operations and it is therefore necessary for operators to receive adequate job related training, either by means of off-site educational or skills related courses for certain types of operation, or hands-on vocational training[3].

Poor or inadequate training and planning activities could result in uncoordinated functioning of the operating units. The training and task planning given to staff in the McDonald's fast food outlets is a good example of the concept in practice. Members of staff know what to do, how to do it, and when to perform their tasks. Although this is also one of the examples criticised as being mechanistic and therefore 'inhumane', customers know what to expect and accept it as good practice. It is also essential in other operating units, such as airline pilots working from set scripts and being fully trained before being allowed to pilot an aircraft, especially a commercial aircraft. One of the areas investigated after aircraft incidents include pilot error, possibly due to inadequate training.

The operating units least likely to be affected by intensive on-the-job training and planning are the verbal units, including sales and marketing departments. Although requiring training in the area of expertise, the operations are more flexible and variable and subjected to immediate feedback loops and corrective activities. From a physiological point of view, these muscle units are less influenced by the subconscious cerebellum than the muscle units in the limbs but under a more direct control of the cognitive brain.

Possible Health Questions for Operating Unit Training and Planning:

- Do the operating units have clear task instructions and guidelines?

- Is the training offered to operators relevant and effective to the type of operation?

- Are operators in supporting operating units as well trained as the operators in the core operating units, and what is the effect on the overall business?

Target Setting and Performance Monitoring

Trained operators and plans of action in themselves are meaningless unless the performance of the activities can be monitored and, if necessary, adjusted to ensure that the units operate efficiently. This function is similar to the stimulation and control feedback loop action of the cerebellum.

Target setting and performance monitoring is not new for operating units and became a source of debate and critique during the twentieth century, focusing on the scope and intensity of targets and control. It is important to identify the different types of targets for different operating units. Endurance units, analogous to the slow muscle units, are more likely to have to work to stable routines and long term targets than operating unit members in the manufacturing and verbal functions where the cycle periods may be shorter.

Target setting and performance monitoring is important but concerns can arise when targets are too tight to achieve or are changing too often to allow for the development of smooth operating processes[8]. This can be compared to uncoordinated moves in the limbs reflected in an inability to move smoothly, or athletes not focused on mastering techniques necessary for competition such as golf swings.

Uncoordinated effort in organisations can be observed in the companies setting ambitious targets for future performance, but then not following through by measuring whether they are on track to meet these targets, or analysing why they did not meet the targets in order to learn and improve. Examples of changing targets are often linked to government institutions and departments. With changes of government, new ministers may try to exert their influence by changing the targets in their departments. In order to comply, operating units focus on the new targets and instead of mastering previous processes, have to change their way of operating, thereby wasting time and effort in the process.

Health diagnostics should focus on the optimum setting of targets for the operating units and the effective monitoring of performance against the targets. Diagnostics should also monitor the frequency of target changes and resulting impact on the performance of the unit.

Possible Health Questions for Target Setting and Monitoring:

- Are targets consistent with the type of operating unit and supportive of their action?

- How effective is the target monitoring process and the performance of the teams against the set targets?

- How often are targets changed, and what has been the observed impact on performance in the past?

While the learning and monitoring of the targets are initiated and controlled by middle management, the actual decision on new products and services are more likely to be set by senior management and include the design and initiating functions as discussed in the next section.

Initiation, Research and Design

Skeletal muscle cell units in living organisms are not only controlled subconsciously by the cerebellum in the central nervous system, but the type of movement is determined and initiated from the motor cortical area in the brain. This demonstrates a direct link between the muscle activity and the conscious and subconscious parts of the brain[9].

An analogy can be found in organisations. Operating units need to receive a steer from senior management about the type of service or product on offer, and from the research and design departments for the process on how this can be achieved as discussed below.

Motor Functions – Motor Cortex Initiation[2]

A map of the motor cortical areas responsible for the stimulation of the skeletal motor units provides an indication of the distorted focus on the stimulation of the different types of motor units within the voluntary brain. Of the different muscle units, the fast muscle units in the fingers, face and tongue have greater representation in the motor cortex than the slow muscle units of the arms, legs and back[8].

The slow muscle units are subject to the standard control feedback loop for skeletal muscle, however, the voluntary impact from the motor cortex is lower than for the fast muscle units. The feedback loop control for the fast muscle units is the same as for the slow muscle units but the feedback cycle initiated by the touch senses in the skin of the finger tips, face or on the tongue, is much stronger than for the other motor units. The higher representation in the motor cortex for the fast muscle units is an indication of the importance of the direct control, especially over the mouth and tongue, used for vocalisation and facial expression. The fast response may be less durable than for the slow muscle units, but can be more intense and targeted.

Initiation and Support

Operating units need to know the services and products on offer and the processes and timescales involved, analogous to the initiation of action required from the skeletal muscle units by the motor cortical areas in the brain. This applies not only to the initiation of a specific operating cycle, but also to changes in cycles and processes, similar to changes required by competitors in the field of sport, crafts or performing arts. Unless these changes are initiated and fully supported at a conscious cognitive level, the subconscious mind will revert to the routine action of the past.

As briefly alluded to in the Different Types of Operating Units section, endurance operating units have longer operating cycles and are less likely to be subjected to senior management involvement than manufacturing, service or verbal units. However, during times of change the success of the outcome depends on whether the change has been initiated and supported by senior management and is accepted by the members of the operating unit. The resistance to change in endurance units seems to be higher than in the other operating units. This finding can be illustrated from unrest and resistance to change in major mining, forestry, transport and other heavy industry organisations, especially when change became essential in enabling the organisation to adopt modern technology and practices to remain competitive[10].

The initiation of new or changed processes in the manufacturing, service and verbal units are more frequent and accepted, analogous to the motor cortical areas being more pronounced for finger and facial muscle units. This can be demonstrated by the importance attached to the development and marketing of new pharmaceutical or electronic products and services in order to compete successfully in a fast changing market.

However, there are also examples of inadequate or unnecessary interference from senior management stunting or disrupting operational effectiveness. This may include the misreading of changes in demand for technology, such as digital or mobile products, resulting in the company falling behind the new market leaders, as demonstrated by Kodak[11]. The opposite is, however, as dangerous to effective performance as demonstrated in decisions to initiate and offer products to market at a stage when the production line has not been implemented or tested successfully, or by continuously changing the product or service offering, whether necessary or not. Examples include the offering of partly tested products such as electronic appliances or cars which have to be recalled shortly after introduction to the market, as well as continuous changes in displays or service offered in shops to the dismay of customers[11].

Health diagnostics should focus on senior management's involvement in the initiation and support for new operating activities.

Possible Health Questions for the Initiation and Support of Changes to Operating Units:

- Are decisions for new or changed products/services in line with external demands, or market and technology developments?

- Are change initiation projects effectively supported and encouraged by senior management towards successful implementation?

- How successful have recent new and change programmes been implemented and accepted by internal and external parties?

Research and Design

New products or services need to be effectively designed and developed to ensure successful introduction. The research and design function, analogous to the learning part of the motor cortex, finds a strong equivalent in research laboratories, as well as the design and development departments of manufacturing and service organisations. While the function is highly relevant to manufacturing and service units, it is also observable in endurance units where the research and development activities are more focused on large fields of operation such as the design and development of new aircraft and major constructions, or prospecting for oil or mineral fields.

Important to the research, design and development function is its cooperation with other functions, including accessibility to relevant information from internal and external sources, and the protection of new designs and findings. This is in line with the need of individuals to be aware of relevant information before deciding on new products or processes and the prevention of patents to be leaked to competitors. The security function covers access protection to the design and development teams in order to protect current and future trade and product secrets such as recipes for processed food, formulae for drugs or prototype designs of products.

Possible Health Questions for the Design and Development Functions:

- Do the research, design and development functions support new and changed operational processes?

- How effective is the use of information to influence the work of research and development departments?

- How good is the cooperation of research with the operating units and supporting functions such as information gathering and protection?

Diagnosing Operations – The Process

Skeletal muscle units can be diagnosed by observing and measuring their ability to operate effectively under normal conditions and during periods of stress or change. A similar process in diagnosing the health of the operating units of organisations is therefore presented in Figure 5.1 in which the operating units are evaluated individually on performance, learning and control and their reliance on the initiation and design of change activities.

Although the diagnostic steps are common for all types of operating units, the health diagnostic questions are mostly unit-specific and should be customised. It is also important to accept that each organisation probably has all four different types of operating units. The core revenue-generating operating unit of a manufacturing organisation will, for instance, be supported by an endurance unit of parts and product transport, a verbal unit of sales and marketing and a personal customer service unit. Each type requires a different approach to detect its level of health.

Figure 5.1   Diagnostic stages for operations functions

Unit Performance

Health questions identified in the Operating Units section of the chapter highlighted the questions which are common to all sections, as well as those that are regarded as more important to a specific type of operating unit. The common diagnostics of training, teamwork and support can be measured by reviewing the availability of skilled operators, resources and supplies to support effective processing.

Measuring the unique health condition of endurance operating units is analogous to measuring the effective status and use of the limbs of living organisms. The focus is especially on the reliance and effective use of machinery and equipment, analogous to tendons and bone structure; and the cooperation and reliance of team members on each other to ensure individual safety by measuring smooth and effective operations. These measures apply not only to revenue creating units, but also to other non-revenue units such as company owned transport for customers or staff.

Measuring the unique health conditions of the manufacturing and service units is analogous to determining whether the fingers and hands are agile and effective in using tools and crafting products, or to operate in direct contact with the customers. The availability of supplies is important, as is the flexibility to perform different tasks and switch from one task to the next without unnecessary delay. Most of this information can be obtained from direct customer survey responses, but also from independent observations, such as mystery shoppers who focus on the customer service and image presented to the customer.

The unique set of diagnostics relating to verbal operating units can also be used to diagnose supporting sales, marketing and the public relations departments. Analogous to the fast moving facial muscle units, these units are concerned with the image projected to the external environment as based on the values of the organisation. The focus should be on the message, its accuracy and the image thus portrayed.

It needs to be emphasised that health diagnostics of operating units are concerned with the ability of the units to perform prescribed tasks, and not aimed at measuring the cost effectiveness or competitive performance of the units. These latter measures of performance are important for competition and winning, but cannot be achieved if the underlying health situation is not supporting the effort.

Learning and Control

Healthy operating units are managed by healthy middle management functions with respect to the setting of realistic targets, effective training, monitoring and an effective feedback system. Analogous to the subconscious control of skeletal muscle units by the cerebellum, training and effective team operations can be observed from the staff records of skills and training, and with respect to the performance interviews of members of staff. It will also be necessary to investigate the type of training programmes offered or skills expected from each member of the different units.

Measuring the performance of operating teams relies on the existence of plans and milestone targets, and on the feedback and action in case of missed targets and schedules. Work targets and performance against these targets are more objectively measurable per unit by checking the consistency and frequency of changed targets, followed by the unit performance and corrective action initiated and implemented for missed targets. The feedback from performance against the targets can also be measured from staff interviews and surveys and the degree of absenteeism or sickness due to target related stress.

Initiation and Change

Management initiation and development guidelines for new products and services, or changes to existing processes, are important elements of guidance to the operating units. It is necessary to ensure that operators are kept informed about new and changed products and services; that sales and marketing teams do not promise or sell undeliverable products or services, and that the support for the operating teams are adequate and timely to ensure effective operations.

Measuring the effect of change on an operating unit is analogous to measuring the ability of an individual to consciously decide on new or changed instructions to skeletal muscle units, and be able to execute and, if necessary, become efficient in learning the modified processes. In order to measure the effectiveness of initiation of new or changed operational process requirements, it will be necessary to analyse reasons for failed attempts to introduce innovative change.

Case Study

A brief summary of the case study history is presented again followed by diagnostic results of the health of its operations functions.

CASE STUDY – THE CORNER SHOP

An independent retail franchise grocery store and bakery, referred to as The Corner Shop, is part of a larger chain. Although the franchisee has the freedom to structure and run the business independently, the holding company is expecting a regular fee from the store as a member of its chain and requires the store to maintain a minimum set of standards. In return, the store owners can use the preferential rates for stock purchases negotiated for the chain and receive advisory assistance from the holding company. The store is in a favourable location in the main street of the town, conveniently situated for a wide range of customers, and the owners have had previous experience and knowledge of retail, finance and accountancy.

The store has been operating for five years. During the first two years it delivered record turnover and profits to the extent that the business was nominated as the 'winning' store in the chain. The customer base was classified as predominantly upper middle-class and the overall image of the store was vibrant and welcoming. The owners went out of their way to satisfy customer needs, for instance, by offering a type of bread made from a special recipe, sought after by many of the local hotels and restaurants, and by ordering and stocking special items on request.

During the third year, the owners decided to expand and diversify by acquiring a butcher shop in the adjacent town. The butchery was at the point of closing and they managed to get it at a reasonable price, including commitments of rental agreements undertaken by the previous owners. They managed to extend their bank loan to finance the deal and one of the owners is spending most of his time running the butchery. The combination of the additional workload for the owners together with mounting repayment burdens of interest and earlier stock purchases are making it difficult to maintain the previous standards of operation. The image of the store and service to the customers has been dropping and resulted in a loss of customers and sales.

The diagnostic tools used to investigate the effectiveness of the operating units of the business include various surveys, measurements and reports presented in Table 5.1 as the summary overview dial of the dashboard method of information presentation[12] and drilled down to detailed levels in Tables 5.2 to 5.4.

The category of operations, in Table 5.1, is subdivided into its functions. These functions are rated in the middle column by indicators as presented in the narrative section of the table, followed by a summary comment of its current observation of health.

Summary Dial of the Operations Functions of the Business		
Narrative of Rating Indicators: First indicator (findings): ○ = acceptable; ◉ = unacceptable; ● = serious Second indicator (trend): ↓ = deteriorating; ↑ = improving; no arrow = unchanged Third indicator (impact): W = warning; S = serious; blank = acceptable		
Operations Functions	**Rating**	**Comments**
Operating Unit performance	○	Good teamwork and willingness of the teams to execute instructions
Learning and Monitoring	○ ↑	Teams are willing and able to learn new processes
Initiation and Development	○	Management is issuing supporting new and changed instructions when required.

Table 5.1   Operations functions summary diagnosis

The high level diagnosis of the health of the operations functions show acceptable levels of performance and an increase in the ability of the operating teams to learn and perform against targets. This seems to be one area within the business that is performing well, and affirms the influence of the management team to draw from their previous experience in the field of retail, sales and marketing. There is, however, a problem at the summary level presentation. While the performance is generally acceptable as applied to the operations in the shop and bakery, the new butcher shop is experiencing staffing and performance concerns, requiring further in-depth analyses of the separate units.

Each of the three functional areas has therefore been expanded in Tables 5.2 to 5.4. Each of these tables offers the latest reports or measurement results in order to present a trend as well as the latest results of issues. Entries are rated in the flag column for their level of health, as explained in the narrative block of the table.

A breakdown of the most recent operating unit reviews and resulting actions are presented in Table 5.2. Most of the reviews and reports were prepared internally by the managers as indicated by the dates (relative to the year of inception) and are offered separately for each of the operating units. In order to obtain further evidence the backup documents of reviews or action should be available on request.

Operating Unit Teamwork Performance History			
Narrative of Flag: W = warning; S = serious; blank = acceptable			
Reports/Reviews	**Date Issued**	**Flag**	**Action**
Store Sales Unit			
-Unit performance review	June 05		
-Staff issue meeting	Aug 04		Issues discussed
-Unit performance review	Jun 04	W	Staff mismatch
Bakery Unit			
-Unit performance review	Jun 05		
-Address workplace	Jan 05		Improve heat issue
-Unit performance review	Nov 04	W	High sickness rate
Butchery Unit			
-Unit performance review	Jun 05	W	Still poorly trained
-Unskilled, inadequate staff numbers	Dec 04	S	Serious staffing problem
Vehicle and Delivery Unit			
-Vehicle and driver checks	Mar 05		Acceptable
-Incident report	June 02	W	Car accident
Marketing Unit			
-New customers gained	June 05	W	Reduction in special customers
- New customer report	June 04		Growing base

Table 5.2   Functioning of operating units

With the exception of the butchery and marketing, all units seem to be functioning effectively as teams. In the case of the butcher shop, the experienced staff left when the butchery changed hands and it was more difficult to recruit and train new staff within the reporting periods. The marketing function, performed by one of the directors of the business, aimed to increase the initial affluent customer base of restaurants and hotels by offering personalised service and product deliveries. The most recent years saw a downturn in this customer base. However, in view of the poor financial situation of the business, it may not have been such a negative result. By repositioning itself with respect to its target market, it may be possible to move away from personal services to a more centralised and general product offering to a new target market.

Staff training, schedules and monitoring procedures were well implemented and maintained in the bakery. However, it is taking an excessive amount of time and effort to find and develop specialist butchers and this area is therefore still a concern. The situation is improving but will take some time to stabilise and operate effectively.

Learning and performance control diagnostics are presented in Table 5.3. Most of the tasks in the store are routine tasks that can be taught and monitored by management and supervisory staff. The two areas requiring specialised staff are in the bakery and butcher shop.

Learning and Performance Control History			
Narrative of Flag: W = warning; S = serious; blank = acceptable			
Reports/Reviews	**Date Issued**	**Flag**	**Issues/Action**
Staff/Skills Training -Skilled operators	July 05 July 04 July 03	W S 	Butchery training Butchery training Fully trained
Targets and Schedules -Working condition evaluation	July 05 July 04 July 03	 W 	 Staff at butchery
Performance Monitoring -Staff evaluation -Staff evaluation -Staff evaluation	July 05 July 04 July 03	W S 	Improving Staff weaknesses Acceptable

Table 5.3   Learning, controls and feedback

On the whole the diagnosis highlights the main area of concern as the butchery, but the prognosis is that the business is heading to a full recovery of the weaknesses identified in the area of operation. Weaknesses in the training of shop and bakery staff in year 04 were addressed and improved. The owners may require specialist support in order to get the butcher shop to operate efficiently, but progress is observable.

Although decisions of innovative changes, such as the purchase of the butcher shop, are often taken and implemented in isolation in young owner-focused businesses, the impact of this isolation can be observed in Table 5.4.

Change Initiation and Development Performance History			
Narrative of Flag: W = warning; S = serious; blank = acceptable			
Reports/Reviews	**Date**	**Flag**	**Action/Impact**
New/Changes to Products/Services			
-Diversified to include butchery	Nov 04	S	New field
-Changes to store layout	Apr 04	W	
Change Support			
-Informal support survey	July 05		70% satisfied
-Informal support survey	July 04	W	45% satisfied
Product/Process Development			
-Not applicable (butchery handled separately by management)			

Table 5.4   New product/service initiation and development

Similar to the health diagnostics of the operations functions presented in Tables 5.2 and 5.3, the diagnostics for new product introduction and development also indicates healthy functioning. Although the acquisition of the butcher shop resulted in serious financial concerns, the managers handled the staffing issues well and continued to ensure that the staff in the butchery are being trained and equipped to the same high standard as those in the store and bakery. Issues were dealt with as and when they arose and regular reviews were conducted at least once a year.

As a young start-up organisation the operating teams are functioning well and are being well managed in their personal and job related tasks. This is often typical of start-up organisations where the owners focus on the core tasks to be performed in order to compete, as well as the people to perform these tasks.

Conclusion

Recommendations addressing the fitness of organisations tend to measure the efficiency and productivity of the operating units in order to ensure that the organisation is not only profitable, but can strive to be a winner in its market. While this is laudable, it may hide underlying health issues which, if not yet visible, could become serious concerns in the future.

The health diagnostics discussed in the chapter therefore addressed the underlying ability of the operating units to function in a coordinated manner. Key common areas to be observed were identified as the ability of the teams to operate in a smooth and coordinated way, be fully trained and equipped with the required knowledge or skills, and be able to perform according to set standards and targets. The units have been identified as the functions which allow an organisation to be mobile, agile and flexible in its relationship to its external environment, analogous to the different skeletal muscle units in the body. The units therefore enable the organisation to compete in its target market, but have also been defined as wider than only the core competitive units, including internal functions of staff transport, sales and marketing, and customer and public relations.

The different types of operating units were addressed separately in order to identify the differences, together with the need for learning, control and initiation of their allocated tasks. This is analogous to the close links among the skeletal muscle units, their initiation of action by the motor cortex in the brain, and the subconscious motor control by the cerebellum.

In Chapter Six the diagnostic focus moves to the gathering and interpretation of information, analogous to the role of senses in the body. Healthy functioning will focus on external and market related information gathering and research, analogous to the use of senses of sight, hearing, smell and taste by living organisms. It also covers internal information gathering compared to the internal perception of pressure, pain and temperature in a body. The chapter will follow a similar format in which each function is compared to its physiological equivalent, how the functions operate within organisations and the best method of diagnosing concerns in their functionality.

Notes

1. Functional structuring and the separation of jobs between managers and workers were key concepts promoted by Classical and Scientific Management theorists in: Taylor, F.W. (1911) *Principles of Scientific Management* Harper & Row, New York; and Fayol, H. (1949) *General and Industrial Management* Pitman, London.

2. Two sources used to explain the physiology of the skeletal muscle units in the human body, including the motor central nervous system control are: Barrett, K.E., Barman, S.M.. Boitano, S., Brooks. H.L. (2010). *Ganong's Review of Medical Physiology*, twenty-third edition. McGraw-Hill Medical, New York; and Barker, R.A., Barasi, S., Neal, M.J. (2008). *Neuroscience at a Glance*. Third edition. Blackwell Publishing, Malden, Massachusetts.

3. Research into the similarities of the functioning of organisations and organisms found focus differences in operating units, as presented in: Dean, C.M. (2012) *The Physiology of Organisations: An Integrated Functional Perspective.* Cambridge Scholars Publishing, Newcastle upon Tyne, pp. 109-119.

4. Reliance on equipment in endurance work is the Piper-Alpha disaster, accessed on www.smd.qmul.ac.uk/risk/yearone/casestudies/piper-alpha.htms; and Freudenburg. W.R., Gramling, R. (2011) *Blowout in the Gulf: The BP Oil Spill Disaster and the Future of Energy in America.* Massachusetts Institute of Technology.

5. Examples of important factors for healthy manufacturing team functioning include: Jaakola, E. and Renko, M. (2007). Critical Innovation Characteristics Influencing the Acceptability of New Pharmaceutical Product Format. *Journal of Marketing Management*, Vol. 23, No. 3-4, pp. 327-346.

6. Concerns based on fast changing targets and unaccepted preparation and training were found by Wilkinson, A., Dundon, T., Grugulis, I. (2007). Information but not Consultation: Exploring Employee Involvement in SMEs. *International Journal of Human Resource Management.* Vol. 18, No. 7, pp. 1279-1297.

7. Misrepresentation of messages to the external environment can be found in the messages following disasters such as in the case of Texaco or Enron in: Pfarrer, M.D., Decelles, K.A., Smith, K.G. (2008). After the Fall: Reintegrating the Corrupt Organization. *Academy of Management Review*. Vol. 33, No. 3, pp. 730-749. The effect of internal misinformation was explored in: Shum, P., Bove, L., Auh, S. (2008). Employees' Affective Commitment to Change. The Key to Successful CRM Implementation. *European Journal of Marketing*. Vol. 42, No. 11/12, pp. 1346-1371.

8. Targets and monitoring can malfunction by being either too tight or changing too often as found in research by: Glover, L. and Wilkinson, A. (2007). Worlds Colliding: The Translation of Modern Management Practices Within a UK-Based Subsidiary of a Korean-Owned MNC. *International Journal of Human Resource Management.* Vol. 18, No. 8, pp. 1437-1455; and Lloyd, C. and James, S. (2008). Too Much Pressure? Retailer Power and Occupational

Health and Safety in the Food Processing Industry. *Work, Employment and Society*. Vol. 22, No. 4, pp. 713-730.

9. Visual presentations of the relative sizes of the motor unit areas in the primary motor cortex can be found in: Barker, R.A., Barasi, S., Neal, M.J. (2008). *Neuroscience at a Glance*. Third edition. Blackwell Publishing, Malden, Massachusetts, p. 84; and Barrett, K.E., Barman, S.M.. Boitano, S., Brooks. H.L. (2010). *Ganong's Review of Medical Physiology*, twenty-third edition. McGraw-Hill Medical, New York, p. 245.

10. Resistance to change in heavy industry was researched in the forestry industry by: Halme, M. (2002) Corporate Environmental Paradigms in Shift: Learning During the Course of Action at UPM-Kymmene. *Journal of Management Studies*. Vol. 39, No. 8, pp. 1078-1109; while the positive impact on change was found by: Ivory, C. and Vaughan, R. (2008) The Role of Framing in Complex Transitional Projects. *Long Range Planning*. Vol. 41, pp. 93-106; and Chreim, S., Williams, B.E., Hinnings, C.R. (2007). Interlevel influences on the Reconstruction of Professional Role Identity. *Academy of Management Journal*. Vol. 50, No. 6, pp. 1515-1539.

11. Classic examples of change decisions which were unnecessarily delayed, or inadequately tested changed procedures are that of Kodak presented by Dr. Munir in 2012 www.jbs.cam.ac.uk/media/2012/the-reasons-behind-kodaks-demise/; inadequate testing caused a disaster on the opening day of Heathrow Airport's Terminal 5 due to inadequate staff preparation or systems testing: Great Britain House of Commons: Transport Committee: *The Opening of Heathrow Terminal 5, Twelfth Report of Session 2007-08*, published on 3rd November 2008.

12. The use of dashboard displays has been widely accepted by organisations to allow a drill-down facility of information to supporting data. A reference, based on practical application in various organisations is: Eckerson, Wayne W. (2011). *Performance Dashboards: Measuring, Monitoring and Managing your Business*. 2nd Ed. John Wiley & Sons, Hoboken NJ.

CHAPTER SIX

INFORMATION FUNCTIONS

*Without healthy information functions an organisation
can lose its way.*

Information functions, analogous to the senses of living organisms, are involved in the observation, interpretation, storage and retrieval of information from various sources in order to enable the organisation to develop an awareness of its environment. These functions include:

External Information

Internal Information

Interpretation, Storage and Retrieval

The general objectives of senses in living organisms are to observe and detect stimuli from their external and internal environments. Different senses include: special senses like sight, hearing, smell, taste and balance which receive stimuli from the external environment; and the somatosensory system of pain, pressure and temperature which receive impulses from receptors in the skin and muscle units. The detection and response to stimuli is accepted as one of the key properties of life and it is in the observation of these stimuli that the senses play a role to inform and thus trigger responses[1]. Similarly, an organisation does not operate in an isolated vacuum and is dependent on information in order to react appropriately. References to the physiology of senses are presented as shaded boxed inserts which can be ignored as additional information and not essential for clarity.

External Information

External information research and interpretation, whether referring to information about the wider environment or a targeted market, can be compared to the use of the special senses by living organisms.

Special Senses[1]

The special senses of sight, hearing, smell and taste are involved in the perception of stimuli from the environment around the body.

The function of the visual sensory system is to observe through sight. The receptor cells in the retina of the eye are responsible for converting light energy into electrical impulses and in transmitting the impulses to the visual areas in the brain where the impulses are analysed and combined into composite pictures. This knowledge is, for instance, important for diagnostic purposes to establish whether an inability to see is related to damage in the eye, such as with cataracts, or as a result of optic nerve or brain damage in transmitting and interpreting the light image, such as in persons with cortical blindness who are capable of receiving the light impulses, but unable to interpret them in the brain.

Hearing is responsible for sound perception from the receptors in the ear where sound waves are detected, converted into electrical signals and transmitted to the associated auditory areas in the brain. These auditory areas interpret sound as well as more complex interpretations of music and language, and eventually transmit to the frontal lobe, responsible for the expression of speech. Hearing disabilities could lead to complications in speech and verbal communication in individuals.

Smell and taste senses are mainly involved in the perception of different chemical stimuli in the form of odours or taste through receptors in the nose and on the tongue, before transmission to the associated sensory areas in the brain. Cells in the sensory areas for smell and taste can change and be replaced throughout life. Taste and smell play an important role in the mouth and nose in detecting food and inhaled air that can either stimulate or be detrimental to the body.

Proprioception is involved in the control and maintenance of balance and posture of the body. Receptors situated in the middle ear monitor balance during walking and standing, resulting in reflexive corrections of balance as and when required.

Tests for the special senses of sight, hearing and smell evaluate an individual's ability to perceive both peripheral and targeted stimuli. Peripheral perception tests focus on the ability of the individual to detect movements, distant noises or smells as warning signals of potential opportunities or danger. The narrower focused checks of visual acuity, directed hearing or smelling determine the individual's ability to be aware of immediate environmental information requiring prompt response. In addition, a test for proprioception should be included to monitor the ability of individuals in maintaining a balanced position in their immediate environment, resulting in reflexive correction of stance when required.

In organisations, wider environmental trends and information, compared to the peripheral sensory tests, refer to information that can have a future positive or negative impact on the organisation and therefore should influence its longer term decisions and strategies. Targeted information, compared to the focused use of special senses and proprioception, is used to measure and monitor immediate environments such as customers, markets, suppliers and competitors. The objective is to react to the stimuli, or to develop and implement short-term tactics and plans either as defensive, collaborative or aggressive actions in the immediate environment.

Diagnostically, it is necessary to evaluate the state of health of the functions involved in environmental data and information research, as well as more targeted market research and positional monitoring of the organisation in its immediate market environment.

External Environmental Information

External information research and analysis can be compared to the ability of an individual to scan the environment for changes by using the peripheral senses of sight, hearing, smell and taste. While this is not always regarded as a feasible separate function in small organisations, it is still necessary for all organisations to detect and be aware of changes in legal requirements, ethical values, technological developments, broad market and competitive trends, and potential physical risks which may impact the future performance and direction of the organisation.

Some of the information can be obtained from official sources or with the help of external information agencies, and include legal and regulatory changes affecting the sector or the organisation directly. The changes often link to 'immunisation' techniques used by governments to address or prevent recurrence of fraudulent or serious unethical practices. By the imposition of laws and regulations, organisations can be impelled to improve their internal controls[2]. It also refers to information on trends and regulatory changes of ethical and ecological issues, such as fair and equal opportunities and treatment of staff in countries of operation or the need for pollution reduction measures.

Environmental information scanning, furthermore, needs to address trends in technological developments which may affect the organisation's operations now or in the future, for example, the tracking of new inventions in the field of products, tools or means of operation that can be beneficial, or a threat to the organisation. This is especially relevant during times of change such as the current fast changing digital age of operation. Established organisations may have been detrimentally affected by not heeding technological advancements of online marketing or improved processing facilities and found their competitive position in the market reduced. However, first movers in new technology may also find that by operating as a beta-test facility in a new field, disastrous results can follow[3]. It is important, not only to detect and collect environmental trends and moves, but to analyse the importance of this information before reporting to senior management for responsive decision-making.

Similar to the wider environmental research function, larger organisations are likely to have functions dedicated to this type of information collection, such as: IT support functions to monitor unwanted data access and hacking; the security departments to investigate warning messages and signals of potential physical access violations; or the product research and development departments investigating new methods to produce improved products. Smaller organisations will either perform this function on an informal basis, or depend on external sources of information and consultation.

In order to diagnose whether an organisation has a healthy information collection and interpretation mechanism for peripheral environmental information, it is necessary to identify the existence of research unit(s) or relevant sources of information, and to determine whether the information thus gathered is relevant, analysed, interpreted and reported for action.

Possible Health Questions for External Environmental Information:

- Does the organisation have the means to detect and interpret relevant new and changed trends, developments or risks?

- Is the environmental information suitably interpreted, analysed and reported to senior management?

- Are there any 'blind spots' in environmental information that caused concerns or issues in the past, what was done about it, and how can recurrences be prevented?

External Market Information

Whereas the initial diagnostic steps of special senses focus on the ability to scan and interpret movements and changes in the peripheral environment, the next area of diagnosis is interested in the ability to focus the senses on the near environment, such as focused reading, the selection of specific sounds, or specific smells and taste. This can be compared to the immediate market research and information gathering of an organisation, covering performances and trends with respect to its customers, suppliers, partners and competitors.

This information research can be performed by the sales and marketing department or dedicated market research functions. It is necessary to be sensitive to customer demands, but at the same time be aware of competitive and new trends in the markets, products, processing technology, availability of supplies, and tools that can be beneficial to the organisation. Concerns arising from inadequate focused information research can impact the competitiveness or continued existence of the organisation and result in the need to reinvent or change its market offer in order to catch up with changed trends[4].

The most immediate and local gathering of market information can be compared to proprioception, the detection of imbalance and the reflexive correction to the positioning of the organism. This information research in organisations refers to collection, analysis and the interpretation of immediate operational, customer and sales data and the ability of local middle management to address immediate concerns. It is not only the sales and marketing departments who are best placed to perform this function, but the customer contact centres as well. The response could also come from local managers to correct immediate concerns.

The focus is on the collection and interpretation of the right kind of information with respect to the organisation's immediate market positioning and performance.

Possible Health Questions for External Market Information:

- Is the organisation aware of specific customer opinions and needs in comparison to the performance of its key competitors?

- What regular action is taken on competitor and market trends?

- What lessons were learnt from poor market information and the action taken to rectify the situation?

- To what extent is middle management empowered to act on immediate complaints or suggestions from customers?

Internal Information

Internal information functions can be compared to the somatosensory receptors in the body, responsible for the detection of changes in pain, pressure and temperature, and resulting in locally induced reflexive action or decisive cognitive response.

Somatosensory System[1]

Somatosensory perception acts through nerve ending receptors in the skin and muscle cells to detect changes in touch, pressure, pain and temperature internal, and on the surface of the body.

The relative numbers of touch receptors are much higher in certain areas of the skin or membranes, thus allowing for greater sensitivity in these parts of the body. Temperature perception and pain is associated with actual or potential tissue damage.

The electrical information transfer from the receptors to the brain only occurs once a threshold of sensitivity has been reached for the receptor. Interpretation and response to the somatosensory stimuli from the body can either be reflexive, initiated at synapses, or take place in the associated somatosensory areas in the brain which then project to the hypothalamus for appropriate response action.

Pathological conditions can lead to numbness and an inability to detect pressure, pain and differences in temperature; or to chronic pain.

Internal information functions, similarly, aim to detect and respond to changes in internal morale and concerns of malfunctions within the organisation in order to decide on, and to initiate corrective action. Action can either be local or the information could be escalated for further action by senior management.

The threshold of severity above which information is communicated to higher levels of management depends on the culture within the organisation and demonstrates the power of local control, but also the atmosphere of openness to complaints, suggestions or warnings available to all staff. Senior management need to be made aware of serious changes in local performance or morale, but should not be inundated with small deviations that can be resolved locally.

Internal information could therefore be discussed and diagnosed under the headings of information requiring executive attention, or information that can be locally addressed.

Internal Information Requiring Executive Response

Each organisation has its own culture to guide staff relationships and an accepted set of operational values. While culture, in its wider sense, can be compared to the hormonal system within living organisms (to be discussed in the next chapter), one aspect of this culture, namely the readiness of the organisation to listen to and heed staff complaints and suggestions, is closer related to the sensitivity threshold of the somatosensory system of organisms.

In small organisations, or organisations with broad informal structures, most concerns or complaints are usually dealt with locally and if possible with minimal senior management involvement. In larger organisations with a more formal structure, the complaints process is more likely to be formal and under the control of a human resource function. The real issues for a healthy functioning response system are to ensure that a complaints and information detection and reporting system is in place, that the transfer of information on issues to senior management is in line with the accepted culture of local control, and that there are no blockages in which individuals do not have access to senior management.

It is, however, possible that the declared level of sensitivity may not reflect actual information transfers, and that parts of the organisation may have blocks on information transfer, either locally imposed or due to blocks in the hierarchical management structure. This may result in areas not receiving due attention to complaints, such as in the cases of poor operating work environments, leading to health issues for the individuals, or localised fraudulent action not being made visible for action[5].

Possible Health Questions for Internal Information Requiring Executive Response:

- Does the organisation operate a complaints system and regularly conducts staff reviews on a free and open basis?

- Is it possible for staff or whistle-blowers to raise issues without fear of reprisal and how good is the staff morale with respect to the issues being listened to and heeded?

- Are complaints and suggestions received from all parts of the organisation, and if not, how was this omission handled in the past?

Internal Information Requiring Local Response

Some internal information may be better addressed at local levels, analogous to reflex responses to internal stimuli. This information can be low key warnings or information requiring immediate local corrective response, for example information signifying staff dissatisfaction or a malfunction in certain areas of the organisation.

Staff dissatisfaction as a result of an undue workload is not uncommon and could be a result of understaffing in certain departments or work peaks imposed by other departments or business activities. Examples include the potential stressful work in call centres, understaffing during times of austerity, or insistence on tight timescales for the completion of tasks. This type of internal information is usually controlled and addressed at a local level, but if persisting, should be reported to senior management.

Information about functional malfunctioning, or fraudulent activities within the organisation, refers to a general disgruntlement either from a widespread section of the personnel, or at a more localised level. Employees could be dissatisfied with the actions of one or a few individuals; their remuneration and work conditions; not receiving the necessary supplies for work; or an unsatisfactory workplace environment. Again, most of the time the responses could be local by expediting the delivery of necessary resources and supplies, or confronting individuals suspected of fraudulent or unethical action. Local managers should, however, report information about serious incidents in order to prevent or limit damage to the organisation[6]. The extent to which senior management is made aware of warnings or complaints remains important.

Possible Health Questions on Local Responses to Internal Information:

- Are pathways available to report and handle work pressure or complaints about malfunction and how effective is the response?

- What is the normal method of response to information offered to management and how does it match the cultural value set of the organisation?

- Were there incidents in which management had to offer an immediate response to information and how was this handled?

Sensory information, whether from the external special senses, or from the internal somatosensory system in the body, can be ignored, immediately acted upon, or stored in memory for future access and utilisation by the brain. It is therefore not only the observations, transmissions and response to information that is important, but also the extent to which lessons learnt from the information can and are used to prevent future similar incidents.

Interpretation, Storage and Retrieval

Since immediate reflex responses to events and requests are short-term, in order to prevent future recurrences, it is necessary for the organisation to be able to remember and learn from experience and to store and utilise the acquired knowledge.

Learning and Memory[1]

"A characteristic of animals and particularly of humans is the ability to alter behaviour on the basis of experience. Learning is acquisition of the information that makes this possible and memory is the retention and storage of that information"[7]. Memory can be split into short term or working memory and long term memories.

Working memory "is defined as the limited capacity (around seven items or chunks of information) to store information in consciousness but that rapidly disappears when attention is diverted"[7]. The effective use of working memory depends on the coordinated activity of the various functions in receiving and executing response to the information. Storage is therefore limited only to the duration of the response. Abnormalities may lead to Huntington's or Parkinson's diseases with a difficulty in resolving problems and coordinated motor reactions.

Long-term memory "is a store of practically unlimited capacity and the memories stored within this system may persist over the lifetime"[7]. These memories can further be divided into explicit memories, i.e. accessible to conscious recall, or implicit memories, such as the motor memories in which case the recall is subconsciously and routinely.

Abnormalities can usually be ascribed to neurodegenerative diseases like Alzheimer's in which case the recall of long-term memories become difficult or spurious or dementia affecting short term memories.

This learning and data/information storage function can be compared to the learning and memory functions in the brain of complex living organisms. It has also been widely promoted through learning organisations, although the concepts involved in organisational learning and application of information differ among the various theorists and supporters of the concepts[8].

The approach to effective storage and recovery of internal and external information will be discussed, analogous to the different types of memory, such as short-term working memory or storage; implicit subconscious learning and memory, and long-term explicit memory.

Short-Term Work Data and Information

Short-term information refers to data and information requiring immediate attention for transaction processing, or is regarded as inconsequential to the functioning of the organisation. Analogous to reflex internal information processing, or the token scanning of the wider and market environments, this information is interpreted and acted upon, and then mostly discarded after the event. Permanent storage is seldom required and action is localised to the area receiving the data and information. Examples, however, of situations when the temporary storage of working information can be crucial include end-of-shift notes to be read by members of the next shift, especially for service, manufacturing or maintenance teams. This could prevent duplication of effort, or more seriously, the omission of steps that still need to be executed by members of the new shift[9].

For the purposes of working memory and learning, the channels of information flow and selection of information for temporary or permanent storage are therefore more important than the actual storage of the information per se. Storage of short-term task related data, for instance worksheets used to calculate prices, can result in excessive data for future manipulation. It may, however, be important to store and be able to retrieve information-driven events and responses for future learning. Examples include responses to the requirements of high value customers for the sales team; responses to access violations of data or physical premises; replenishment of supplies and/or assistance for functions unable to perform their tasks due to inadequate support; or immediate response to image-damaging events within the environment.

Diagnostics should therefore focus on: the availability and use of task related data; the ability to differentiate between short-term temporary data to complete specific tasks; and the data and information that need to be stored for future referencing and analysis. It is also necessary to be aware of how and where this data and information can be recorded and stored to become part of the implicit or explicit long-term memory storage and learning facilities within the organisation.

Possible Health Questions for Short-Term Working Data and Information:

• How is day-to-day work data and information acted upon and stored, and are the processes adequate and safe?

• Is it possible for individuals to access day-to-day data and information essential for their work?

• Are programmes in place to teach and encourage cooperation among workers with respect to data and information transfers?

Stored Information to Facilitate Learning

Long-term memory and learning in living entities can be compared to the recording of event or fact-based data and information in a format that allows it to be recalled, analysed and used in support of future decisions or actions. Whereas other types of information recording and learning are process related, long-term recording focuses on historic performance, events, trends and analysis results. In the past storage used to take the form of paper based archives, this form has now been largely replaced by the electronic recording and storage of data and information. This creates better access to the data and information stored in the relevant databases of the organisation.

The functions most closely linked to data storage and information interpretations are the IT department for the database processing and access, and a management information or data analysis section to retrieve, analyse and interpret the stored information for reporting to senior management. A research team in 2007 interviewed directors of 40 organisations in the UK with respect to their roles in the formulation of strategic decisions. In addition to defining their importance as strategic decision-makers at executive and board level, they emphasised that the executive group "monitored, reviewed and, if necessary, amended strategy in the light of changes in the organisation's internal and external environment relative to when the strategy was first formulated"[10]. This demonstrated the importance of accessibility to information by senior managers as and when required.

Not all information recorded and stored as long-term information is, however, effectively used in the making of executive decisions. In their plea for evidence-based information to support business decisions, Pfeffer and Sutton referred to the many management decisions based on the previous experiences, values and beliefs of the managers instead of on actual information gathered, interpreted and applied to the relevant decisions[11]. Similar to the difficulty in accessing and analysing archival information in the past, the vast amount of electronic data and information currently available to management does not mean that this information is analysed and heeded.

Diagnostics should focus on the availability and maintenance of electronic and other data storage facilities of relevant long-term data and information based on past performance and consequences of action, and the impact that these may have on decisions for the future. Especially in the global environment of operation, these facts and event-based lessons are becoming essential to successful operations.

Possible Health Questions for Long-Term Information and Learning:

- How is long-term data and information recorded and stored and is it possible and accessible to retrieve and use this information in the future as and when required?

- Are the storage databases and facilities secure and protected against incidents of damage and can they be restored?

- Is this stored information ignored, or referred to and used in decision-making processes?

Diagnosing Information – The Process

Diagnosing the state of health in an organisation's ability to scan, detect and interpret external and internal environmental signals can be compared to an individual's ability to effectively use his or her senses to recognise stimuli that denote opportunities, dangers or threats from the external environment or from internal organs in the body. Healthy means of observation rely on the existence of functions or individuals performing the scanning process; and the effectiveness of the analysis, interpretation, storage and learning processes. Diagnostic steps can therefore follow the sequence as presented in Figure 6.1 by checking for the existence and effective functioning of the information collection functions, followed by the extent to which the information is interpreted, stored and retrieved in the organisation.

Figure 6.1   Diagnostic stages for information functions

External Awareness

External information research and analyses functions are analogous to the existence and effective functioning of the special senses of sight, hearing, smell and taste in living organisms. To be effective, it is necessary to check for the ability of a person to scan and identify peripheral movement, as well as be able to focus on specifics, such as focused reading or tone detection. Within organisations the first step will therefore be to determine whether it has access to information from its own or external research bodies for wider environmental and immediate market related information.

Measurement of the first diagnostic category can be partially tick-box related. It may be sufficient to identify the existence of separate departments involved in the relevant areas of research and data collection. The types of information, their relevance and the extent of the research and analysis should however form part of the measurement.

The existence of information functions or access to external research bodies does not mean that the information thus collected is relevant, or addresses essential topics.

A good question to ask could be whether the organisation is aware of (or has performed) informational risk analysis exercises to identify the areas of vulnerability on which information will be required, or else be beneficial. This could include the tracking of: essential legal and regulatory information; trends in ethical attitudes; indications of new technological or processual developments; and specific customer or competitive trends in its target market.

Internal Awareness

Unlike the functioning of its special senses which enables a living organism to position itself within its immediate and wider environment, the internal somatosensory system warns the organism of potential or imminent areas of concern, danger or damage within itself. This function in organisations is usually performed through observations, meetings or surveys conducted by a human resources department or by managers as part of their staff relations remit.

Diagnostic tools to ensure healthy collection of internal information should address: the use of staff surveys on morale and concerns; the availability of channels for complaints; and the availability of historic information and trends of damaging incidents in the past and how these were addressed with lessons learnt.

Similar to the effectiveness of the external information functions, a key question with respect to the gathering of internal information needs to consider the seriousness with which the internal information is gathered and heeded by management. It is not enough to tick a box saying that staff surveys or meetings are conducted regularly if the information is not analysed, passed on and actioned at relevant levels of management.

Interpretation, Transmission and Storage

Analogous to incidents of cortical blindness or selective deafness in individuals where the stimuli are reaching the senses but are not transmitted to the brain, or when the stimuli cannot be interpreted, the information collected by organisations need to be interpreted before it can meaningfully be used to support decision-making by senior management.

This diagnostic step, therefore, requires action wider than a tick-box for information collection. Evidence should be available of information collected, but also presented for further action, and effectively stored for future retrieval and action. Specific information related health diagnostics could include:

- An acceptable list of the relevant legal, regulatory, ethical and ecological categories of information being collected, interpreted and reported to management.
- Evidence of correct and relevant interpretation of wider environmental trends and their potential impact on the organisation.
- Evidence of suitable interpretation of market related information as applied to existing and new products, customers and suppliers.
- Evidence of the recording and learning of quality operating processes.
- Evidence of the recording and learning from crisis incidents and lessons learnt to prevent recurrences.

Data and interpreted information should be available for immediate decision-making, or for future utilisation, analogous to the use of the short-term and long-term memory areas in the brain. To ensure that data and information remain accessible for analysis in the future, the data recording, archiving, retrieval and utilisation of information is as important as the collection. The role of IT to manage and provide access to various data storage facilities and tools is important in today's electronic environment and this function therefore requires the same amount of diagnostic checks as the collection functions. Areas to investigate include: data storage tools; their security; accessibility; and recovery after incidents of the loss of the facilities.

As a stimulus of opportunity, warning or danger, information is important and should be taken seriously by all members of the organisation. It is also important that this information is transmitted to the relevant users, mostly senior management, as a foundation for decisions on action to be taken by the organisation.

Case Study

A case study of a retail store is used throughout the book in order to demonstrate the applicability of a health diagnostic process for organisations. The brief summary of the case study history and overall image performance is presented again in the shaded insert, followed by additional diagnostic findings of the information functions.

In the case study of The Corner Shop, broadly based on a real five year old franchise retail store, the initial diagnosis in Chapter Two identified financial concerns as a serious survival issue together with image concerns which could point to additional issues. The store owners requested a survey to determine whether a health check diagnosis of all functional areas could highlight other issues which could then be addressed to prevent a potential closure of the business. This formed the basis of the case study.

Chapters Three to Five explored health issues in the survival, protection and operations functions of the business. The diagnostic tools used in this chapter investigated the effectiveness of the information functions in order to contribute to the full health check of The Corner Shop.

CASE STUDY – THE CORNER SHOP

An independent retail franchise grocery store and bakery, referred to as The Corner Shop, is part of a larger chain. Although the franchisee has the freedom to structure and run the business independently, the holding company is expecting a regular fee from the store as a member of its chain and requires the store to maintain a minimum set of standards. In return, the store owners can use the preferential rates for stock purchases negotiated for the chain and receive advisory assistance from the holding company. The store is in a favourable location in the main street of the town, conveniently situated for a wide range of customers, and the owners have had previous experience and knowledge of retail, finance and accountancy.

The store has been operating for five years. During the first two years it delivered record turnover and profits to the extent that the business was nominated as the 'winning' store in the chain. The customer base was classified as predominantly upper middle-class and the overall image of the store was vibrant and welcoming. The owners went out of their way to satisfy customer needs, for instance, by offering a type of bread made from a special recipe, sought after by many of the local hotels and restaurants, and by ordering and stocking special items on request.

During the third year, the owners decided to expand and diversify by acquiring a butcher shop in the adjacent town. The butchery was at the point of closing and they managed to get it at a reasonable price, including commitments of rental agreements undertaken by the previous owners. They managed to extend their bank loan to finance the deal and one of the owners is spending most of his time running the butchery. The combination of the additional workload for the owners together with mounting repayment burdens of interest and earlier stock purchases are making it difficult to maintain the previous standards of operation. The image of the store and service to the customers has been dropping and resulted in a loss of customers and sales.

Feedback on the diagnostic findings of the health of the information functions within the business is presented in a simplified dashboard display format. This approach commences with a summary set of 'dashboard dials'[12] to cover the main findings at summary level in Figure 6.1, followed by a drill-down facility that supports and presents additional detailed functional reports and evidence in tables 6.2 to 6.4.

The category of information functions presented in Table 6.1 is subdivided into its functions of external information, internal information and the storage and retrieval of the information. The functions are rated in the middle column by indicators as presented in the narrative section of the table and supported by summary comments in the right hand column.

Summary Dial of the Information Functions of the Business		
Narrative of Rating Indicators: First indicator (findings): ○ = acceptable; ◉ = unacceptable; ● = serious Second indicator (trend): ↓ = deteriorating; ↑ = improving; no arrow = unchanged Third indicator (impact): W = warning; S = serious; blank = acceptable		
Information Functions	**Rating**	**Comments**
External Information	● ↓S	Informal market and legal requirement research
Internal Information	◉ ↓W	Informal, and from staff meetings or reviews
Information Recording and Analysis	◉ ↓W	Mostly held on personal computers or paper

Table 6.1   Information functions summary diagnosis

The diagnosis of the health of the information functions indicates deterioration in all aspects of information gathering and interpretation, especially those focused on market information. Although not critical for the immediate survival of the company, they have to be highlighted as warnings for the business. Some of these impact concerns have already occurred as will be discussed below.

Each of the areas of information diagnostics have been expanded in Tables 6.2 to 6.4. The idea is to offer at least the latest report or measurement results and comment on the trend as well as the identified concerns or issues. The flags next to the results rate each finding as presented in the narrative section of the table.

A breakdown of the effectiveness of external wider and market related information gathering, reporting and utilisation is presented in Table 6.2, covering regulatory and ecological information; market and sales related reports and information.

The handling of legal and regulatory information proved to be satisfactory. External customer and market related information was either gathered on an informal basis or developed internally, and the quality of some of this information was either not very good, or was not reacted on in a timely manner.

Environmental and Market Related Information History			
Narrative of Flag: W = warning; S = serious; blank = acceptable			
Reports/Reviews	**Date Issued**	**Flag**	**Action**
Wider Regulatory and Legal Information -Legal and tax changes -Employment regulation changes	Jun 05 Mar 05		Latest obtained, implemented
Ecological Information -Changes in retail health issues -Latest ethical issues and regulations	Aug 05 Jan 03	W W	Need risk analysis of impact on sales
Market Related Information -Customer demand analysis	Jun 05	S	Still addressing original market
Sales Reports -Sales analysis reports	Jun 05	S	Sales report not by product type

Table 6.2   External environment and market related information

As demonstrated by the acceptable flags in the availability of legal information, the company regularly obtained the latest changes to taxation and staffing regulations, and implemented the changes and requirements successfully. Due to work pressure the owners did not really collect or heed any wider environmental or general ethical trends and information. While this may not be a problem at the moment, it should nonetheless be seen as a warning. Future regulatory changes based on these trends may result in major changes in the operating procedures which could, at that stage, become costly.

The information which could have made a difference to the dire financial situation of the company was the market information on customers and their needs compared to the sales analysis reports. Customer needs were not collected formally, and the owners relied more on their own observations and direct contact with the customers than on formal analyses. In the beginning, this resulted in procurement of products required by the more affluent customers in order to cultivate this market.

As the more affluent customers moved away, the owners did not accept or realise that their customer market was changing and that the product purchasing pattern had to change as well. This lack of awareness was compounded by the fact that the sales reports were not produced by product category, but on total turnover and profitability. It was not possible to identify which products were leaders or not selling at all, and this impacted stock replenishment and therefore a further loss of customers.

The diagnostic findings of gathering, interpretation and reporting external information was therefore mixed. For legal and regulatory information it operated well, but customer and market related information was gathered and interpreted subjectively and in general with the result that it was not possible to detect early warning triggers.

Internal Information History			
Narrative of Flag: W = warning; S = serious; blank = acceptable			
Reports/Reviews	**Date Issued**	**Flag**	**Action/Impact**
Staff Morale Surveys -Staff morale surveys	Apr 05	W	Morale lower in second survey
Suggestion/Complaint Procedures No formal process is in place. Concern are discussed during one-to-one interview sessions. -Informal staff survey		W	Possible to overlook concerns
Incident Reports -Staff theft report -Staff dissatisfaction report	Jun 05 May 04		Fired individual Addressed complaints

Table 6.3   Internal information

The ability to detect and monitor warning signals from staff, as demonstrated in Table 6.3, can be compared to the sensitivity of the brain to identify, interpret and react to pain, pressure or temperature changes within any part of the body. The brain can be sensitive, but it is also possible that it can be over or under-sensitive in its awareness or reactions to these stimuli. The analogy in the case study is the sensitivity of the owners and management team to staff concerns and damaging incidents within the business. During its five years of existence, the owners of The Corner Shop, for instance, only conducted two formal staff morale surveys. The first one was a year after the opening of the store and the morale of the staff was high. During the second survey, some dissatisfaction could be identified as the pressure of work increased and the focus switched from performance to survival. Although the concerns were raised in staff meetings, it was also an indication that more needed to be done to address general and individual concerns.

A more comprehensive method of presenting internal information, for instance internal complaints, is presented as a mosaic graph in Figure 6.2.

Narrative: Black = Serious; Dark Grey = Unacceptable; Light Grey = Acceptable; White = Good					
		Bakery	**Butchery**	**Shop**	**Owners**	**Back-office**
Finance	Profit		Black	Black		
	Remuneration				White	
	Investments		Black			
Logistics	Replenish			Dark Grey		Dark Grey
	Storeroom					
Workplace	Utilities	Light Grey				
	Cleaning			Dark Grey		
	Equip. maint.	Light Grey	Black	Black		
Security	Physical			Dark Grey		Dark Grey
	Fraud/theft			Black		
Operations	Sales		Dark Grey	Dark Grey		
	Customer			Dark Grey		
Information	Compliance					White
	Market				Dark Grey	
	Morale	Light Grey		Dark Grey		
Language	Image			Dark Grey		
	Staff comms		Dark Grey	Dark Grey		
Strategy	Development				Dark Grey	
	Expansion				Black	

Figure 6.2   Internal complaints by section and type of complaint

A better alternative presentation of the financial status of the business in Chapter Three was found to be the use of graphics. Similarly, complaints and concerns identified from internal information collection can be meaningfully presented as a mosaic of findings. This approach is popular (as coloured maps) in presenting population densities or weather patterns, and can also be used to pinpoint areas of concern as detected from staff surveys or reported incidents in the business.

The mosaic display in Figure 6.2 highlights the butcher shop as the area with the most serious complaints, while the bakery is performing best on image, sales and profits. The store had no formal methods for staff to complain or whistle-blow anonymously or without fear of reprisals with the result that a member of staff was able to remain undetected of product pilfering for a period of time before being caught by the manager. It was easier to report on petty theft by customers and children than to pinpoint areas of concern from within.

Table 6.4 presents the extent to which organisational information was stored and analysed in order to assist management in meaningful decision-making activities.

Information Storage and Retrieval History			
Narrative of Flag: W = warning; S = serious; blank = acceptable			
Reports/Reviews	Date Issued	Flag	Action/Impact
Incident Response and Learning -Crisis management reports		W	No formal reports Incident reports filed.
Operations Processes and Learning -Written/learnt processes -Training procedures and learning	Jun 03		None written Hands-on training
Archive and Trend Analyses -Regulatory archives -Environmental/market trend analyses	Jul 05	W	Regulatory files kept for 7 years No formal trend analyses

Table 6.4   Information storage and retrieval

The learning, storage and retrieval of information, analogous to the successful application of working and long-term memories in the brain, seem to be addressed informally and not as well-established procedures in the business. Regulatory and legal documents were stored for the required number of years, but the other types of information were either dealt with immediately, or often stored without further action or learning from the contents. Task processes have been developed on-the-job and although summarised in the job descriptions, have not been officially recorded to demonstrate the best practice of essential tasks. In a retail store this may not be too serious, but a record of best practice with respect to stacking and other tasks can make a difference to the image of the store as observed by customers, and in contributing to the overall efficiency of staff.

Management decisions were therefore based on informal experience instead of on lessons learnt from previous incidents or information obtained from sources internal or external to the business and the subsequent learning process.

Conclusion

Diagnosing concerns in the survival, protection and operations functions, as discussed in the previous three chapters, can provide pointers to serious concerns in areas that can be either fatal or debilitating to organisations. It is essential to follow sound financial processes and controls; protect the assets, people and information of the organisation against damage or intrusion; and to ensure that the operating units perform at an acceptable level in order for the organisation to operate healthily.

The ability to collect, interpret, analyse, store and learn from external and internal information, analogous to the effective use of senses by the brain, may not be essential for immediate survival but will affect the ability of the organisation to observe and react to stimuli from its environment, and therefore plan and/or change direction in order to meet its aims and objectives and persist in its environment.

Although management decision-making will only be discussed in Chapter Eight, the collection of information as discussed in this chapter should form the basis for the decisions and it is therefore important for organisations to collect the right information, interpret the knowledge in a meaningful way, and use these reports and analyses to ensure that the organisation is still on the path it has set for itself in its strategic goals and plans. Communicating the response to the collected information and subsequent actionable decisions is presented in Chapter Seven.

Notes

1. The important role of senses to detect and interpret stimuli from external and internal to organisms has been recognised and discussed by authors such as: Silver, B.L. (1998). *The Ascent of Science*. Oxford University Press, pp. 321, 322; Barker, R.A., Barasi, S., Neal, M.J. (2008). *Neuroscience at a Glance*. Third Edition. Blackwell Publishing, Maldem, Mass.; and Barratt, K.E.,

Barman, S.M., Boitano, S., Brooks, H.L. (2010). *Ganong's Review of Medical Physiology*. Twenty-third Edition, McGraw Hill Medical, New York.

2. Examples include the introduction in the USA of the Sarbanes-Oxley Act 2002, requiring organisations to improve their internal controls after the Enron scandal, evaluated by Chhaochharia, V. and Grinstein, Y. (2007). Corporate Governance and Firm Value: The Impact of the 2002 Governance Rules. *The Journal of Finance*. Vol. LXII, No. 4, pp. 1789-1825.

3. Examples of companies not embracing new technology for online trading were researched by: Birch, A., Gerbert, P. and Schneider, D. (2000). *The Age of E-Tail: Conquering the New World of Electronic Shopping*, by, ISBN 1-84112-092-8, accessed in: http://www.computerweekly.com/feature/Retailers-dont-delay-go-online-today. Companies who embraced technology too soon are the various Dot.com companies who failed due to hastily-made moves: Skillings, J. (2002). *Explaining the "Dot-Cons"*, ZDNet.com.au, 8th March 2002.

4. Kodak and US car manufacturers ignoring market and technological development trends were discussed by: Locke, R.R. and Spender, J-C. (2011) *Confronting Managerialism: How the Business Elite and Their Schools Threw our Lives out of Balance*. Zed Books, New York, pp. 106 – 132; and the Kodak incident: Eastman Kodak Company, *The New York Times*, May 30, 2013.

5. The need for channels for whistle-blowing and complaints is covered in: Linstead, S., Fullop, L., Lilley, S. (2009). *Management and Organization: A Critical Text*. Second Edition. Palgrave MacMillan, London, pp. 381-385.

6. Internal damage can occur in various functions and levels of an organisation. Examples include: Swartz, M. and Watkins, S. (2003) *Power Failure: The Inside Story of the Collapse of Enron*, New York, Doubleday; Report of the Board of Banking Supervision Inquiry into the Circumstances of the Collapse of Barings, 18 July 1995, *The Bank of England Report*, accessed on www.numa.com.

7. Memory is discussed in Barker, R.A., Barasi, S., Neal, M.J. (2008). *Neuroscience at a Glance*. Third Edition. Blackwell Publishing, Maldem, Mass. P. 289; and Barratt, K.E., Barman, S.M., Boitano, S., Brooks, H.L. (2010). *Ganong's Review of Medical Physiology*. Twenty-third Edition, McGraw Hill Medical, New York pp. 102–103.

8. Concepts used for learning organisations combine the use of memory and learning as promoted by: McMaster, M.D. (1995) *The Intelligence Advantage: Organising for Complexity*. Knowledge Based Development Co. Ltd, Douglas, Isle of Man; and Cybernetics by Norbert Wiener and explained in: Morgan, G. (2006) *Images of Organization*. Updated edition. Sage Publications Inc., Thousand Oaks, California pp. 81-87.

9. The importance of competency and message transmission during shift changes have been highlighted as potential reasons for disasters due to poor maintenance of aircraft or large drilling equipment http://news.aviation-safety.net/2010/04/07/poor-maintenance-started-accident-chain-that-resulted-in-learjet-high-speed-runway-excursion/ and
http://iveybusinessjournal.com/topics/leadership/bp-and-public-issues-mismanagement#.U0zxdvZOXIU

10. The research of the roles of company directors was conducted by Kelly, J. and Gennard, J. (2007). Business Strategic Decision Making: The Role and Influence of Directors. *Human Resource Management Journal*. Vol.17, No. 2, pp. 99-117.

11. Pfeffer and Sutton published some myths and truths on the use of management information in: Pfeffer, J. and Sutton, R.I. (2006). *Hard Facts, Dangerous Half-Truths, and Total Nonsense: Profiting from Evidence-Based Management*. Harvard Business School Press, Boston, Mass.

12. The use of dashboard displays has been widely accepted by organisations to allow a drill-down facility of information. A reference, based on practical application in various organisations, can be found in: Eckerson, Wayne W. (2011). *Performance Dashboards: Measuring, Monitoring and Managing your Business*. 2nd Ed. John Wiley & Sons, Hoboken NJ.

CHAPTER SEVEN

LANGUAGE AND COMMUNICATION

Without healthy communications functions an organisation cannot change

In order to adapt, an organisation needs to be able to observe information about challenges and concerns from within or from its external environment. This information will, however, be meaningless unless the organisation is able to understand how to respond to these stimuli and communicate the responsive action to the relevant areas and audiences. Organisations need to understand and remain healthy with respect to their:

Internal Communications

Communicating to Adapt and Change

External Language and Communications

Living organisms use their endocrine or hormonal system to communicate with cells by means of chemical hormones produced in various glands. This method of communication is continuous at an innate base level of hormonal production, but can be enhanced in crisis or special situations by increasing or suppressing the production in specific glands. Cell communication can also be direct through electrical impulses from the nervous system. External communication can be initiated by the emotional system in the brain, developed in the language area, and expressed through the use of language and emotional facial expressions to the external environment.

Organisations, analogously, display an innate culture developed and maintained by internal communications; a framework to communicate or motivate staff in case of change; and its own external language, public relations and image building procedures. While culture may influence external communications, the differences between the internal and external use of language and communications forms the focus for the diagnosis of healthy functional processing in this chapter.

Internal Communications

The internal communications function is compared to the endocrine system producing hormones as the chemical messengers for cellular impact and action[1]. The shaded insert of the physiological comparison offers additional and not essential information, and can be ignored.

Endocrine System[1]

Hormones act as messengers, produced by various endocrine glands and with actions at distant sites. The role of the glands is to produce both stimulating and suppressive messages to increase or decrease cell activity in order to achieve a balanced innate method of cell functioning. Many different types of hormones have been identified with a few examples presented.

The thyroid produces hormones to optimise metabolism by stimulating oxygen consumption in cells; regulating fat and carbohydrate metabolism; and being essential for normal growth and maturation. Pathological functioning either results in hypo-production leading to the slowdown of metabolic rate and lethargy, or to hyper-production resulting in hyperactivity. The parathyroid gland is similarly responsible for the production of calcium regulating hormones required for effective development of bones. Malfunction can lead to vitamin D deficiency and bone ailments such as rickets or osteomalacia resulting in weak and deformed bone structures.

The pancreas produces insulin and other digestive hormones which regulate efficiency of the intermediary metabolism of fat and carbohydrates, an absence of which can lead to diabetes and the resulting symptoms of inadequate energy production for normal cell operation.

The adrenal cortex produces adrenalin (also known as epinephrine). Adrenalin prepares the body for a fight or flight situation by mobilising the availability of nutrients through increased metabolic and heart rates. Examples of the impact of adrenalin include changes in the strength and contraction of the heart rate and muscle units, changes in the diameter of airways, and a reduction in intestinal mobility.

The pituitary gland produces growth hormones. The hormones stimulate growth, especially young growing bones, and muscle growth in adults. Excess production of the growth hormone could result in gigantism in young adults or the development of enlarged body parts e.g. hands or heart (acromegaly) in adults. Reproductive or sex hormones result in the maturation of the sex organs in adolescents and prepare the adult body for reproduction.

Hormonal production by the endocrine glands is a continuous process based on a standard innate rate of production of both stimulating and suppressing hormones required for normal functioning, or in cases of need, the selective increased production of stimulating hormones. Internal communications in organisations, analogous to the endocrine system, therefore refer to formal and informal communications functions which determine its innate value set or culture – adaptable during times of change.

Why use the word culture in organisations if the hormonal system in living organisms is about communication? Although there is no uniform definition of culture in organisations, a definition which has been widely accepted is that culture is the way things are, or are done in organisations, therefore, the values and attitudes as developed and accepted through internal communication. Johnson and Scholes used the concept of a cultural web to describe the way in which an organisation views itself within its environment, including elements of organisational and power structures; control systems; rituals, myths and symbols[2]. Of these elements the organisational and power structures and control systems define the value set of the organisation and 'how things are done', while the rituals, stories, myths and symbols reflect the culture based on internal formal and informal communications. However, as in the case of living organisms, innate does not mean permanent, and organisations may display different complementary or even opposing cultures in different parts of the organisation and can change them if required. It is necessary to understand the current and/or historic cultures before diagnosing its state of health.

Innate Culture

Defining the innate culture of an organisation is one of the more difficult tasks within any organisation. The standard method of using questionnaires or group discussions on organisational values often reflects individual opinions, or the preferred opinions of senior management, rather than organisational reality. Although values, beliefs and aspirations are a standard part of any organisation's public statement of vision and strategy, this may reflect the culture and values used by management to demonstrate the desired and therefore external image for the organisation. The reality in organisational functioning may be different as can be demonstrated by organisations officially promoting a caring or cooperative value set while the employees present a total disregard for these values in their actions[3].

A published set of values do not necessarily offer wider information on 'what the organisation is', in other words the innate mode and standards of its functioning. From a physiological point of view, factors to be included to expand the above model can be derived from the types and functioning of hormones produced by the endocrine glands. The various hormonal glands can, for instance, be summarised as addressing: effectiveness of metabolism and bone maintenance (thyroid and parathyroid); efficiency in the use of sources of energy and nutrients (pancreas); inclination to aggressiveness in fight or flight situations (adrenal cortex); organic growth (pituitary gland); reproduction for mature organisms (sex hormones); and emotional response to external stimuli (limbic system).

In combining the physiological framework to the alternative options of other cultural models[4], health diagnostics should therefore consider the criteria of:

- Attitude towards the effective use of resources.
- Efficiency in task fulfilment and interrelationships.
- Level of staff motivation (can do attitude).
- Commitment to balanced organic growth for the organisation.
- Attitude towards expansion through mergers or divesting of units.
- Sensitivity to external perception and changing signals.

Plotting the culture from the expected and observed sets of values will help to understand the innate organisational functioning and values. It does not mean that specific patterns are not healthy, as each organisation will have its own unique culture. It can, however, point to areas of significant deviation from other similar organisations, or areas that could cause problems in the future. It can also identify areas where the actual and published sets of values are different or split within the organisation. In the absence of a conscious understanding and decision to change, the organisation's innate culture becomes the default driver of action and decisions.

Sources and Channels of Internal Communication

If the values and ethos of an organisation is analogous to the impact of an innate level of hormonal production in a living organism, then the beliefs, rituals, myths and stories can be compared to the general or targeted messages being communicated through various channels within the organisation. In physiology the channels of communication is either remote by transmitting hormones from the glands through the bloodstream or plasma to be recognised and interpreted by the target cells; or it can be direct from nerve cell to individual cell by means of electrical impulses. The main sources and channels of communication can therefore be either direct or remote, including:

- Training and development programmes (effectiveness, efficiency, motivation).
- One-to-one or group discussions of supervisors and managers with staff (efficiency, motivation).
- Meetings and team discussions within operating teams on the task at hand (effectiveness, efficiency).
- Project team or wider notification of major changes (expansion, growth).
- Direct mail or email correspondence (efficiency).
- Networking either on a one-to-one basis, through social media or in groups, used by managers and teams to discuss and learn about specific events or topics (sensitivity, effectiveness, cooperation).

Organisations are likely to use multiple channels depending on the type of message to be communicated. The health concern is whether the channel used and messages transmitted are effective or whether some of these channels have been blocked or under-utilised. Are personnel informed about important organisational decisions directly by managers or does the information reach them via the grapevine?

Internal communication is the essential glue that binds together all the members of the organisation, whether through formal or informal means. Understanding this culture can help management to learn and improve by changing messages or exploring better and more effective channels of internal communication.

Possible Health Questions for Internal Communications:

- Does the organisation have a published set of values?

- Does internal culture reflect and support the published set of values?

- Do internal communication messages offer a good balance between encouragement and moderation, in line with the published values?

- Are the channels appropriate for the messages transmitted?

Communicating to Adapt and Change

Analogous to the hormonal system of a living organism, communication contributes to the development of an innate culture of structure, values, beliefs and conduct within organisations. What has also been demonstrated in both living organisms and organisations is that the innate culture and value set is not static, relies on feedback controls, and can temporarily or permanently be changed by adjusting certain messages.

Feedback Controls of the Endocrine System[1]

Hormonal production normally operates in response to a feedback control loop system. Information about changes in the functioning of cells is transmitted from various sources to the hypothalamus in the midbrain from which the stimulating responses are transmitted via the pituitary gland to different hormonal glands. Not all glands are affected by this feedback control loop. Adrenalin, for instance, is released in response to sympathetic nerve stimulation from the spinal cord and affects all cells.

One of the feedback cycles is via the central nervous system. Somatosensory nerve cell receptors pick up stimuli from cells as warnings of damage to cells. The response in the central nervous system includes stimulation of the limbic system and then via hypothalamus to endocrine glands to ensure increased hormonal production to assist healing, or as in the case of adrenalin, to prepare the different organs for a fight or flight response.

Reduced feedback and response to concerns relating to hormonal functioning can lead to illnesses such as diabetes or growth abnormalities.

The changes impacting organisational processing are usually either incremental or innovative changes. In a research project on the factors influencing changes within organisations it was found that communication played the most prominent role towards the successful implementation of change, both incremental and innovative[5]. The origin and channels of communication however differed for the two types of changes.

For a healthy internal communications function, the feedback mechanism and its effectiveness will be explored both during normal operations, but also during periods of incremental and innovative change within the organisation.

Communication Feedback Controls

By comparing organisations to living organisms, the importance of a close link among functions becomes obvious in the feedback control loop applicable to the production of hormones. In organisations this feedback control loop can be described as:

Function → Information → Management → Communications → Function

Information is collected from all functions about concerns or changes, transmitted to various levels of management and the reflex or initiated responses communicated back to the operating functions. This important feedback loop method that controls and monitors the effectiveness of communications has been widely promoted by organisational supporters of Cybernetics and the concept of the Learning Organisations[6]. However, it is often overlooked, resulting in potential misunderstandings or a lack of essential information to benefit processing.

It is necessary to know whether an effective feedback loop is in place to receive and communicate response to complaints – and for all members of the organisation to receive information about decisions to either change existing processes or to introduce major innovative changes. It is furthermore necessary to ensure that members are aware of the effective functioning of this feedback loop. Do they trust managers to listen and take action in regards to their concerns? And are they informed about the decisions or action taken?

Communicating for Change

Communicating for change can be separated into messages to incrementally improve existing processes, or messages to inform and facilitate the introduction of major innovative changes to the organisation.

Incremental changes do not alter underlying processes but address improvements to one or more of the processes, the levels of productivity or the levels of efficiency of the processes. They can be compared to routine response to cellular performance by adjusting the internal hormonal production, or by introducing changes to the lifestyle and/or diet of a person to address a hormonal imbalance. The target areas of these changes are usually specific and the direct sources and channels of communications localised.

Characteristics of effective communication to promote incremental changes in procedures, motivation and efficiency are likely to:

- Originate from design or implementation teams of improved systems, and can be effectively communicated by using local training methods.

- Rely on general communication with respect to benefits, or can alternatively be linked to a performance monitoring system, both as a stimulus and reward.
- Be transmitted via managers to promote individual performance, teamwork or group-work as motivational messages.

However, the change is often temporary and only for the duration of the flow of the motivational communication. Permanent changes may either require continuous motivational messages to be issued or more severe action to be imposed.

Innovative changes may affect a particular part or all members in the organisation and usually involves changes such as mergers, take-overs or a change in competitive direction. From a physiological point of view, this can be compared to: a major imbalance or lack of production of essential hormones such as insulin; attempts to prevent a potential rejection of transplanted organs; or preparation for pregnancy. In addition to assisting healing, drugs can be prescribed to suppress functioning of selected organs and systems, for example to calm a state of aggression or anxiety.

Communications for innovative change, analogous to the taking of additional hormones and drugs, differ from communication during incremental change in that:

- The decision to change is usually deliberate, taken and supported by senior management to ensure successful implementation of the radical change programmes.
- The main messages should originate from senior management to demonstrate their positive support.
- Affected departments are made to feel part of the intentions and action and if possible, accept ownership of the planned changes.
- Effective messages are likely to continue after completion in order to assist in the effort to adjust to the change and to develop a new culture and value set.
- The regular process of feedback is important in improving and addressing lessons learnt.

The focus of diagnosis for both incremental and innovative changes should be on the types of messages to be distributed, the involvement and backing of senior management to the changes, and the regular monitoring and adjustment of messages based on feedback of their impact.

Although periods of change are not necessarily part of the normal functioning of organisations, and can therefore be argued to be part of cures rather than a health diagnostic tool, it is necessary for an organisation to be able to adapt to changing circumstances in its environment, analogous to evolutionary and adaptive changes required by living organisms in order to survive and persist. It is already widely accepted that internal communication plays a critical role in the success of the normal balanced functioning of an organisation as well as the successful implementation of change programmes and for this reason it is necessary to ensure that both the sources and types of communication messages are healthy.

Possible Health Questions for Communicating Change:

- Have change programmes been effectively communicated to relevant members of staff?

- Has management offered and communicated visible backing to innovative change programmes?

- How effective is the information and communications flow loop in the organisation?

- What lessons were learnt from successful or failed incremental or innovative change programmes?

External Language and Communications

Internal communication shapes the culture, value set and operational conduct of an organisation. Being internally focused, it affects all members, and forms the glue that binds together the individuals and functions in the organisation. There is, however, another method for an organisation to communicate, this time to and with its external environment. Analogous to the limbic system and language area in the brain, it is reliant on information received from external sources, but then links this to its own interpretation and understanding of the meaning of the information, and responds through the use of language and image presentations. Diagnostically, the comparative areas for observation by medical practitioners include the aspects of projected appearance, mood and speech as part of the examination of the mental state of a patient.

Language and the Limbic System[7]

The limbic areas, such as the hippocampal complex and the amygdala in the brain, perform high-level processing of information received from the sensory cortices and pass information on to the planning areas and the frontal cortex for decision-making; the hypothalamus for hormonal production; and the motor cortical areas for muscular response. The limbic system is, however, also the location of emotion and mood, and its role can therefore be interpreted as adding behavioural and emotional significance to responses to stimuli. Damage to these areas may result in impairment of the individual to recognise facial expressions of, for example, fear in other individuals and therefore inability to interpret and respond empathetically to external sensory stimuli.

The secondary auditory cortical and language areas in the brain respond to external complex sounds of language and music and respond by links to Broca's area in the frontal lobe, responsible for the expression of speech. These two areas enable the individual to respond to external stimuli through speech and mostly facial, but also bodily expressions of intention. Damage can result in the inability to vocalise or express language and emotions, and displays a degree of bluntness in communications and actions.

External communication offers the external environment an insight into the internal functioning of an organisation, including its culture, code of conduct and value set. It is, however, important to realise that this insight is limited to what the organisation is willing, or able to disclose. It is conceivable that the image could be deliberately different from the reality of the internal value set, or be inadvertently influenced by potential signs of deteriorating or improving health. Similar to diagnosing concerns related to the internal culture of an organisation, the health of external communications functions should include current observations, compared to historic or independently verified observations.

Many theories have been developed around the dichotomy of disclosed versus actual meanings behind external communication messages. Visual communication messages encompass the organisation's use of corporate image and brands to present its internal set of values for the purpose of competitiveness. From a verbal perspective we focus on the ability of the organisation to present its views through its public relations functions, but also its ability to negotiate, and therefore communicate with its external partners and other players in the environment.

Corporate Image and Market Branding

Non-verbal communication in a competitive environment relies heavily on the image portrayed by the organisation to its customers and the wider market about its status and values, analogous to the appearance and mood presented by a patient during a health check. This image develops over a period of time, similar to the internal culture of the organisation, and encompasses the image of the organisation's integrity, quality and ethos as well as individual product brands. The image, like the culture, can be changed or re-invented, especially after major innovative programmes of mergers or a change in competitive direction.

A reliable method in using the image of an organisation as an indication of areas of concern is to observe and compare its current image to past history in order to detect changes or a trend with respect to physical appearance and atmosphere or mood on contact. The physical image presented to external observers can be checked for being: professional and well maintained; run-down and neglected; or old and uncaring. Similarly the mood or atmosphere as detected by customers or observers could be: professional; friendly and understanding; aggressive; laissez faire; or not interested or caring. A change in image portrayed can be an early sign of serious concerns in the operations or the management of the organisation, or of improving conditions of health. This change of image is especially significant for retail and service organisations or call-centres and can impact the willingness of customers to continue supporting the business.

Branding, on the other hand, refers to the remote messages linked to specific products, product ranges or services, such as Heinz Baked Beans. Regular customers of the brand will instantly recognise the brand and prefer it to other similar products, even though these may offer better value for money. However, a brand offers little or no information about the organisation owning this brand, and may result in a front for the organisation rather than a benefit to customers. Through mergers and selling of brands, it is not so easy to know, for example, which organisations produce certain brands of cars; how the value set of the current owners differ from the original owners who developed the brand; and whether the brand can still be trusted.

In order to develop or maintain the healthy status of the image and product brands of the organisation, diagnostics should focus on changes to the ownership of the brand; current history of consistency of brand performance and the link between individual product brands and organisational image.

Possible Health Questions for Image and Brand Presentation:

- Is the public image of the organisation consistent with its published and practiced set of values and ethos?

- Has the image of the organisation changed over time as a sign of improved or deteriorating performance?

- Is the brand image of products or services reflective of the organisation's value set and unchanged from historic values?

Negotiations and Public Relations

Organisations have to negotiate with various partners and peers in their external environment in order to survive and strive. This occurs at various functional levels, such as: negotiations for the best price and value of supplies and parts; negotiations with clients for an optimal selling price; and negotiations with governments for favourable tax and benefit deals.

Various negotiating approaches and styles include: persuasion; confrontation or avoidance; concessions; or the statement of initial positions from which to negotiate. Similar to the effective use of language and speech, the differences in negotiating styles can be linked to the innate style of the organisation or demonstrate an ability to be sensitive to and flexible in their response to the negotiating challenges. It is therefore necessary to determine the organisation's ability to read and respond to the messages put forward by partners and be able to negotiate from a mutually beneficial position instead of one-sided gains.

Public relations communication offers the organisation a one-sided opportunity to state its desired message to the external environment. Unlike negotiations when the organisation is responding to mutual and equal arguments from partners in the environment, the public relations messages, similar to internal hormonal communications, are offered remotely to target wider external audiences. These messages could be in response to changes in the public's opinion, or in support of organisational activities which might be misconstrued by the public. In this case the signs of health should be in the organisation's ability to read the intended audience, especially if it is a hostile audience or foreign culture in the case of multi-nationals. Various public relations successes or blunders can be linked to organisations that quickly accepted mistakes and explained corrective action taken, versus organisations that preferred to pass the blame for incidents or mistakes on to others, thus losing the trust of their peers or the public[8].

Possible Health Questions for Negotiating Skills and Public Relations:

- Do the organisation's public relations statements reflect a clear understanding of its audience's mood and offer acceptable responses when required?

- Is the organisation able to negotiate mutually beneficial deals with various parties?

- Have there been any changes in the organisation's ability to negotiate or offer public relations statements and what lessons were learnt from these incidents?

Analogous to the testing of an individual's ability to understand and clearly express responses to questions, public relations and the ability of an organisation to negotiate appropriately can be measured by evaluating past incidents in its ability to read the audience and to communicate to the benefit of all parties.

Diagnosing Language – The Process

Closely linked with an organisation's ability to receive and interpret information from its internal and external environments is its ability to use language and communications to find and navigate its way in its environment. Various questions were suggested in this chapter as part of a health checklist to determine what to diagnose for in the language and communications functions.

Diagnostic steps used for checking the hormonal balance and mental acuity of an individual can be used to determine how to diagnose organisational health by examining: published versus observed values and culture (health of hormonal functioning); impact of internal communications (changes in hormonal functioning); changes in company or brand image as observed by the public (the general appearance and mood of the patient); and the ability of the organisation to present itself in public relation statements or in negotiations (the person's mental and verbal acuity).

Figure 7.1   Diagnostic stages for communications functions

Values and Culture

In order to determine the status of health in an organisation with respect to its internal culture and communications systems, it is necessary to focus on the actual observed values and conducts within the organisation as compared to the published sets and how members (including managers) of the organisation communicate formally and informally within the organisation.

Measurement entails either questionnaires to managers, or reviews of the written set of values, policies, procedures and codes of conduct of the organisation. The published and/or desired set of values of the organisation may indicate areas of concern, but only by observing the difference between the actual and desired values will it be possible to pinpoint concerns of mismatch, or of a split in the values, and therefore areas where the innate culture and communications are ineffective. To prevent biased or concealed responses, observations should be performed by independent observers, using the same checklist compiled for the previous step.

The identified areas of concern where the internal culture of conduct and values differ from the published set, or are split into different sets of values, should be further submitted to diagnostic evaluation focusing on understanding why this occurred, and especially whether it could be due to inadequate or blocked channels of communication. Independent observations should be made with respect to the channels used for formal and informal communications.

Internal Communications

Response to information about concerns and imposed trends is important for organisations to survive and persist in an ever changing environment, and internal communications is one of the essential tools to enable this adaptation. Diagnostic tools will therefore consist of an analysis of previous incremental and innovative change programmes in addition to addressing shortcomings in current methods of internal communication and culture.

Incremental change messages are likely to originate from local management, closely related functions, such as IT, the design and development teams, or the training/HR departments. Health measurement is therefore concerned with historical events of incremental change and reasons for success or failure, focusing on local communications.

Measuring the impact of communication on innovative change programmes relies on the same method of analysing success, but the sources and types of information could be significantly different. Principally, the supporting role of senior management should be determined and evaluated as part of successful implementation.

External Communications

Healthy functioning of the external communication skills of an organisation demonstrates its ability to interpret and respond to external stimuli and to present itself to the external market and partners in a manner sensitive to their expectations and consistent with its internal culture and values. This is analogous to the ability of individuals to communicate vocally and through body language with other individuals and be sensitive to their moods and attitudes. Diagnostics should focus on image, branding, public relations and negotiating skills.

Image and brands are readily determinable for well-established organisations through searches in market and commercial publications or on the internet and social media. For new or young organisations the personal or independent observations and opinions from partners, peers, customers and the public may offer a better understanding of how the organisation is viewed in its immediate environment.

Because the effect of concerns due to complaints or crisis events affecting the organisation usually leads to a public relations response, it is necessary to determine how the organisation handles adverse opinions from the public or its market. A healthy response will be in line with company values, timely and sensitive to external opinion.

Case Study

A brief summary of the case study history and overall image performance is presented again followed by additional diagnostics on the health of its language and communications functions.

CASE STUDY – THE CORNER SHOP

An independent retail franchise grocery store and bakery, referred to as The Corner Shop, is part of a larger chain. Although the franchisee has the freedom to structure and run the business independently, the holding company is expecting a regular fee from the store as a member of its chain and requires the store to maintain a minimum set of standards. In return, the store owners can use the preferential rates for stock purchases negotiated for the chain and receive advisory assistance from the holding company. The store is in a favourable location in the main street of the town, conveniently situated for a wide range of customers, and the owners have had previous experience and knowledge of retail, finance and accountancy.

The store has been operating for five years. During the first two years it delivered record turnover and profits to the extent that the business was nominated as the 'winning' store in the chain. The customer base was classified as predominantly upper middle-class and the overall image of the store was vibrant and welcoming. The owners went out of their way to satisfy customer needs, for instance, by offering a type of bread made from a special recipe, sought after by many of the local hotels and restaurants, and by ordering and stocking special items on request.

During the third year, the owners decided to expand and diversify by acquiring a butcher shop in the adjacent town. The butchery was at the point of closing and they managed to get it at a reasonable price, including commitments of rental agreements undertaken by the previous owners. They managed to extend their bank loan to finance the deal and one of the owners is spending most of his time running the butchery. The combination of the additional workload for the owners together with mounting repayment burdens of interest and earlier stock purchases are making it difficult to maintain the previous standards of operation. The image of the store and service to the customers has been dropping and resulted in a loss of customers and sales.

In the case study of The Corner Shop, the initial diagnosis in Chapter Two identified financial concerns as a serious survival issue together with image concerns which could point to additional issues. The financial status of the company has already reached a stage in which there seems to be little chance of rescuing the company from its liquidity problems. It was deemed advisable to determine whether a health check diagnosis of all functional areas could highlight other issues which could have prevented this serious situation. The diagnostic tools used to investigate the effectiveness of the language and communication functions followed the suggested steps and questions discussed in this chapter and the results have been presented in a dashboard display style[9] in Tables 7.1 to 7.4.

The functional category of language and communications in Table 7.1 is subdivided into its functions. These functions are then rated in the middle column by three indicators, explained in the narrative. The diagnosis of the health of the language and communications functions indicates deterioration in external communications and during times of change, although internal communications seems to be acceptable.

Summary Dial of the Language and Communications Functions		
Narrative of Rating Indicators: First indicator (findings): ○ = acceptable; ◉ = unacceptable; ● = serious Second indicator (trend): ↓ = deteriorating; ↑ = improving; no arrow = unchanged Third indicator (impact): W = warning; S = serious; blank = acceptable		
Communications Functions	Rating	Comments
Internal Communication	○	Informal communications, but acceptable morale and ethos
Change Communication	● ↓W	Limited communication to staff of major changes e.g. butcher shop
External Communication	● ↓S	External image deteriorating and messages ignored by customers

Table 7.1   Language and communications functions summary diagnosis

Each of the areas of communication diagnostics has been expanded in Tables 7.2 to 7.4. The idea is to offer the latest reports or measurement results in order to present a trend as well as the latest results of concerns or issues. Table 7.2 addresses observations, evidence and results of health checks performed on the internal communications functions in the business. The flags next to the results rate each finding as explained in the narrative block.

As a new start-up business, the initial proposal and business plan included the usual mission, targets and value sets envisioned for the store. This included values of equal opportunities within the organisation, reward for productivity, teamwork and an attitude of support and friendliness to customers. These values are in line with general value sets proposed for new companies, and are therefore fairly general and only offer a general picture of the envisaged culture for the business.

Internal Communications History			
Narrative of Flag: W = warning; S = serious; blank = acceptable			
Reports/Reviews	**Date**	**Flag**	**Action**
Actual versus Published Values and Conduct			
-Observation of actual value set:	Aug 05		
Attitude to work			OK
Attitude to growth		S	Ambitious
Attitude to people/environment		W	Neutral
-Published or implied values	June 03		Part of initial plan
Channels of Communications			
-Observation of use of channels	Aug 05		
One-to-one interviews			Regular annual
Meetings/ presentations		W	Crisis times only
Staff informal functions		W	Christmas time
Communications Feedback			
-Observation of feedback methods	Aug 05		
Management meetings		W	Reasonable
Suggestion or open door policies		S	Informal only

Table 7.2   Internal communication

No mention was made of the attitude of the owners to competitiveness (although the vision statement was to be the best in the area), or to the attitude to growth, as demonstrated in the purchase of the butchery. The dashboard approach to information presentation offers various methods of display, and in this case, similar to the graphic display used for the financial status of the business and the mosaic display to present areas of complaints or concerns, culture can be better presented in the form of the web diagram presented in Figure 7.1.

Observations conducted in year 05 showed that the actual attitudes of the staff supported most of the published values. This is an indication that the selection process of staff based on their values and ability to match the organisational values and internal culture is healthy. The one area which showed discrepancies between the observed staff attitudes and the desired values and aspirations of the owners is in the area of competitiveness and growth for the organisation. While the staff showed acceptable attitude to work and customers, they were neutral with respect to the environment, and not aware or concerned about the need to excel in order to be competitive, or showed any interest in the further growth of the business. This discrepancy resulted in staff not going the extra mile to retain the original market customers.

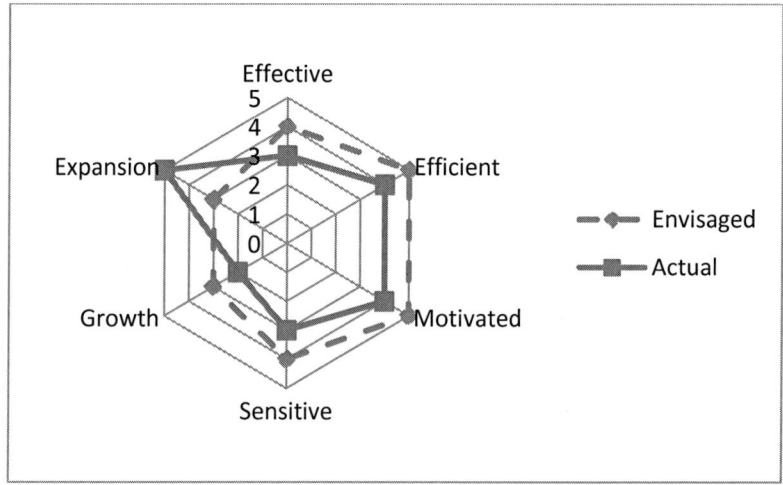

Figure 7.2   Envisaged versus actual culture of The Corner Shop

Communications with and amongst staff were limited to one-to-one performance or disciplinary meetings as and when required. Informally the staff benefited from the usual facilities at work and an office celebration before Christmas. Due to the small size of the organisation this was not regarded as unusual for the type of business or unacceptable to the staff, as demonstrated by the accepted culture of sensitivity and cooperation during normal daily activities.

The main concern of this low key and informal method of internal communication was the inability to detect early signs of discontent among the staff as part of a feedback control loop. This was already identified as a shortcoming in the section on internal information in which early warning whistle-blowing was ignored, resulting in a financial loss to the organisation and the need to discipline one of the members of staff when knowledge about the incidents of theft became known.

Unlike normal day-to-day communications which were conducted and accepted according to the stated value set, the communications during times of change, presented in Table 7.3, were less successful.

Communication During Times of Change			
Narrative of Flag: W = warning; S = serious; blank = acceptable			
Reports/Reviews	**Date**	**Flag**	**Issues/Action**
Incremental Changes			
-Change store layout	Nov 04		Staff informed
-Install tills at exit	Apr 04		Staff consulted
-Move office to overlook store	Apr 04	W	No communication
Innovative Changes			No communication
-Acquire butchery	Jul 04	S	with staff. Concern about staff shortage and stress

Table 7.3   Communication during times of change

The business operated along the lines of an owner-directed business, in other words, decisions to change are taken by the owners with no consultation or communication to staff and implemented with minimal communication or preparation. While this is not uncommon or unusual for start-up and small businesses, the impact on the staff and therefore the company as a whole was negative and affected its overall performance.

Incremental changes were mostly aimed at changes in the store to cut down on pilfering and to improve its image, especially after it became necessary to reduce stock because of financial constraints. Except for the moving of the tills to the exit of the store, members of staff were not consulted and only realised what was happening when the changes were implemented. Most of the changes were accepted by the staff. However, the decision to move the office to overlook the store from an elevated position caused some anxiety amongst members of staff.

The lack of communication with respect to the innovative move to acquire a butcher shop in a nearby town had a more serious impact on the members of staff as well as the customers of The Corner Shop. There was no intention from the owners to be secretive about the acquisition, but the financial, staffing and operational concerns following the acquisition required at least one of the two owners to move on a full-time basis to the butcher shop. This left the store not only short-staffed, but often with reduced leadership and resulted in an observable drop in morale and attitude to work. While innovative changes often need to be kept confidential until the move can be certain of success, the sharing of the information with the staff during the implementation and even while addressing some of the problems, could have helped to improve morale.

Diagnostics on the state of health of the store's ability to successfully communicate externally evaluated the image of the business, the brand of service and products, its success in convincing the public and market after periods of change and the company's negotiating skills. Findings of the diagnostic results are presented in Table 7.4.

External Image and Promotional History			
Narrative of Flag: W = warning; S = serious; blank = acceptable			
Reports/Reviews	**Date**	**Flag**	**Action/Impact**
Corporate Image			
-Public survey	Jul 05	S	Image of neglect
-Public survey	Nov 03		Best in franchise
Product/Service Brands			
-Feedback on bread	Jul 05		High quality
No earlier specific brands			
Public Relations and Marketing			
-Announcing butcher shop	Jan 05	S	Scepticism
-Promote new store approach	Oct 04	W	Cautious
Negotiating Skills			
-Deal for purchase of butcher shop	Jan 05	S	Poor deal
-Deal for product purchases	Jun 03		Good deal with franchise chain
-Bank loans for business	Yr 03, 04	S	Poor status

Table 7.4   External image and communications

Surveys were conducted with the customers and members of the local public. The company image was first surveyed shortly after start-up, and the public image was good, as was its image within the franchise chain of businesses. The store was awarded a prize for the best performing store in the chain, and the local community supported the business. This image deteriorated over the years and during the final survey in year 05 the public described the image as one of neglect. This was a serious turnaround of the general image of the business.

The store did not really have a separate brand image to offer the public with respect to service. However, as a result of a special recipe for bread, it did achieve a brand image for the best bread in the area, in particular, restaurants and hotels placed regular orders. This caused another concern for the cash-strapped store. These customers were scattered around the town and in neighbouring towns, and expected the bread to be delivered to their premises. The additional cost of the transport resulted in the bread becoming a loss leader and management was seriously considering not only discontinuing the bread as an own brand product, but also closing the bakery in order to save money. Although the store could rely on a good own brand image for one of its products, it came at a price which was difficult to sustain in the long run.

The management of the store had a few occasions during which they announced changes to the organisation, thereby offering and developing a public relations message to bond with their customer base. The initial public relations and marketing announcement before the store opened was well received, albeit more in anticipation than commitment from the public. As the service deteriorated and the layout of the store had to be changed, another public relations announcement was issued, this time to attempt to recapture the original customer group by assuring them that The Corner Shop was serious about a good service. The reception was cautious and did not result in many customers returning to the store. The final announcement of the purchase of the butcher shop was received with scepticism by the current market audience and with caution by potential customers in the neighbouring town where the shop was situated. The reason for the latter was the fact that the previous owner of the butcher shop did not succeed with the business. Although the attempts to communicate with the public in all of these cases were genuine, the statements did not tie up with the reality of the deteriorating image, service and shortage of products. There was not much more management could do but to admit that they either have to reposition their target market or close the store.

With respect to negotiating skills, management had better success in negotiating a deal with the franchise chain to assist them in setting up the business and allowing them to use the discount system to purchase their stock. This success did not continue in the negotiations for the purchase of the butcher shop. Although the shop came at a reasonable price, they did not complete a due diligence on the status of the business or get all the information on previous commitments of long lease periods and other debts before completing the deal. Inexperience in negotiating skills had a serious negative effect on the business. The difficulty in negotiating good financial deals with the bank was also a concern, although in this case it was more due to their credit rating than to negotiating skills.

In conclusion, the internal communications of the business did not show serious health concerns, but communications during times of change was more under the control of the owners and could have been handled better in order to reduce some of the anxiety, stress and concerns which were felt by staff. External communication was handled in the standard method known to management with respect to changes in the store and the acquisition of the butcher shop. However, since the messages were not backed up by reality of operations in the store and butcher shop, the messages were ignored by the target public.

A serious health concern was the lack of experience in negotiating skills of the management with respect to major deals. The managers were able to negotiate: a good replenishment deal with the franchise; reasonable deals with staff in their employment; limited deals with the bank; but failed to negotiate an acceptable deal on the butcher shop, thus aggravating their dubious financial status.

Conclusion

Diagnosing concerns in the survival, protection, operations and information functions as discussed in the previous four chapters can provide pointers to serious concerns in areas that can be either fatal or debilitating to organisations. It is essential to follow sound financial processing and management; protect the assets, people and information of the organisation against damage or intrusion; ensure that the operating units perform at an acceptable level; and observe, interpret and heed internal and external information in order for the organisation to survive and operate at an acceptable level.

In order to respond to information received from either within or external to the organisation it is, however, necessary to be able to communicate. Internal communication consists of a regular flow of messages from various formal and informal sources and channels building up to an innate culture over time. An understanding of this culture and values within the organisation is necessary in order to be able to diagnose areas of concern, but more importantly, to be able to introduce change programmes to enable the organisation to adapt and improve. If some of these communications channels or sources are inadequate, the organisation could have problems in changing their current means of operation. However, motivating messages may change performance or culture temporarily, but once the messages are being discontinued the organisation is likely to revert back to a default position of its innate way of operating.

Organisations also need to be able to respond to, and communicate with, members in its immediate customer and wider external environment by means of presenting a realistic image. Unless the external messages are accepted by this wider audience and regarded as credible, they may result in a backlash that can cause harm to the organisation. External negotiating skills are also important, especially in the case of the young or smaller organisation that do not always have the advantage of size or history to back up its side of the negotiations. This may result in many young organisations not being able to get out of financial danger zones.

The diagnostic process at this stage addressed the internal survival and protection functions, essential to the survival of the organisation, but under local control. Senior managers were recognised in their role as initiators of products and services, receivers of information and formulators of messages to be communicated in response to the information. A combination of management functions, including their responsibility for decisions regarding the future direction of the organisation are covered in Chapter Eight, which also concludes the initial health check for the organisation.

Notes

1. The role of the hormonal system to communicate messages throughout the body is covered in: Barratt, K.E., Barman, S.M., Boitano, S., Brooks, H.L. (2010). *Ganong's Review of Medical Physiology*. Twenty-third Edition, McGraw Hill Medical, New York; and Greenstein, B. and Wood, D. (2006). *The Endocrine System at a Glance*, Second Edition. Blackwell Publishing Ltd. Exford.

2. For the cultural web see Johnson, G. and Scholes, K. (1999). *Exploring Corporate Strategy*, Fifth ed. Pearson Education Ltd. Harlow, pp. 73-78. Various definitions and discussions around the concept of culture have been offered in: Linstead, F., Fulop, L., Lilley, S. (2009). *Management and Organization: A Critical Text*, Second Edition. Palgrave Macmillan, Basingstoke, Hampshire, p. 157.

3. A research in the differences between actual behaviour versus value statements was conducted by Linda Smircich, as referred to in Morgan, G. (2006). *Images of Organization*, Updated Edition. Sage Publications Inc., Thousand Oaks, California, p. 126.

4. Hofstede's approach on how to observe culture is presented in Linstead, F., Fulop, L., Lilley, S. (2009). *Management and Organization: A Critical Text*, Second Edition. Palgrave Macmillan, Basingstoke, Hampshire, p. 178.

5. Research conducted on the functions impacting the outcome of incremental and innovative change was conducted and presented in: Dean, C.M. (2012). *Physiology of Organisations: An Integrated Functional Perspective*. Cambridge Scholars Publishing, Newcastle upon Tyne, pp.123-140.

6. Concepts used for learning organisations combine the use of memory and feedback loop learning to apply communication as part of training in the double-loop learning method promoted in Cybernetics by Norbert Wiener and explained in: Morgan, G. (2006) *Images of Organization*. Updated edition. Sage Publications Inc., Thousand Oaks, California pp. 81-87.

7. Functioning of the limbic system and the use of the language area of the brain are covered in: Barratt, K.E., Barman, S.M., Boitano, S., Brooks, H.L. (2010). *Ganong's Review of Medical Physiology*. Twenty-third Edition, McGraw Hill Medical, New York; and Barker, R.A., Barasi, S., Neal, M.J. (2008). *Neuroscience at a Glance*. Third Edition. Blackwell Publishing, Maldem, Mass. Checklists of steps to diagnose mental health are stated in: Turner, R. and Blackwood, R. (1997). *Lecture Notes on Clinical Skills*, Third Edition. Blackwell Science, Oxford, p 100.

8. A research into methods used by organisations to recover after disasters was published in: Pfarrer, M.D., Decelles, K.A., Smith, K.G. (2008). After the Fall: Reintegrating the Corrupt Organization. *Academy of Management Review*. Vol.33, No. 3, pp. 730-749.

9. The use of dashboard displays has been widely accepted by organisations to allow a drill-down facility of information. A reference, based on practical application in various organisations can be found in: Eckerson, Wayne W. (2011). *Performance Dashboards: Measuring, Monitoring and Managing your Business*. 2nd Ed. John Wiley & Sons, Hoboken NJ.

CHAPTER EIGHT

STRATEGY AND GUIDANCE

Without healthy strategy and guidance functions an organisation cannot strive.

Living organisms can and do survive by acting reflexively on internal and external stimuli. More complex life-forms, such as predators and primates, however, need to be able to interpret stimuli, plan ahead and act decisively in order to compete and persist. In order to strive, equivalent functions lie with the executive management team and will be discussed in terms of:

Knowledge and Understanding

Strategy and Planning

Direction and Guidance

By comparing organisations to the physiological functioning of living organisms, it became clear during the previous five chapters that the functional categories are guided in their operations by: a specific purpose of contribution; prescribed processes of functioning; controls to monitor smooth performance; and links to other functions. There is, however, one area in complex living organisms (and especially in higher primates) where the functioning is different. The cognitive part of the brain has no clear physical activity to perform. It receives information as electrical impulses from all parts of the body via the other cortical areas and, together with this knowledge and a sense of self-awareness, decides and initiates longer term actions to sustain life. These decisions are transmitted back to the relevant cortical areas for action. Although understanding of the complex links in the brain is still being explored, a person's mental state forms an integral part of the general health diagnosis of the individual. A shaded insert in the chapter briefly summarises the physiological functioning of the cognitive brain. This insert is offered as complimentary and not essential reading for the diagnosis of organisational health.

In Chapter Seven, the mental state was diagnosed by observing appearance, mood and speech. The focus in this chapter is on the cognitive areas of understanding, thinking and reasoning[1]. The analogous functions in organisations performed by the owner, executive management team and directors are therefore to understand and know, to decide and plan, and to guide longer term activities for the organisation. This can be determined by evaluating their knowledge, beliefs, decisions and guiding instructions.

Higher Functions of the Brain – Cognition[1]

The association cortices in the brain are unique in that they have no primary motor or sensory roles, but react to information from the other cortical areas in order to understand, learn from memory and initiate action in response to the stimuli received. They consist of the posterior parietal and the prefrontal cortical areas, are the most evolutionary advanced parts of the brain, and allow higher primates to be aware of their self-consciousness and be involved in purposive behaviour.

The awareness of self-consciousness and the control of emotion, also referred to as 'the theory of mind', allow an individual to interpret and predict intentions from the actions and tone of speech of other persons. The content of consciousness therefore refers to the objects and events of which individuals are aware, and shapes their most complex social interactions. Damage to this part of the brain could lead to the inability to 'read' intentions of others and can result in anti-social behaviours such as autism or schizophrenia.

The prefrontal cortex is involved in purposive behaviour through the planning of responses to the stimuli received from the other cortical areas, including memory, the sensory and the motor cortices. Damage can lead to changes in the ability to formulate and pursue goals, emotional responsiveness, difficulty in judging risks, and becoming blunt, apathetic or aggressive.

The posterior parietal cortex enables the use of tools, ability to develop collaborative plans and the development and use of language. Input and guiding response links are especially strong from and to the sensory areas, proprioception and sensors in the skin, as well as visual acuity. Damage can therefore lead to insensitivity to collaborative partners, failure to recognise tactile objects through touch and problems in reading, writing or the use of language.

Knowledge and Understanding

It is important for an individual to be conscious of the intention of other people, be aware of his or her own abilities and be able to decide on appropriate responses. It is similarly important for an organisation to know its own abilities, be aware of its position within the immediate market environment and understand the challenges, opportunities and threats posed by the wider environment in order to formulate balanced executive decisions. The data research and information functions can collect and pass the information on, but the executive needs to interpret and place the knowledge within context, or the essence of the information is lost.

Knowledge and understanding are two diagnostic steps used by medical practitioners to determine the mental state of an individual by asking basic questions about the person, immediate environment and state of mind. For example, asking a patient's name, age, the current day or date and how the person is feeling. From the point of view of diagnosing the 'mental health' of the organisation, it is therefore necessary to distinguish between the available pool of information and the executive's knowledge and understanding by asking and exploring similar questions.

Know the Organisation

Analogous to knowledge about 'self', it is important for the executive team to be in possession of, and understand information about the health status of organisational functions. The information forms the core of the organisation's health diagnostics and for effective prognosis and healing action to be initiated, it is necessary that the status is adequately interpreted by the executive team.

Various analysis tools have been suggested to management, including the identification of the strengths and weaknesses as part of a SWOT (Strength, Weakness, Opportunity, Threat) analysis, or the internal process evaluation section of a BSC (Balanced Scorecard)[2]. The internal information obtained from these tools is, however, focused on the organisation's ability to compete in its market, rather than offering a balanced view of healthy functioning.

Performance and morale trends in all functions, including the survival functions are important, as is information regarding potential risks in protection, and about areas of disgruntlement or malfunctioning that may not be identified and recognised. It is especially important to be aware of operational blockages in the organisation, as well as potential ineffective decisions with respect to the essential supplies and workplace suitability to ensure efficient action towards the survival and competitiveness of the company.

- The executive's knowledge of the organisation needs to include the normal information about processing performance, but also knowledge about potential or actual areas at risk.

Know the Organisation in its Environment

Similar to the need for an individual to detect and understand the intentions of friends or competitors, knowledge about the organisation's immediate and wider environments is important for its survival, but also in order to determine its competitiveness. This is the one field which is very well covered by business schools and management theorists.

Tools for external evaluation can be found in the opportunities and threats sections of the SWOT analysis, the customer and market sections of the Balanced Scorecard, and other tools such as Porter's Five Forces (Suppliers, Buyers, Potential entrants, Substitutes and Competitors), and Kotler's STEP (Sociological, Technological, Economic and Political) factors[2]. Again, these tools are valuable but mostly aimed at competitive positioning of the organisation in its environment, and may lack external information of risk, trends or changes which could result in unplanned or unanticipated threats. For example, information about trend changes in the public's ethical expectations of organisational governance and ethical behaviour may be of greater importance to organisations than their competitive position. The impact of misreading public opinion can be demonstrated for firms who decided to cut cost by outsourcing their manufacturing function to countries with limited regard for working conditions of their staff; or whose operations triggered environmental disasters of chemical spills[3]. These incidents invariably resulted in serious public backlash and a reduction in sales and image.

- Understanding the environment is more than only the competitive environment, it must include the understanding of wider intentions and trends of the public as well.

Understand and Utilise the Information

Information may be provided to the executive team from various sources, but then ignored by the team. This is analogous to checking the healthy mental state of an individual by exploring the person's beliefs or perception of reality. From an organisational point of view, internal and external knowledge allows the executive to make balanced decisions both on the health and the competitiveness of the organisation. However, analogous to individuals, knowledge does not necessarily translate into optimum decisions with respect to their future health. Individuals who participate in long distance running without a previous health check and appropriate training are more likely to damage their health by believing that intention alone can ensure success.

This neglect of understanding as the basis for successful executive decisions was highlighted in research into various executive decisions based on the personal experience and beliefs of the executive managers rather than on the information offered[4], and that these decisions often led to damage for the organisation.

- Available and interpreted information needs to be heeded and form part of balanced decisions, and not ignored in favour of instinctive decisions or short term profits and image adjustments.

Understand Cultural Differences

It is possible for a published set of values, beliefs and attitudes to differ from the culture and attitude to values observable within the organisation. This can be compared to an individual's intent on self-harm or neglect to bodily health, or by imposing aggressive changes such as crash diets or excessive exercise. Suitable observations in organisations would include the value set and attitude of the executive team as presented to the public, compared to the already established actual culture, with respect to the organisation's role and conduct within its environment.

The culture of a young and small business unit is often dictated by the aspirations of its owner or executive team, subsequently to be replaced or enhanced by developing its own internal value set over time. In the case of established organisations this may be different. It is possible for a new executive team to decide on new values and the development of a supportive culture, but in order to succeed, it will be necessary for the team to understand the current culture and realise the obstacles ahead in trying to change it. The promotion of a cooperative and sensitive ethos to the external environment, for instance, needs to be supported by caring processes and staff – not by a culture of aggressiveness in order to win. Research into failures can be linked to this dichotomy in the promoted versus actual cultures of organisations[5].

Diagnosing healthy executive functioning should therefore focus on the availability of the necessary balanced information in a format acceptable to, and useable by, the executive and the inclination of executive management to base decisions for action on relevant information rather than on tradition, personal beliefs and aspirations.

Possible Health Questions for Executive Knowledge and Understanding:

- Is the executive team provided with essential information about performance, culture, concerns and risks?

- Do external information reports cover the market, trends in technology developments, ethical processing and public concerns?

- Is the reported information used to underpin understanding of the organisation and decisions to react to stimuli within the reports?

Strategy and Planning

A key cognitive function in higher primates, and especially in human beings, is the ability to be conscious of their own consciousness. They are aware of who they are and their distinctiveness from other living beings. However, purposive consciousness in humans evolves and should therefore also be linked to age. Children are more likely to have unrealistic visions and plans for their futures; adults could be more realistic, but over-ambitious; while older people could have become complacent and either gave up on goals, or are still hoping to live and realise the dream of their past.

Based on information about the internal functioning of the organisation within perspective of what is required to survive and persist in the external environment, executive management should be able to offer a clear expression of the purpose, ethos and value set of the organisation, summarised in its vision, mission, goals and strategic plans. Questions of where the organisation is going, why and how it plans to achieve its goals can establish the level of healthy functioning of the executive team. Similar to humans, the questions may have to be linked to the size, age or development phase of the organisation for clarity.

Vision, Mission and Goal

The vision, mission and goal of an organisation portray an indication of its self-awareness and aspirations. For small and young start-up companies, this is often informal and a reflection of the owner's ambitions, while in established organisations it is more likely to be published statements that form a permanent part of the organisation's long-term strategy.

The diagnostics of the culture and internal communications functions of an organisation addressed the questions of whether the internal culture and code of conduct are in line with any published set of values and the goals or vision of the organisation. In diagnosing the health situation of the executive function in organisations, the opposite question has to be addressed, namely: are the organisation's vision, mission and goals realistic and based on current cultural values, or achievable without major changes to the culture? Written or published ambitions may not reflect reality, or may be historical and no longer valid, either when compared to internal culture or external changed circumstances. The danger is that companies express their wishes for the future of the organisation without sufficient consideration of whether they are realistic and achievable.

The impact of unrealistic visions can be detected in young start-up companies, especially during the dot.com boom on the internet. Many of these companies had vastly unrealistic expectations without realising what was involved, or else the objective of the entrepreneur was to make money as quickly as possible and then to sell out to another interested party. Failures include online order companies that could not deliver, as opposed to companies who arranged distribution and support warehouses before commencing their online retail offerings[6]. On the other hand, a well-established organisation may have achieved its original ambitions to be the best in its established core market only to be leapfrogged by competitors taking advantage of changing market and technological trends[7]. In order to evaluate the health of the consciousness of the executive function, the diagnosis should focus on the reverse tests which were found to be relevant for internal communications and culture of organisations.

- Explore whether the published or intended vision, mission and ethos are supported by the actual culture and work ethics in the organisation and address the changing reality of the external environment.

Strategy

Having a clear self-awareness and an uncompetitive vision for the future is acceptable and healthy if matched by internal culture – and the vision and strategy is one of stability and continuity. This is not unusual and can be detected in village shops, or manufacturing businesses with dedicated and loyal customers. Not all organisations want to be winners in highly competitive markets, and as long as they keep an eye on changes in the environment, such as new shops or supermarkets close by, or changes in the needs of their customers, they are likely to be accepted with their current ethos and level of service.

However, whether the goals are business as usual, competitive winning, or directional change, they can only be achieved if the organisation has a clear picture of the path or strategy it needs to follow in order to reach the goal and 'live' the mission. This direction may vary if impacted by changing circumstances, but without a clear strategy, it is more likely that the organisation will drift into an unintentional position from which it may be difficult to emerge. This drift could especially affect young companies. As part of their initial justification plans to attract start-up financing, the entrepreneurs are often required to submit an official set of goals, strategies and plans. This may be realistic at the initial stage of development, but most of the time the strategy documents are filed and not considered again until too late to address changes which impacted the performance of the company. The strategy, similar to the mission and vision, may be ambitious, but also realistic, achievable and regularly reviewed for relevance over the intended period of implementation.

Analogous to determining whether the lifestyle of individuals are healthy and relevant to their goals and ambitions, it is necessary to diagnose whether the organisation has a set of formal or informal strategies in support of its vision, mission and goals. The existence of a strategy does not mean that it is feasible or followed-through.

- Strategies should be available, realistic and in support of the stated vision and goals of the organisation.

Plans, Policies and Procedures

Strategy offers a broad direction which an organisation can follow to achieve its goals and implement its vision and mission. The timespan is usually five to ten years but can be longer. In order to achieve the organisational goals, the strategy must be supported by shorter term plans, forming the tactics and interim targets to be met if the strategy is to be successful. The involvement of executive at this stage will be to approve and sign off rather than to develop the plans. The actual plan development and implementation is more likely to be tasked to a project team or operational management.

The two dominant types of tactical plans are the operational plans, to modify or improve internal and operational functions, and the innovative change plans to introduce new or different strategic directions. This compares to the action decisions by the brain to decide on a response to immediate stimuli of concerns, or deliberate decisions to, for example: change the lifestyle; introduce an exercise programme; or introduce necessary medical procedures towards healthier living.

Policies and procedures define the code of conduct in the organisation and therefore form part of its culture and value set, whether formally published or informally accepted. It is a function of the executive to recognise and approve or tacitly accept the policies and procedures and ensure that they either reflect the existing internal culture and work ethos, or support the new strategy that the organisation is introducing.

- Plans, policies and procedures should be available, regularly monitored and checked for planned progress and support to the stated mission, goals and strategies.

Without a clear direction and plans to meet their vision and goals, organisations cannot strive to achieve.

Possible Health Questions for Strategy and Planning:

- Is there a clear awareness of realistic vision, mission and long term goals for the organisation?

- Does the organisation have a clear strategic direction and plan, and is there evidence that this plan is still valid and being followed?

- Is the strategic plan supported by a set of shorter operational and innovative change plans, and are these plans regularly monitored?

- Are the published or declared policies and procedures in line with the actual culture of the organisation?

From a diagnostic point of view, it is necessary to determine that the executive team has a clear view of the mission and goals of the organisation; the strategy the organisation should follow in order to achieve these goals; supporting and executable tactical plans; and a set of policies and procedures which accurately present its culture and value set.

Direction and Guidance

Analogous to the cognitive functions in the brain, executive functions do not include action, but stop at initiating and guiding the action of the other functions in the organisation. Decision, plans and programmes are passed on to the relevant functions or implementation teams and only guided and/or supported by executives. While this is a healthy and ideal situation, it may not always be the case. Competitive decisions such as running a marathon may be taken by the cognitive part of an individual's brain, but if the individual decides that success only depends on taking additional energy boosting drugs, more harm can be done to the individual than planned preparation for all parts of the body. The role of power may impact decisions and impose instructions to functions to the detriment of the organisation.

Guide and Direct

Guiding an organisation when the long term goal, strategy and plans are in line with internal culture and ethos will mainly consist of evaluating the feedback of progress and regular performance of the operating units. Guiding an organisation during times of innovative change such as mergers, organisational crises or directional changes in the market can be more challenging.

Research shows that the most important guiding and directive action from executive management during the implementation of innovative action consists of visible and clear support for the change and the communication of messages to allay fears and concerns about the change[8]. The executive function of guidance must also include the initiation and transfer of the messages to all relevant departments and parts of the organisation in order to ensure full involvement and support from all functions. In addition to the communications and visible support, reverse transfer of information should include progress reports to the executive management in regards to major innovative programmes. Progress should be regularly reported and reviewed together with the impact of deviations and modifications to plans, in order to ensure that the strategic direction is followed towards the long term goal.

Areas of concern in guiding innovative strategies arise when imposed change programmes are introduced with minimal regard to the cooperation of staff, or when innovative change programmes are not supported by executive management. In both cases the change effort may fail, either because the operating units do not accept imposed changes to their regular way of operating, or because they do not regard the initiation of the change as important. This failure in successful guidance to support innovative programmes is often linked to the role of power invested in and used by the executive management[9].

- Diagnosing the health of executive guidance and support should focus on the visibility of the executive team in their support of innovative programmes and the extent to which they are involved in the progress evaluation of performance and change.

The Role of Power

A potential area of concern with respect to the executive functions of organisations is the role and possible misuse of power by the executive management. Some organisational theorists accept Robert Dahl's definition of power as the ability to get another person to do something that he or she would not otherwise have done. This power can come from various sources, including: formal authority; scarce resources; use of organisational structure, rules and regulations; control of decision processes; control of knowledge of information; ability to cope with uncertainty; interpersonal alliances and the use of networks[10].

From an organisational point of view the guidance and directive functions of the executive management place them in a position of power over the internal functioning and health of the organisation as well as over its environment. The health questions should explore how they use this power to the benefit of the organisation and the environment, analogous to evaluating the psychological state of mind of an individual. To have strong convictions and use power to impose them on others is not in itself a health failure, but to use the power to benefit only specific individuals or functions to the detriment of the rest of the organisation or the environment requires further investigation and, if necessary, action.

The impact of the use of power by internal functions has already been covered as part of the health concerns of the functions. Examples include the non-acceptance of a new or different electronic system when the operators regard it as an imposition and do not use it; or strike action by members of staff against unacceptable conditions or terms of employment.

The power of the executive over internal functions is as valid and important for the organisation. Incidents of executive impositions on internal functions could include, for example: the enforced introduction of sub-standard supplies in the manufacturing of products; or the decision to outsource essential survival functions such as accounting, supply, distribution, or cleaning and waste management to external organisations. The decision could have been taken in order to reduce cost, but due to an increase in external pressure or power exerted by outsourced companies, it may turn out to be unsustainable in the long run[11].

Power from external influences over executive management demonstrates the degree to which the organisation can be manipulated by external stakeholders such as their shareholders, sponsors, suppliers, customers or the public. Examples include the decisions by shareholders to replace directors either because of negligent or illegal activities or to influence the direction the company should take in order to increase profit, regardless of harm elsewhere. Organisations with a poor corporate social responsibility image, or guilty of environmental pollution, often become the target of pressure groups. They may find that they are compelled to comply with the universal or accepted standards, and if the executive does not initiate an acceptable response, the action would be regarded as token compliance with little impact on the pressure groups.

Possible Health Questions for Executive Direction and Guidance:

- How effective is the evaluation and guidance offered by the executive to the performance and change activities in the organisation?

- Is there evidence of misuse of power by the executive over the functioning of the organisation or its external environment?

- Is the executive team able to counter or adequately respond to impositions of power from external sources on the organisation?

- How did the executive team succeed in guiding the organisation in the past and what lessons were learnt?

The diagnosis of health with respect to the guiding and directing functions of executives should focus on the internal effectiveness of executive actions, and include the external impact of these actions on the environment. It is also necessary to strike a balance between power and realism in the execution of the functions.

Diagnosing Strategy – The Process

Diagnosing the state of health of the executive function, analogous to the cognitive functions in the brain, does not only involve checks for the healthy functioning of information delivery to the executives, but also for the psychological level of understanding and use of this information as the source of knowledge for purposive decisions about the future of the organisation.

Steps advised to medical practitioners to diagnose the cognitive mental state of an individual include questions to explore his or her thinking, beliefs, perceptions and cognitive functioning. These questions were discussed in this chapter, and for organisations, the similar steps should therefore be to evaluate the way in which the organisation is guided by strategies and plans, based on sound knowledge and understanding of the internal and external environments of the organisation.

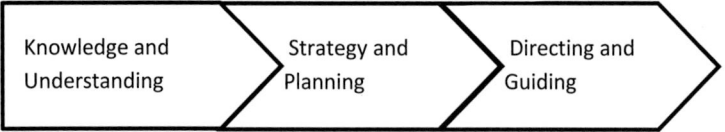

Figure 8.1   Diagnostic stages for strategy and guiding functions

Knowledge and Understanding

It is important for the executive team to be able to display knowledge and understanding of the organisation. Interviews or available reports should confirm whether they have access to relevant information to offer a perspective about the functioning of the organisation in an acceptable format. However, further evidence of events based on poor decisions for which information has been presented and discarded, or not presented, must also be evaluated for impact and lessons learnt.

Strategies and Plans

Diagnosing the strategic capabilities of an organisation is analogous to checking the self-awareness and ambitious intentions of an individual. It is necessary for executive managers to have an understanding of the organisation's position in its environment, and to have an idea of where it wants to be in the future.

In order to be healthy, the executive functions of organisations should be evaluated by reviewing their formal or informal strategic and tactical plans:

- The existence and awareness of the organisation's vision, mission and ethos should be tested against existing culture and work ethics.
- The long term strategies need to be realistic, periodically reassessed and monitored.
- The tactical plans, policies and procedures should be checked for support to strategy, milestones, risk evaluations and back-up plans.

For healthy executive functions, managers need to be able to vocalise their long term intentions and offer plans on how to achieve them as a suitable guidance to the rest of the organisation.

Direction and Guidance

Diagnosing the ability of the executive team to effectively direct and guide an organisation can be compared to diagnosing the psychological decisions and actions of individuals. It is not only necessary to check for consistency and effectiveness in the particular action, but also for the potential of either self-harm or harm to others as a result of their actions. In organisations, areas to address should include:

- The effectiveness of the guidance and directives offered to all relevant functions, especially during times of innovative change.
- Evidence of harmful instructions to internal functions directly contributable to actions and directives from executives.
- Evidence of harm done to external parties or the environment directly contributable to actions and directives from executives.

The executive team, analogous to cognition, has the freedom to guide organisational activities, but it also has a social corporate responsibility to act for the common good of the organisation as well as its environment.

Case Study

A brief summary of the case study history is presented again, followed by additional diagnostic findings of the strategy and guidance functions.

CASE STUDY – THE CORNER SHOP

An independent retail franchise grocery store and bakery, referred to as The Corner Shop, is part of a larger chain. Although the franchisee has the freedom to structure and run the business independently, the holding company is expecting a regular fee from the store as a member of its chain and requires the store to maintain a minimum set of standards. In return, the store owners can use the preferential rates for stock purchases negotiated for the chain and receive advisory assistance from the holding company. The store is in a favourable location in the main street of the town, conveniently situated for a wide range of customers, and the owners have had previous experience and knowledge of retail, finance and accountancy.

The store has been operating for five years. During the first two years it delivered record turnover and profits to the extent that the business was nominated as the 'winning' store in the chain. The customer base was classified as predominantly upper middle-class and the overall image of the store was vibrant and welcoming. The owners went out of their way to satisfy customer needs, for instance, by offering a type of bread made from a special recipe, sought after by many of the local hotels and restaurants, and by ordering and stocking special items on request.

During the third year, the owners decided to expand and diversify by acquiring a butcher shop in the adjacent town. The butchery was at the point of closing and they managed to get it at a reasonable price, including commitments of rental agreements undertaken by the previous owners. They managed to extend their bank loan to finance the deal and one of the owners is spending most of his time running the butchery. The combination of the additional workload for the owners together with mounting repayment burdens of interest and earlier stock purchases are making it difficult to maintain the previous standards of operation. The image of the store and service to the customers has been dropping and resulted in a loss of customers and sales.

In the case study of The Corner Shop, the initial diagnosis in Chapter Two identified financial concerns as serious survival issues together with image concerns. Although it may be too late to save the business, it was felt necessary to determine whether a health check diagnosis of all functional areas could highlight other issues which can be addressed to prevent a closure. The diagnostic tools used to investigate and present the effectiveness of the executive functions are based on similar diagnostic steps recommended to medical practitioners, and the findings are presented in a dashboard dial format[12] in Tables 8.1 to 8.4.

The strategy and guidance functional category in Table 8.1 is subdivided into its functions. These functions are rated in the middle column by indicators as described in the narrative section of the table.

Summary Dial of the Strategy and Guidance Functions

Narrative of Rating Indicators:
First indicator (findings): ○ = acceptable; ◉ = unacceptable; ● = serious
Second indicator (trend): ↓ = deteriorating; ↑ = improving; no arrow = unchanged
Third indicator (impact): W = warning; S = serious; blank = acceptable

Executive Functions	Rating	Comments
Knowledge and Understanding	● ↓S	Critical information not available or understood
Strategy and Planning	◉ ↓W	Plans prepared for initial set-up but not updated
Direction and Guidance	○	Informal guidance to the relevant staff only

Table 8.1 Health summary of executive functions

Diagnostics of the health of the executive strategy, planning and guiding functions indicate weakness in the knowledge and understanding of information necessary to inform decisions to guide the business towards achieving its desired goal. Strategies and plans were prepared as part of the initial justification plan. These plans were not reviewed and updated, thus resulting in a strategic drift rather than clear plans and direction.

Each of the functional areas of knowledge, strategy and guiding has been expanded in Tables 8.2 to 8.4. The idea is to offer the latest findings as reports or measurement results in order to give a trend as well as the latest results of concerns or issues.

Table 8.2 presents the diagnostic findings of the executive knowledge and understanding functions. A diagnostic observational flag is offered in the third column and described in the narrative block of the table.

With respect to information about internal performance, the only formal management analysis reports available to the owners were the annual financial statements, mainly prepared for tax purposes and legal requirements. These statements were produced on time and in accordance with legal requirements – therefore satisfactorily addressed. Knowledge about staff misconducts, however, was collected and presented informally and resulted in late action and loss to the business which could have been prevented if there were channels for the owners to find out about the crisis events at an early stage.

Knowledge and Understanding Performance History			
Narrative of Flag: W = warning; S = serious; blank = acceptable			
Reports/Reviews	**Date Issued**	**Flag**	**Action**
Internal Performance Management Information			
-Financial statements	Apr 05 Apr 04 Apr 03		Financial reports as required
-Morale and crisis reports	No formal	W	Informal knowledge
Sales and Marketing Management Information			
-Sales analysis reports	No separate	S	As part of finance
-Market analysis reports	No formal	W	Informal
Environmental Issues Management Information			
-External environmental reports	No formal	W	Broad knowledge
Unsupported Decisions/Action			
-Butchery acquisition	May 04	S	Unsupported and
-Stock replenishment	Regular	S	damaging action

Table 8.2   Knowledge and understanding

Sales and marketing information were not prepared separately, but gained from the financial statements. These reports indicated the current financial position, but offered no in-depth trend or sales analysis conclusions to indicate the turnaround and profitability of the various sales and product categories. The statements also did not include any forecasts about outstanding debts or future sales, with the result that today's debt with respect to the replenishment of stock was expected to be paid by tomorrow's revenue and profits, causing problems with the drop in sales. The lack of meaningful interpreted information and understanding of the consequences resulted in the inability of the owners to decide and guide the replenishment of stock, either to match the changing market or to address the customer demand and lower their expectations.

Interpreted information and knowledge about the wider environmental and ecological issues had a lesser effect on business decisions. The owners were generally aware of political and ethical issues and incorporated them in their decisions and guidance towards a supportive culture and ethos in the store.

Although small and start-up businesses often operate on a more informal basis with respect to information reporting and knowledge, the lack of meaningful information to support decisions in the critical areas of replenishment and business expansion proved to be problematic for the owners.

Diagnostic results on the strategy and planning function are presented in Table 8.3.

Strategy and Planning Performance History			
Narrative of Flag: W = warning; S = serious; blank = acceptable			
Reports/Reviews	Date	Flag	Issues/Action
Vision, Mission and Ethos -Stated mission and aspiration	Year 00		Part of initial business plan
Long-Term Goals and Strategies -Strategic statements	Year 00	W	Part of initial business plan
Measurable and Justified Tactical Plans -Measurable plans		W	No tactical plans

Table 8.3 Strategy and planning

As a new start-up organisation, the initial proposal and business plan included the usual mission, targets and value sets envisioned for the store. This included values of equal opportunities within the organisation, reward for productivity, teamwork and an attitude of support and friendliness towards customers. These values underlie the general value set proposed for retail companies and were therefore fairly general. No mention was made of the attitude of the owners to competitiveness or growth, although the mission – to be the best in the area – implied competitiveness.

The strategies underlying the mission were vague and did not contain any detailed and measurable implementation plans. This is not unusual in young start-up companies, but the plans were not reviewed and activities were based on informal and personal aspirations rather than to follow a broad strategic path towards the eventual goal. Strategy revision could have indicated the necessity to switch to alternative plans to prevent the strategic drift or damaging decisions.

With respect to the guidance and support given by the owners during times of change and the potential misuse of power either within or external to the organisation, as presented in Table 8.4, the diagnosis showed no undue health concerns.

Direction and Guidance Performance History			
Narrative of Flag: W = warning; S = serious; blank = acceptable			
Reports/Reviews	**Date**	**Flag**	**Action/Impact**
Guidance and Support for Innovation -Extend to include butchery -Change in store layout	Jul 05 Nov 03	W	Directives top-down with some support
Awareness of Internal Concerns -Shortage of funds for operations	Jul 05	W	Financial damage
Awareness of External Concerns -Ethical concerns	None		None observable

Table 8.4   Direction and guidance

Not keeping staff informed in all innovative changes was not damaging since the main change of the purchase of the butchery did not directly affect the staff in the store and only reduced the time spent by management in the store. Damage to the organisation as a result of this decision was the reduced funds to replenish stock and this was also due to incomplete information offered by the financial reports.

Ethically, the store operated in line with the accepted political and ethical standards, and damage to the external environment and people was minimal.

Health concerns in executive functioning of The Corner Shop were found to be a lack of knowledge and experience of what is important on behalf of the owners rather than deliberate misconduct or misguidance to the staff. Mission, long term goals, strategies and some plans were included in the initial justification report, but not reviewed. This resulted in a strategic drift as a result of early successes. Instead of getting and relying on realistic information and a revision of the strategies and plans, the owners believed that the business would continue to thrive and provide financial support for all the informal expectations and decisions, such as: the belief that the initial affluent customer base can be retained; the trust that today's replenishment debts can be repaid out of tomorrow's profits; and the belief that the time is right to expand the business and that the acquired business will be similarly profitable to repay the additional loan required for this expansion.

This over-optimism of entrepreneurs in start-up businesses that are doing well in the beginning is not uncommon, but should be tempered by deliberate activities of discipline, learning and building up of experience.

Conclusion

Diagnosing organisational health concerns, as discussed in Chapters Three to Eight, can provide pointers to serious shortcomings that can be either fatal or debilitating to organisations. It is essential for organisations to: follow sound financial processing and distribution management; protect assets, people and information against damage or intrusion; ensure that the operating units perform at an acceptable level; interpret and heed internal and external information; effectively communicate intentions to internal and external audiences; and plan and direct long term activities in order for the organisation to survive, strive and operate successfully.

In order to strive, compete and meet the long term ambitions for an organisation, the executive team needs to be provided with analysed information about internal performance, market and wider environmental trends and issues as a balanced pool of knowledge and perspective. The role of executive managers is not to act, but to rely on and interpret this information and then to decide on, and guide, future action. Health diagnostics of executive functions should focus on the extent to which the executive managers are aware of the direction for the organisation, and the method of guidance which will not result in harm to the organisation or its environment, in other words, to the psychological state of mind of the executive as the cognitive part of the organisation.

In diagnosing the survival, protection, operations, information, language and strategy functions (SPOILS model) in Part II, it was possible to develop an overview of the health status of organisational functioning. This is analogous to the general diagnostic checklist used by medical practitioners to determine the health of an individual and be able to recommend additional in-depth diagnoses or treatment. Diagnostics in these six chapters are initial indicators, and serious concerns may have to be addressed by getting a better integrated perspective on the interactions among the functions or address the affected function in professional detail.

Part III explores the value of a holistic health diagnostic process as a prerequisite for competitive participation. In Chapter Nine the functional diagnostics will be interlinked and possible steps for further action discussed before an organisation can be declared healthy and ready to become competitive in its selected field of operation. Chapter Ten addresses the different competitive programmes available to organisations and the concepts of health and fitness are combined in Chapter Eleven.

Notes

1. The physiology of cognition is covered in: Barker, R.A., Barasi, S., Neal, M.J. (2008). *Neuroscience at a Glance*. Third Edition, Blackwell Publishing, Malden, Mass., pp. 72-73 and 98-99. Steps to diagnose the mental state of patients are presented in: Turner, R. and Blackwood, R. (1997). Lecture Notes on Clinical Skills. Third Edition Blackwell Science Ltd. Oxford, pp. 100-104.
2. Various analytical tools are presented to management to prepare for strategic planning. Summaries and references to well-known tools are presented in: Middleton, J. (2003). *The Ultimate Strategy Library: The 50 Most Influential Strategic Ideas of All Time*. Capstone Publishing Limited, Oxford.
3. Examples on unethical decisions by organisations include Nike's outsourcing of production to companies with poor work conditions in Barnet, R.J. and Cavanagh, J. (1994). *Global Dreams: Imperial Corporations and the New World Order*. Simon and Schuster, New York; or soil pollution from chemical or oil companies.
4. Pfeffer and Sutton commented on executive decisions made on experience rather than factual information in: Pfeffer, J. and Sutton, R.I. (2006). *Hard Facts, Dangerous Half-Truths, and Total Nonsense: Profiting from Evidence-Based Management*. Harvard Business School Press, Boston, Mass.
5. Research into the differences between cultures and sub-cultures by Linda Smircich, and other examples, are presented in: Morgan, G. (2006). *Images of Organization*. Sage Publications Inc., Thousand Oaks, Calif., pp. 125-134.
6. Reasons for the failure of start-up companies, including the limited knowledge and understanding of the owners are presented on the internet: www.businessknowhow.com/startup/business-failure.htm accessed March 2013; www.cnet.com/1990-11136_1-6278387-1.html for the top 10 Dot-Com failures, accessed January 2012.
7. Kodak and US car manufacturers ignoring market and technological development trends were discussed by: Locke, R.R. and Spender, J-C. (2011) *Confronting Managerialism: How the Busines Elite and Their Schools Threw our Lives out of Balance*. Zed Books, New York, pp. 106 – 132; and the Kodak incident: Eastman Kodak Company, *The New York Times*, May 30, 2013.
8. Research conducted on executive's role in successful implementation of innovative change programmes is presented in Dean, C.M. (2012). *Physiology of Organisations: An Integrated Functional Perspective*. Cambridge Scholars Publishing, Newcastle upon Tyne, pp. 131-133.

9. The impact of executive's firm support to the implementation of innovative programmes is presented in researched conducted by: Halme, M. (2002). Corporate Environmental Paradigms in Shift: Learning During the Course of Action at UPM-Kymmene. *Journal of Management Studies.* Vol. 39, No. 8, pp. 1078-1109.

10. The use of power by and within organisations is discussed extensively in: Morgan, G. (2006). *Images of Organization.* Sage Publications Inc., Thousand Oaks, Calif., pp. 166-194.

11. Executive decisions to outsource support functions were explored by: Augurzky, B. and Scheuer, M. (2007). Outsourcing in the German Hospital Sector. *Services Industries Journal.* Vol. 27, Issue 3, pp. 263-277.

12. The use of dashboard displays has been widely accepted by organisations to allow drill-down facilities of information. A reference, based on practical applications in various organisations is: Eckerson, W.W. (2011). *Performance Dashboards: Measuring, Monitoring and Managing your Business.* Second Edition. John Wiley & Sons, Hoboken, NJ.

PART III:

THE VALUE OF HEALTH AND FITNESS

The objective of PART III is to combine Health and Fitness of an organisation into a single applicable approach.

- In Chapter Nine, health diagnostics offer a holistic prognosis of the health of an organisation – acknowledging that while the diagnostic process is common for all types of organisations, the most common concerns could be linked to their age or phase of development.

- Chapter Ten evaluates competitiveness and fitness programmes for organisations, concluding that the programmes are sector specific rather than linked to a phase of development.

- The two approaches are combined in Chapter Eleven to emphasise that it cannot be only fitness or only health that should be addressed for an organisation, but a mutual supportive combination of both.

CHAPTER NINE

HEALTH PERSPECTIVE

Before offering a health prognosis for an organisation, it is necessary to place the diagnosis into full perspective. This includes: a perspective on functional interaction; the life cycle phase of the organisation; its health history; and its general lifestyle culture. These steps are discussed in this chapter as:

Functional Integration

Case Study Prognosis

Likely Prognosis by Organisational Life Phase

Prognosis Summary

In order to be able to compare an organisation to a living organism from the point of view of its functioning, it was necessary in Chapter One to delimit and define an organisation as a business unit responsible for the maintenance of its own functional structure and mode of operation. This definition categorised conglomerates as families with each subsidiary or independent business unit being a member of the family. Start-up entrepreneurs were defined as infant businesses. A global organisation can either operate as a conglomerate or an individual business. If the foreign branches are under the direct control of the central head office in the same way that its local branches are being controlled and supplied by central support functions, the global organisation has to be accepted as a single independent business. This definition allows all independently functioning organisations to be categorised by age group for the purpose of health diagnostics.

Within each independently operating organisation an overall prognosis can be reached by evaluating concerns and interrelationships among the functions, analogous to in-born or acquired defects in the functioning of organs, and by being aware of health concerns that are most commonly associated with the different development phases of an organisation's existence.

Functional Integration

Diagnosing individual functional categories offers an indication of the functions requiring special health attention. Despite this being helpful, the corrective action may turn out to be too function-specific while not covering the interrelationships required among functions. It is necessary to place the various functional diagnostics into perspective by considering their interdependencies as indicated in the SPOILS functional framework (survival, protection, operations, information, language, and strategy functions), developed in Chapter One and presented in Figure 9.1.

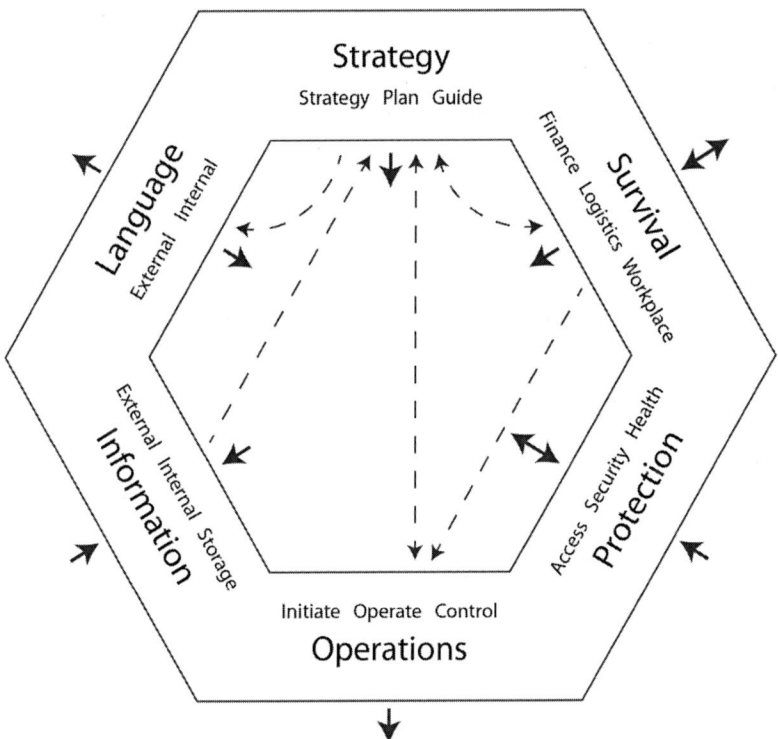

Figure 9.1   Functional interrelationships – the SPOILS model

Functions do not operate in isolation, but perform tasks in close cooperation with, or by impacting other functions. The most dominant relationships have been highlighted in Figure 9.1 with arrows and can be grouped in relationships of internal support and external positioning.

Internal Support Relationships

As demonstrated by the inward pointing arrows, optimal functioning of an organisation requires each member or employee to be adequately supported by the various functional categories.

Survival functions can ensure that employees are remunerated, have access to necessary and well maintained equipment, supplies and material, and operate in an environment which is conducive to the tasks being performed. Protection functions, analogous to an immune system, offer independent protection, security, health and safety support to all members of the organisation. Next to the importance of survival function support, is the need for guidance from the strategic executive function and the effective operation of internal communication channels, analogous to the hormonal system, to develop and if necessary assist in changing the culture within the organisation.

However, in order to offer clear guidance, it is also necessary for the executive to be aware of internal performance and concerns from all parts of the organisation through the internal information systems:

- Without the interrelationships of support, protection, guidance and communication, individual employees or groups are likely to operate ineffectively, become disgruntled and leave.
- Without good feedback systems on performance and morale, decisions on guidance and support become dictatorial and ineffective.

External Positioning Relationships

Survival and internal communications functions need close links with all members of the organisation through their internal focus. Protection and information functions also have a wider view of the internal functioning and external environmental trend changes and are therefore more risk aware by viewing the organisation in totality. Guiding and positioning the organisation in its external environment can be achieved through the close interrelationships between the strategy, operations and the language and communications functions.

Strategy functions, executed by senior management, require close links with information, survival and the operations functions for decision-making support. Executive also requires close links and interrelationships with the operations functions to position the organisation and compete externally and, with the language and communications functions, to be able to negotiate and build a favourable image.

Operations, analogous to skeletal muscle units, require guidance from the executive on which products and/or services to offer to the external market. In living beings the limbs are not essential for survival but without them individuals may be incapable of movement and therefore limited in ways to compete or persist in their environment. The close link between the executive strategic direction for the organisation and the ability of operations to perform, is therefore one of the interrelationships essential for competitive participation in the market and a relationship which is receiving significant attention in the field of strategic management:

- Interrelationships between information, strategy, operations and communications are necessary for the organisation to determine and achieve its goals and to establish its product or service position in the market.
- Close links between strategy and the external language and communications functions enable the organisation to develop its external image and be able to negotiate preferable deals towards successful operations.

Health diagnostics should address the effective integration of organisational functions. Individual operators throughout the organisation are unable to perform their tasks effectively without required support, and external communications could be meaningless when offered out of context of external information on changing trends.

Case Study Prognosis

A single case study, broadly based on a real start-up business situation, was used to demonstrate the diagnostic procedures in the book. For legibility, the insert block is a repetition of the background to the case study business referred to as The Corner Shop, and Table 9.1 presents the full functional diagnostic dashboard summary as developed in Chapters Three to Eight.

CASE STUDY – THE CORNER SHOP

An independent retail franchise grocery store and bakery, referred to as The Corner Shop, is part of a larger chain. Although the franchisee has the freedom to structure and run the business independently, the holding company is expecting a regular fee from the store as a member of its chain and requires the store to maintain a minimum set of standards. In return, the store owners can use the preferential rates for stock purchases negotiated for the chain and receive advisory assistance from the holding company. The store is in a favourable location in the main street of the town, conveniently situated for a wide range of customers, and the owners have had previous experience and knowledge of retail, finance and accountancy.

The store has been operating for five years. During the first two years it delivered record turnover and profits to the extent that the business was nominated as the 'winning' store in the chain. The customer base was classified as predominantly upper middle-class and the overall image of the store was vibrant and welcoming. The owners went out of their way to satisfy customer needs, for instance, by offering a type of bread made from a special recipe, sought after by many of the local hotels and restaurants, and by ordering and stocking special items on request.

During the third year, the owners decided to expand and diversify by acquiring a butcher shop in the adjacent town. The butchery was at the point of closing and they managed to get it at a reasonable price, including commitments of rental agreements undertaken by the previous owners. They managed to extend their bank loan to finance the deal and one of the owners is spending most of his time running the butchery. The combination of the additional workload for the owners together with mounting repayment burdens of interest and earlier stock purchases are making it difficult to maintain the previous standards of operation. The image of the store and service to the customers has been dropping and resulted in a loss of customers and sales.

The business found itself in a serious financial situation and the reason for the comprehensive diagnosis was to determine whether the functions of the business are operating at an acceptable level so that a recovery solution could be considered. In this chapter the diagnostic results from the tests considered in Chapters Three to Eight are presented and evaluated in order to reach a prognostic conclusion.

The comprehensive health diagnostic results in Table 9.1 cover all functional categories, subdivided into their identified functions. The functions within each category are rated for health as determined during the health checks in Chapters Three to Eight and the interpretation of the rates is covered in the narrative block of the table.

Summary Dials of the Functional Categories of The Corner Shop

Narrative of Rating Indicators (second column):
First indicator (findings): ○ = acceptable; ◉ = unacceptable; ● = serious
Second indicator (trend): ↓ = deteriorating; ↑ = improving; no arrow = unchanged
Third indicator (impact): W = warning; S = serious; blank = acceptable

Survival Functions		Protection Functions	
Finance & Accounting	● ↓S	Access Control	● ↓S
Logistics	● ↓W	Legal Compliance	○
Workplace Maintenance	◉ ↓W	Health & Wellbeing	◉ ↓W

Operations Functions		Information Functions	
Operating Performance	○	External Information	● ↓S
Learning and Control	○ ↑	Internal Information	◉ ↓W
Design and Development	○	Information Recording and Analysis	◉ ↓W

Language/Communications Functions		Strategy/Guidance Functions	
Internal Communication	○	Knowledge and Understanding	● ↓S
Change Communication	● ↓W	Strategy and Planning	◉ ↓W
External Communication	● ↓S	Direction and Guidance	○

Table 9.1   Comprehensive overview of organisational health

An interpretation of the results, including the lifestyle and functional interrelationships, are viewed holistically in order to reach a prognosis and recommendations for the business.

Health Dashboard Interpretation

Functional diagnostics on the dashboard dials in Table 9.1 show that the operating units in the shops are functioning satisfactorily, and with respect to learning and control the functions have actually improved over recent years. Members of staff have been well selected and are being regularly monitored on performance, resulting in a dedicated and satisfied team under adverse circumstances. They are willing to learn and change and can therefore be an asset during times of recovery. Other functions operating at acceptable levels or deteriorating to a warning status are workplace maintenance and the protection functions of regulatory compliance and staff wellbeing.

In addition to the already critical financial status, the functional categories that were diagnosed with serious concerns are the strategy and guidance, information, logistics, and communications functions.

Finance and Accounting

The highest and potentially most lethal health concern of the business is its serious financial situation. The share funding of the business was based on the owners committing to high personal loans. In addition, the initial running costs could only be financed by obtaining loans from the bank. This adverse debt situation was eased during the initial years of good performance and profitable sales, and the future appeared promising. However, instead of consolidating their financial position by reducing their debts, the owners decided to take advantage of the sales performance and to extend the business by acquiring a butcher shop.

The acquisition was not well investigated, due to inadequate due-diligence research, and resulted in further over-extension of the financial commitments and management time at a stage when the sales already showed signs of decline. In addition, the original targets and standards set by the franchisor, when it accepted the business as a franchisee, are tight and not that easy to maintain when the business is not doing well. The owners were under increased pressure to either perform according to the targets, or leave the chain store family.

Strategy and Guidance

The functional category of strategy and guidance was also diagnosed with serious concerns. The diagnosis of the health of the executive strategy, planning and guiding functions indicates weaknesses in the knowledge and understanding of information necessary to guide the business towards the desired goal. Strategies and plans were prepared as part of the initial justification plan but were not reviewed or updated, resulting in a strategic drift rather than clear direction. This was indicative of the lack of experience of the owners, escalated by inadequate information and how to use the information. The previous roles of the owners were in marketing and academic finance and accounting. In theory, this combination offers a strong and positive level of expertise for starting a business, and the success in the functions of staff management, initial sales, and regulatory adherence proved that they were aware of the basic requirements for a successful business. Financial problems, lack of information, and reliance on self-instincts instead of evidence-based reasons for decisions, however, resulted in management decisions which were detrimental to the long term health of the business. Eventually the owners became immersed in fire-fighting to survive, rather than planning and guiding the business.

Information

Serious information concerns included the lack of meaningful operating performance information and the lack of suitable analysis of available data and information. Operating performance and profitability were deduced from regulatory tax returns in which sales revenue and costs were identified and recorded at overall summary level. Performance reporting contained minimal information by product category or forecasts for replenishment and other future debt repayments.

This basic level of financial recording and analysis offered a false sense of security to the owners during the early flourishing years of the business. While sales were increasing, it was relatively easy to repay replenishment orders from the increased sales and profits. However, with the slowing of business sales, the available information only offered a summarised historic view of performance instead of incorporating forecasts of impending concerns or opportunities. It became easier to focus on today's serious problems, thus losing overall perspective of future prospects and/or concerns.

Logistics

Another negative influence of the basic level of product performance information is the lack of knowledge about which products are profitable, desirable or not selling. This affected the re-order process as well as the storage and workplace maintenance functions. Reorder was based on stock counts and the informal knowledge and opinions of management about which of the products were selling or required by customers. No consideration was made with respect to slow or fast moving stock, with the former taking up space in the storeroom and the shelves, and the latter having to be purchased locally at a higher price between the regular order dates, or not appearing on the shelves.

This short supply of fast moving stock further affected the workplace maintenance in the store in which empty shelves offered a poor external image to customers, thus resulting in a declining customer base and low staff morale.

External Communications

Inadequate information can also be linked to the poor diagnostic findings with respect to the health situation of the external communication function of the business. Even though one of the owners has a marketing background and has excelled at attracting the initial client base to the business, the change in sales patterns resulted in a change in the numbers and types of customer to the store. This should have acted as a warning sign and encouraged the owners to consider the possibility of changing direction with respect to their target market.

Instead of re-appraising the target market the managers tried to 'reinvent' the store to attract the initial customers back into the business. However, the communication messages offered to the original customers were not supported by sufficient improvements in the internal image of the store and performance of the staff, with the result that they were ineffective.

Interrelationships

Regardless of the fact that individuals in small organisations are often expected to perform multiple functions, a holistic view of the effectiveness of functional interrelationships indicated an acceptable level of mutual support by the survival functions, some concern with risk evaluation and prevention and the tendency of the owners to arrive at subjective decisions with limited support or understanding of information.

The question to be addressed is whether the business can survive and recover in the future or should fold.

Prognosis and Treatment Recommendations

Analogous to individuals with serious breathing problems who are offered oxygen support, the question is to determine whether the business has the potential to recover if it is to be offered some cash injection to continue operating in the short term, while the other functional concerns are being addressed and improved.

Based on the balanced view of health diagnostics, the prognosis in this case study has to be that there is hope for the business to recover and succeed, provided that it is possible to find a sponsor to inject cash for monthly expenses for a period, preferably at a low interest rate or in exchange for shares in the business. It must also be possible to implement the essential health changes at a reasonably low cost and be fully supported by the owners. Various recovery models are already available and could be followed to benefit the business. However, the recommendations should at least address the following functions which were identified in the dashboard diagnosis:

- Offer advice, training and mentoring guidance to the owners about the interpretation of knowledge and information in order to plan and guide the business (Strategy and Information functions).
- Develop a strategy and tactical plans for the target market and direction of the business and how to achieve a sustainable model (Strategy function).
- Improve the stock control, accounting and financial reporting systems to offer the necessary performance information required for planning (Information, Procurement and Workplace Maintenance functions).
- Implement adequate risk management and protection procedures to minimise future damage to the assets (Protection function).
- Get assistance and support to renegotiate the debt of the business, including the contract and financial constraints introduced by the purchase of the butcher shop (Survival – Finance function).

While the health diagnosis and prognosis cannot guarantee the future health of an organisation, it offers a good perspective on its overall functioning in order to identify areas of concern to be addressed before focusing on its competitive position. Health treatment plans can, however, be improved when health concerns, common to the stage of development of the organisation, are included as part of the prognosis.

Likely Prognosis by Organisational Life Phase

The most vulnerable age groups in humans are from infancy through childhood and then again in old age. Mature adults are found to be less susceptible to illness, but the health concerns of this group can be more severe than for the other two groups. Applying this analogy to organisations, the preferred categorisation for health prognosis will therefore focus on the development phases in preference to the type, size, global spread or product sector as is the norm for competitive advice. Young start-up and growing organisations may be more prone to the absence or neglect of some of the essential survival functions due to innate weakness in the structure or a lack of experience and knowledge by the owners. Ageing organisations on the other hand may have become complacent about what worked in the past, while mature and thriving organisation may be prone to crisis events impacting their effort to remain competitive in their market environment.

Start-Up and Small Growing Organisations

New start-up businesses are most likely to fail within the early years of their existence[1]. This can be compared to a higher death rate among infants and children, especially in the countries and the times where not enough attention was given to the reasons for high mortality in this age group. Infant mortality showed a significant drop in countries where the causes have been researched and preventative action introduced[2].

Using the analogy of the main reasons for infant mortality on organisations, the types of concerns to be identified and addressed for young start-up organisations would include: innate structural weaknesses analogous to birth defects; imposed constraints, analogous to treatment from carers due to unhygienic conditions or the lack of clean water and nutritious food; damage due to weaknesses in protection, analogous to inadequate immune systems against infectious diseases; and damaging events or actions due to lack of understanding and experience, analogous to childhood accidents. Most of these can either be addressed or averted if diagnosed early or if the level of severity is not too high.

Innate Weaknesses and Imposed Restrictions

Innate weaknesses refer to the absence or poor performance of some of the functions necessary for healthy operations of an organisation, as discussed in the previous six chapters. This occurrence of innate weakness is understandable since many entrepreneurs tend to focus on their field of interest in the market while ignoring the essential supporting functions necessary to ensure the survival and persistency of the business. The lack of balanced functioning may show itself early and be corrected, but there is the possibility that weaknesses may only become apparent after a period of fast growth or when the possibility of failure seems inevitable. In this case the impact is likely to be more severe and enduring with less chance of successful treatment.

One of the most serious health concerns for start-up companies is a lack of funds needed to obtain necessary assets and resources. It is an accepted requirement today that sponsors like banks or investment fund managers insist on well-argued business plans before agreeing to finance asset acquisition and the running of the business. Whereas the plans may appear realistic when submitted, it is not always obvious whether the entrepreneur has a clear idea about the consequences of non-repayment or the danger of an escalating increase of the debt burden when more money is required. Furthermore, sponsors are likely to expect unrealistic returns on their investments which could exacerbate the situation.

Other innate concerns refer to inadequately operating survival and support functions such as ensuring the business can get hold of suitable supplies, or has implemented well-functioning distribution, workplace maintenance and protection functions for growing as well as failing business situations. During the initial enthusiasm to make a business succeed, these support functions are often ignored. Lessons should be learnt from historic success stories or failures, for example stories of online businesses that succeeded or failed[1]. Formal structures may not be necessary, but it must be possible to demonstrate healthy operation and integration of all functions.

Start-up Common Concerns Due to Potential Innate Weaknesses and Imposed Restrictions:

- Financial concerns due to problems in obtaining or using funds, together with restrictive conditions.

- Inability to source and distribute essential supplies to all parts of the business due to blockages or inadequate setup of supply and distribution channels.

Weaknesses in Protection

Another potentially serious health concern of young start-up organisations could be intentional acts of damage to the organisation, analogous to underdeveloped immune systems in young persons and therefore the inability to defend against these attacks. Most common of these concerns affect legal or regulatory compliance required by the business, data security concerns or the possibility of theft and physical damage to its assets.

From a legal or regulatory point of view it is important for owners to have a sound understanding of the financial and regulatory requirements for businesses. Most of these regulations were developed over the years to prevent recurrences of damaging activities by organisations, analogous to mass immunisation programmes by nation states to eliminate serious epidemics. By heeding these regulations the young business can prevent prosecution, but also deal with industrial or pressure group interferences in case of unethical behaviour.

However the business also has its own data and information to protect such as trade secrets, research and development information about its products and plans, and protection of people and customer information. In today's electronic world it is easy for hackers to obtain organisational secrets, or to block website access to customers. Preventative action is required to protect against serious damage to the data and information in the organisation and to identify warning signals.

An additional health concern for young growing companies is the possibility of physical damage to property, equipment or people in the business. Since it is difficult to plan in advance for incidents of deliberate or natural accidental damage, it is better to ensure that the protection function is well established and that suitable risk analysis and disaster planning programmes have been developed and are regularly tested to limit damage.

It is also advisable to make sure that the business can respond in a suitable way after damaging events in order to regain an acceptable level of internal functioning and external image as viewed by external markets.

Start-Up Common Concerns Due to Inadequate Protection:

- Legal or regulatory concerns due to non-compliance.

- Loss of sensitive data as a result of inadequate access controls.

- Physical damage and loss due to theft, deliberate or natural disasters.

- Inadequate procedures with regards to damage limitation or restorative action after incidents of damage.

Lack of Experience/Understanding

However, research showed that in addition to being manipulated by power players such as fund providers and suppliers of essential material, the lack of personal experience of the entrepreneurs can also develop into serious concerns. Entrepreneurs are enthusiastic about their ideas and may attempt to succeed in sectors in which they have little or no personal experience, or by using short-cut attempts to succeed. Typical concerns can be ascribed to the setting of unrealistic goals, strategies and plans, and the inability to observe and interpret external and internal information necessary for realistic decisions. An analogy can be found in the underdeveloped or inadequate use of senses in young children.

In order to attract suitable funding to start a business, most fund institutions today require business plans, including the goals, strategies and tactical plans for the business. Proforma frameworks are on offer on the layout and contents of these plans. However, the lack of experience in developing realistic plans can be marred by the enthusiasm of the entrepreneur, resulting in over-optimistic forecasts and unrealistic supporting plans. Even if the funds have been acquired, the plans are often filed as having served their purpose and the daily functioning of the business starts to rely on instinctive decisions by the owners, regardless of the impact these decisions can have on the future of the business.

Poor performance often result in bigger unrealistic expectations for the future of better times to come, while good performance can lead to wasteful investments in areas which could cause problems, such as: premature expansion of the business; high dividend payments to shareholders; unrealistic internal salary increases; unnecessary workplace improvements; or no action at all. The most common advice to new entrepreneurs is to gain the necessary knowledge and expertise from qualified independent advisors, mentors or peers that will offer objective truthful advice, and to learn and improve.

Part of this inexperience also lies in the difficulty to read early warning signals, either from within or external to the organisation, even if this information is available. Owners and employees in small businesses have to perform more than one function each and it is quite possible for the owners not to delegate but to get too involved in the daily operations of the business. Extensive hands-on involvement may deprive owners and managers of the time or ability to observe shortcomings in services provided, or deterioration in the quality of the support functions. Signs about declining services may be obvious, but could require independent outsiders to detect and spell out the potential consequences.

Most of these shortcomings were found in the case study enterprise as major causes for potential failure of the business. As a young start-up organisation, the selected experience of the owners in only the functions that matter to them resulted in a cumulative financial health concern. A wider understanding of the functions necessary for a business to effectively operate comes with time, experience and training.

Start-up Common Concerns Due to a Lack of Experience/Understanding:

- Unrealistic strategies due to over-optimism in the ability to achieve the goals of the business.

- Reflexive or poor decisions and plans due to inexperience in collecting and interpreting external and internal information and identify warning signs.

- Damage to the image of the business due to inexperience in effective external and internal communications.

Health Recommendations

As the most vulnerable group of organisations the recommendation for entrepreneurs and young organisations during the initial years of their existence is to ensure that they are aware of the potential health concerns. Most of the time suitable advice and research can help to overcome shortcomings in the set-up of the business but if the concerns affect innate shortcomings in any of the functions or management teams, more serious action may have to be taken.

Established, Mature Organisations

The dominant group of organisations, as well as the group least likely to have serious health issues, is the group of organisations which have established themselves as viable independent entities and are active in a competitive market, analogous to adults participating in their selected careers, lifestyles or sporting activities.

This is also the group of organisations receiving most attention from organisational theorists and gurus on suggestions of how to compete effectively and become or remain winners in their fields of operation. Whereas this is laudable, it is still advisable to conduct regular comprehensive health checks to ensure that the organisation can withstand the continuous pressure of competition and receive assistance when health concerns do occur. Concerns most likely to instigate the need for a check-up or advice include: accidental or self-inflicted damage, analogous to injuries; imposed damage, analogous to infections and/or poor lifestyles; or serious internal damage to individual functions from individuals or groups of employees, analogous to cancerous growths in the body.

Externally Inflicted Damage

Externally inflicted damage, analogous to accidents or injuries to individuals, can occur in any of the functions performed by an organisation. The damage can occur either as a result of unplanned events such as theft or power failures, or as a result of natural disasters affecting a specific function or the organisation as a whole. Some of the functions most affected are the protection functions and their inability to prevent or respond to the damage; survival functions of supply and distribution; the work environment maintenance function; and therefore the operating units who rely on these support functions.

Damage impacting supply and distribution chains can be attributed to natural disasters, serious financial or ethical concerns about the suppliers or disrupted means of product distribution. Tsunamis, earthquakes or other major natural disasters can lead to the closure of businesses, but also to disruption in remote businesses responsible for the sourcing of essential production material and supplies[3]. Another type of damage, analogous to infections, are the deliberate and malicious attacks on an organisation from external forces and bodies with the main purpose of causing physical, ethical or financial damage to the organisation. Deliberate damage to premises and people can often be attributed to actions of pressure groups, saboteurs, individuals with a grudge against the organisation, or people within the organisation itself. These types of attacks are either personal against the specific organisation in the form of negative advertising campaign used by competitors, or generic against the sector such as attacks by animal rights campaigners against organisations involved in using animals for medical research.

Generic attacks, analogous to epidemics, require wider attention for organisations in the sector or all organisations in the market. It is as a result of these types of incidents that governments may have to intervene with laws and regulations to prevent or reduce the possibility of damage. Examples include criminal laws against wilful damage; data protection acts; and currently the effort by various governments to make sense of any laws that can regulate online information, hacking and data theft. Recommendations to organisations preparing for this kind of attack, or having been subjected to attacks in the past, will be to stay informed about governmental regulations to prevent similar recurrences and offer recourse that can be taken after the events in courts of law. By ensuring that they comply with preventative processes, similar to mass immunisation action, the organisation can at least limit potential damage.

The above incidents are mostly outside the control of the organisation, although from a healthy living point of view, it will help if the organisation takes regular precautionary risk checks and measures about how to prevent, or deal with similar situations.

Mature Common Concerns Due to Externally Inflicted Damage or Natural Disasters:

- Damage due to inadequate risk management plans to cover potential natural disasters or deliberate acts of destruction.

- Inability to recover after a disaster due to ineffective damage limitation procedures to address the impact on image and internal processes.

Self-Inflicted Damage

There is however another type of damage prevalent in mature organisations, namely the self-inflicted damage caused by over-ambitious decisions in an attempt to win in a competitive environment, or the lack of attention or care by executive about the healthy functioning of the organisation. Functions most likely to be affected by over-zealous self-inflicted decisions are the operating units.

In an attempt to win in the market environment either by matching competitors, or appeasing and increasing a customer base, the operating units may be subjected to ever changing and tighter targets to achieve. Since performance is measured against targets, the units will direct their attention and effort towards meeting these, sometimes to the detriment of other related activities required for healthy operations. Examples include the impact of targets which are too tight to meet, resulting in shortcuts in production and poor quality manufacturing products, or are changing too often, thus creating an image of disorder or indecisiveness, especially in the service organisations[4].

Self-inflicted harm to survival functions has become popular over the past decades with the notion that in order to win, organisations have to focus on their core competencies and, if necessary, outsource other 'non-core' functions. Non-core has however been interpreted to be various different functions, including the support functions of logistics and workplace maintenance including cleaning, IT processing, buildings and equipment maintenance. While the original justification for these decisions could have been motivated and justified on financial grounds, many organisations may not have considered all the possible longer term implications. Outsourced organisations may have different and potentially clashing cultures, or may be purely interested in their own financial gains which could become a crippling burden to the organisation in the future. In addition, the organisation may find a lack of control over the services, especially in times of stress. This incompatibility, analogous to relying on machinery such as dialysis equipment for kidney failures, motivated some organisations which could afford it, to reverse their outsourcing decisions and took the essential survival services back in-house[5].

Similar to outsourcing, the non-investment in new and potentially helpful technology and operating procedures may result in a short term cost cutting and competitive advantage while the technology is being tested by other organisations, but catch-up cost in productivity could lead to longer term financial concerns. It is important to be able to evaluate a balanced moment for entry or changes to processes and equipment.

Mature Common Concerns Due to Self-Inflicted Damage:

- Inability of operating units to excel in their tasks due to overambitious and too tight, or ever-changing operational targets.

- Loss of adequate support to operating units due to outsourcing of 'non-core' functions or badly planned cost cutting procedures.

- Loss of productivity due to unwillingness to take advantage of new technology and/or processes.

Internal Damage

One of the basic assumptions of the classical Systems Theory was that if you can improve the processes in an organisation, you will automatically improve performance and profitability. This was proved to be incorrect – employees are not machines that can be improved technically, and not all employees adhere to the ideal work ethics or codes of conduct necessary for a harmonious, healthy and productive operation. Some may find the culture detrimental to their idea of how an organisation should operate and rebel against it, or they may find the protection functions easy to breach and take advantage of this flaw to cause internal damage to the organisation, especially through theft. This is a serious health concern analogous to the development of cancerous growths in living organisms.

Dissatisfaction can be detected in internal information measuring the morale and productivity levels in all parts of the organisation. It is necessary to be able to identify signs of internal dissatisfaction or external peer concern and act on them to prevent unnecessary industrial action. While this will help to address areas of dissatisfaction analogous to infections, cancer in humans is not referred to as the 'silent killer' without justification. It is not always easy to detect individuals or sections within organisations who act with the deliberate intention to cause harm such as financial damage, and early warning signals may have to come from whistle-blowers who became aware of the subversive attempts.

These signs of potential damage from within organisations therefore refer to internal attacks by staff who can pilfer away data, funds or assets as a result of out-dated or poorly implemented protection regulations and processes. The relevant health concern can manifest itself in any type of organisations, in any phase of their lifecycles, and at any level in the organisation[6]. Health checks to deter internal damage is therefore necessary for all organisations.

Mature Common Concerns Due to Internal Damage:

- Damage or loss of finance, assets, or sensitive information due to inadequate internal protection functions.

- Inability to prevent serious damage or loss due to a timely inability to detect or respond to internal signals of malpractice or morale changes.

Health Recommendations

Mature organisations have reached the stage of development in which most of the initial health concerns have been addressed and eliminated. Their concerns therefore tend to be as a result of accidents, self-inflicted harm or deliberate damage. There is, however, still the possibility of serious innate functional concerns as identified in young start-up organisations.

The health recommendations will have to be case specific, but with some general guidelines. Accidents and natural disasters may not be preventable, but the potential damage can be reduced by good protection and preventative risk analyses and procedures. It is also necessary for information about regulatory requirements to be available and to ensure that the organisation complies with them. This requires integrated action from the protection, information, communications and executive functions in conjunction with potential effected functions such as operating units.

Internal damage, either self-imposed through top-down decisions or as a result of internal subversion can only be stopped by means of early-detection systems, regular health check-ups, and the existence of good early warning systems such as the acceptance of whistle-blowing and complaints by staff. This will allow treatment to be activated early enough to prevent serious damage.

Ageing and Declining Organisations

After the start-up companies which are regarded as the most vulnerable health risk organisations, ageing and declining organisations form the next category of companies with high incidents of health concerns. The concerns, however, do not necessarily affect the survival of the organisation as in the case of the young start-up companies, but are the types of concerns that can be closely linked to age: namely failing functions and processes analogous to the onset of arthritis; failing of organs; infections due to inadequate immune protection; or complacency analogous to signs of dementia.

Although these concerns may not result in the demise of the organisation, they can be debilitating and the onset of a steady decline.

Failing Functions or Processes

Failing processes in ageing organisations can be compared to the slow and crippling malfunctioning of joints and muscle as a result of arthritis, osteoporosis or muscle wastage. Functions most likely to be affected by ageing and consequently failing processes in organisations are the operating units responsible for product manufacturing or the offering of services to the external market environment. This is likely to be reflected in declining sales performance due to customers moving towards newer product or service offerings.

A major source of failing processes can be attributed to the continued use of ageing equipment or systems requiring more and expensive maintenance, thus resulting in an inability to compete with organisations using the latest equipment, technology or processes in their operations. Examples include airlines relying on old aircraft and mining organisations using old equipment, not because it is part of a strategic plan, but because they did not adequately plan for replacement, or still believe that the existing equipment is satisfactory, a possible sign of complacency.

Whereas failing equipment and processes are health concerns, they are unlikely to cause the inevitable demise of the organisation. Organisations may be able to continue to operate in their niche environments and the concerns can be treated over time by replacements or by improved processes. If, however, the organisation used to be in a prime competitive position, it may have to accept that it is unlikely to regain this position against competitors who leapfrogged into the lead with the latest technology, equipment, innovations and processes.

Ageing Common Concerns Due to Failing Processes:

- Drop in competitive productivity and market share due to old and ineffective processes, technology or equipment.

- Drop in productivity due an inability to source components or supplies required by old processes or equipment.

Complacency

A more serious and debilitating concern of ageing individuals is the onset of dementia and its effect on the daily lifestyle of the person. This is not common to all individuals, but does affect the memory, interpretation and decision-making skills of the person. They can still recall early historic events from their long-term memory but short term working memory may be unable to record recent actions. Analogous to this ageing concern in the human body is the onset of complacency within ageing organisations, whereby the focus becomes more on the way it used to be, thereby ignoring a need to adapt to changing circumstances.

Typical functional concerns are likely to be detected in the gathering, interpretation and utilisation of information and knowledge as part of the decision-making processes by the executive. One of the often quoted examples is the strategic decision by Kodak to ignore the digital camera threat and to stay with film cameras and film development as their key product offering. The result was that the organisation eventually had to sell most of its subsidiary functions in order to survive and is unlikely to repeat its historic prime position in the market[7].

In addition to not heeding external and internal warning information, the culture of ageing and declining organisations is often one of satisfaction and complacency. Based again on what worked in the past, the organisational ethics and code of conduct could be one of 'we know what is right, even for the customer' or an attitude of friendly promises without much sign of fulfilling the promises. Image presentations to the market are likely to be token promises rather than action, including commitment and compliance to ethics in the environment. Similarly the protection functions are likely to operate using outdated means of protection which are not really suitable for the current digital environment.

The advice of mentoring and training to improve the strategic management of start-up companies will not be applicable as a treatment in a culture of complacency since the executive team is unlikely to accept outside help if they are under the illusion that past practices and experiences are better than external advice. The options open to the organisation will be to: be accepted in a reduced niche market; change or replace the executive team in order to change the ethos and culture; or drastically restructure the organisation through sell-offs or take-overs in order to re-emerge as a new organisation.

Ageing Common Concerns Due to Complacency:

- Business decline due to an inability or unwillingness to read and adapt to environmental changes.

- Loss due to a reliance on historic goals, values and procedures to retain their relevance in a changing competitive market.

Discontent and Internal Damage

Working in a complacent organisation is, however, not acceptable to all employees. Similar to all types of organisations, some may find the culture detrimental to the persistence of the organisation and rogue members may find the relaxed protection functions easy to breach, thus enabling them to inflict asset and financial damage on the organisation. This is more serious in ageing organisations, analogous to cancerous growths in individuals, especially the elderly who may be more at risk.

Dissatisfaction is likely to occur in the operating units who have to deliver on promises made by management and sales staff to customers with inadequate or ageing equipment and supplies. Unless the dissatisfaction can be dealt with to the satisfaction of the employees and pressure groups, serious damage can be done to the organisation, both financially as well as to its image in the market.

Another sign of potential cancerous growth in ageing organisations is the internal attacks by staff who can defraud the organisation as a result of out-dated or poorly implemented protection regulations. While this type of concern also applies to all types of organisations, ageing organisations should be aware of breaches because of inadequate protection.

Ageing Common Concerns Due to Discontent and Internal Damage:

- Damage or loss due to inadequate internal protection functions.

- Inability to prevent serious damage or loss due to an inability to detect or respond to internal signals of malpractice or fraudulent activities.

Health Recommendations

Except for damage and internal dissatisfaction, most of the health concerns of ageing organisations are unlikely to result in the immediate demise of the organisation. The organisation can continue to operate in a reduced capacity by making step-wise improvements to the areas of concern such as the ageing equipment, outdated processes and a culture of complacency. Even if these changes are not fully successful, it will be possible for the organisation to operate with an element of success, although less competitive than in the past. Alternative treatments will include restructuring, including down-sizing, sell-offs, mergers or folding.

Recommendations for internal dissatisfaction and damage must, however, focus on speedy treatment of the causes, by either addressing points of dissatisfaction, or by removing the elements of perversion. In these cases, similar to their occurrence in other types of organisations, the treatment must be swift and transparent to prevent further damage to the status and image of the organisation.

Common Concerns by Organisational Life Phase

Table 9.2 presents a summary of common causes for health concern in organisations by their life cycle phase.

Functional Categories	Types of Causes Resulting in Potential Serious Health Concerns in Organisation by Life Cycle		
	Young	Established	Declining
Survival -Financial -Logistics -Workplace	Restricted funds Innate weakness Innate weakness	Accidental	Failing processes
Protection -External threats -Internal threats	Inadequate protection	Damage	Internal damage
Operations -Operating units -Monitor, control -Design, initiation		Self-inflicted Over control Self-inflicted	Failing processes Complacency
Information -External -Internal -Interpret/ store	Inexperience Inexperience		Lack of attention
Language/ Communication -Internal -External	 Inexperience		
Strategy/ Guidance -Strategy -Planning -Guidance	Over-optimism Inexperience	Over-ambitious Driven	Complacency

Table 9.2   Causes of main health concerns by life cycle phase

Analogous to human health checks, the prognosis and therefore healing recommendations for organisations are affected by their age and life cycle phase. The common causes of health concerns for organisations in the different phases of their life are presented in Table 9.2 but it is necessary to accept that they only highlight the most common concerns and exceptions can occur in any organisation at any time during its existence.

Of the three life cycle phases, the deductions summarised in Table 9.2 show that health concerns for young start-up organisations can be closely linked to:

- Functional defects in the original set-up of the business. A focus on operations and how to make money out of an idea may lead to inadequate attention to the need for supporting survival, protection or information functions.
- Most of the other health concerns in young start-up organisations can be ascribed to the enthusiasm and lack of experience or relevant knowledge by the owner.
- The main accepted 'killer' of young start-up organisations has however been recognised as cash-flow concerns. The start-up business requires own capital, loans or other funding which come with strings attached. If the pay-back requirements or the pre-arranged objectives linked to the funding cannot be met the business may have no alternative but to fold.

It is therefore also accepted that the best advice to ensure healthy functioning of start-up organisations is for inexperienced owners to obtain honest advice from independent external parties such as peers, mentors or advisors and to learn about healthy functioning of similar organisations. Experienced owners of new start-up companies may still have to check that the functions operate effectively.

Most organisations, analogous to mature adult individuals, may not have the same level of health concerns as young organisations. At this stage of development most of the innate structural problems would have been resolved and the executive team has enough experience and knowledge to ensure smooth and healthy functioning of the organisation. As a result of a relentless focus on performance and competitiveness, the health concerns when they arise, may have serious consequences for the financial status and image of the organisation. Causes can usually be traced to:

- Accidents or external events impacting supply chains or organisation as a whole.
- Efforts of damage whether from external or internal sources.

- Self-inflicted damage as a result of the executive team being over-ambitious and therefore interfering too much with the execution or manufacturing of the services and/or products.

From a health point of view it is necessary to ensure that adequate risk analyses and provision have been made for serious incidents, accidents or damage from external or internal sources, and that the organisation is not becoming dominated by an executive team more interested in winning than in health.

The third life cycle organisations, namely the ageing and declining businesses, unlike the competitive mature organisations, are more likely to be diagnosed with:

- Elements of complacency and failing processes and functions. The culture from executive throughout the organisation can usually be observed as comfortable and relying on past successes and operational processes.
- External warning signs are either not picked up by the information functions, or ignored as part of executive decisions with the result that the organisation is withdrawing into an ever decreasing niche market.
- A susceptibility to external or internal damage as a result of lax protection processes or shortcuts.

While niche markets do not necessarily point to health concerns, the organisations will have to accept that their time as a winner in their current market is in the past unless they are willing either to change significantly, or break up and start again as part of another independent organisation through sell-offs or mergers.

Conclusion

Chapter Nine presented a summary of the case study findings to bring all the diagnostic results into perspective and contemplate the prognosis and possible recommendations of treatment towards its healing. Each organisation must be regarded as a unique case but the SPOILS model, discussed in Chapters Three to Eight and presented in Figure 9.1, offers a framework broadly based on the checklist and guidelines used by medical practitioners in determining the health of a person. It aims to check all the essential functional categories for meeting acceptable standards for healthy functioning.

Healthy functioning is important for all organisations. It is even more important for mature competing organisations to be aware of their general underlying health before preparing for competitive winning. This can be compared to the popularity of professional medical health support offered to competing individuals. In the next chapter the focus is on health for fitness and competitiveness and the health needs are explored within separate competing operating sectors analogous to the difference in health regimes for singers versus athletes. This reinforces the conclusion that, although general health is applicable to all organisations based on the commonality of their functions, a 'one size fits all' approach to health may be different when it comes to active competitiveness in a selected market.

Notes

1. Various books, research papers and internet websites address reasons for young companies to fail and how to address these concerns, including: Lynn, Richard (ed.). (1974). *The Entrepreneur: Eight Case Studies*; Allen and Unwin; www.businessknowhow.com/startup/business-failure.htm and http://boss.blogs.nytimes.com/2011/01/05/top-10-reasons-small-businesses-fail/ accessed (11/03/2013); Top 10 dot.com flops, http://www.cnet.com/1990-11136_1-6278387-1.html (accessed on 05/01/2012).

2. References on infant mortality can be found in studies and statistics on the internet: www.who.int/mediacentre/factsheets/fs178/en/ ; www.thelancet.com/journals/lancet/article/PIIS0140-6736(12)60560 ; www.nlm.nih.gov/medlineplus/ency/article/001915.htm and other sources.

3. Examples of external incidents affecting the supply, distribution or operating functions are regularly making headlines in newspapers or research papers, including: Japan Quake, Tsunami Take Heavy Toll on Toyota, www.forbes.com/ dated 8 Apr. 2011; Building Sustainable and Ethical Supply Chains, www.forbes.com/ dated 9 Mar 2012.

4. Examples of research into the impact of this potentially distorted focus of operations can be found in work done on tight or changing targets by: Lloyd, C. and James, S. (2008): Too Much Pressure? Retailer Power and Occupational Health and Safety in the Food Processing Industry. *Work, Employment and Society*. Vol. 22, No. 4, pp. 713-730; and Nayak, A. (2008): Experiencing Creativity in Organisations: A Practice Approach, *Long Range Planning*. Vol. 41, pp. 420-439.

5. Outsourcing 'non-core' functions should consider all the known and hidden costs and potential pitfalls, such as clashing cultures, inadequate controls over creeping costs or quality of service. Various research projects were conducted in this area, including: Augurzky, B. and Scheuer, M. (2007): Outsourcing in the German Hospital Sector. *Services Industries Journal*. Vol. 27, Issue 3, pp. 263-277.

6. Internal damage can occur in various functions and levels of an organisation and, analogous to cancerous growths can cause severe damage if not addressed early enough. Examples include: Swartz, M. and Watkins, S. (2003) *Power Failure: The Inside Story of the Collapse of Enron*, New York, Doubleday; on RBS: Brown, G. (2010) *Beyond the Crash: Overcoming the First Crisis of Globalisation*, Simon & Schuster; Banking Crisis: 'Nothing short of chronic recklessness powered by unchecked greed' in The Guardian of 07 Dec. 2010; on Icelandic Bank: Sigurjonsson, T.O. (2010) The Icelandic Bank Collapse: Challenges to Governance and Risk Management. *Corporate Governance,* Vol. 10, No. 1, pp. 33-45.

7. Examples of complacency resulting in organisation falling behind peers include Kodak and others as demonstrated for the US car industry by: Locke, R.R. and Spender, J-C. (2011) *Confronting Managerialism: How the Busines Elite and Their Schools Threw our Lives out of Balance.* Zed Books, New York, pp. 106 – 132; and the Kodak incident: Eastman Kodak Company, *The New York Times*, May 30, 2013.

CHAPTER TEN

WHAT ABOUT FITNESS
AND COMPETITIVENESS?

Diagnosing health issues in organisations can help to address them in an effective and timely manner to ensure sustainable functioning. However, these checks cannot predict or ensure success and winning in a highly competitive market environment. Unlike health concerns which can be commonly diagnosed in all organisations regardless of their sector of operation, factors impacting competitive fitness differ by sector similar to, for example, the fitness required for athletes versus professional singers. These differences will be explored as:

Why Differentiate between Health and Fitness?

Endurance Sector Fitness

Manufacturing Sector Fitness

Service Sector Fitness

Verbal Sector Fitness

Health to Support Fitness

It is important to recognise that not all organisations want to be winners or compete aggressively. Many businesses may only want to compete to the extent of existing as a business in their field of operation. The section exploring the differences between health and fitness identifies the steps to ensure competitive readiness, analogous to the preparation and fitness programmes recommended separately for athletes, craftsmen, carers or singers.

These areas of focus on mental and physical preparation are expanded within each sector of operation in order to determine similarities and differences.

Why Differentiate Between Health and Fitness?

The general health of an individual is concerned with the person as a whole and the integrated acceptable functioning of the organs in his or her body. The focus is inward. It is not necessary for all functions and organs to operate and integrate perfectly, but the individual needs to know whether functional concerns: can be corrected internally through natural healing; require external attention such as medical treatment; need to be compensated for by other functions or through transplants.

Fitness programmes towards competitive participation, on the other hand, focus on the skeletal muscle units that enable the individual to be mobile and agile enough to participate and compete externally in his or her selected activity. Although fitness programmes are likely to be tailor-made for different types of competition, they recommend the participants to[1]:

- Know the game.
- Become mentally prepared.
- Obtain relevant support.
- Become physically prepared.

This is also applicable to organisations, as noticeable in the academic debates around competitive theories. Various theories, models and tools offered to management identify the key components in a winning formula for organisations in a capitalist market by focusing externally on how to beat the competition by, for example, offering better and more innovative products at better profit margins. However, innovation is not relevant to all organisations and managers should accept that there are differences based on the operational sectors, analogous to the differences in the use of muscle units in a body. The generic phases of fitness preparation, as discussed below, may be common to all organisations, but their implementation would be unique per sector.

Know the Game

Knowledge of the sector in which the organisation is competing can make the difference between professional or amateur competitiveness. The focus is external and organisations need to understand the business, know the customers and their demands, know the strength of the competition and how easy or difficult it is to participate and compete in the selected sector.

Knowledge of the dominant sector can offer an insight into the strength of the competition. This can be strong with many competitors, or else consisting of only a few players with either niche markets or delimited areas of operation. In the latter case the barriers of entrance for newcomers to the market may, however, be high due to a need for extensive initial capital investments, or due to legal or monopolistic restrictions. Strong competition, on the other hand, may be an indication of ease of entry and participation in the sector, but this could have the disadvantage that it is just as easy to be eliminated by the competition.

It is necessary to be aware of the type of competition, both from the point of view of the participant, and of the customer that will benefit from the competitive offering. The customers may be few and selectively dedicated to the organisation or many and indiscriminate except with respect to the purchase of products for their own satisfaction. The type of competition can be event/project-specific, or based on a personal relationship between the organisation and its customers. Relationships could also be remote, easily changeable, and rely on continuous innovative new ideas to attract necessary customers.

Models to acquire knowledge about the external environment for competition have been widely promoted to businesses, such as the classical models of[2]:

- Kotler's STEP used for environmental analysis.
- Porter's Five Forces to determine competitiveness.
- The external dimension of Kaplan and Norton's Balanced Scorecard.

In each of these models managers are encouraged to study their external environment with respect to competitors, customers, suppliers, society and the ecology. The models are useful to determine the sector, competitors and customer before starting with a fitness programme.

Know the Game – Generic Steps to Consider for Fitness:

- Understand the selected sector of operation.

- Know the strength of the competition and barriers to entry.

- Know the customers and type of competition.

Become Mentally Prepared

Knowledge of the market, competition and environment can only be meaningful if it is used to prepare the organisation 'mentally' for competition. The mental preparation, analogous to deliberate decisions made by individuals to compete, can be embodied in the choices made in the goals, strategic and tactical plans of an organisation. The initial choice will be to establish the specific area of focus, or competency, of the organisation, and to set its long-term ambitions and goals to achieve within its market. Similar to the external scanning models for organisations, strategic planning models and theories have been widely presented to managers, covering the identification and definition of its mission, vision, goals, strategies and plans.

Some existing models to determine capabilities and develop strategies within the preferred areas of competition include[3]:

- SWOT (strengths, weaknesses, opportunities and threats) analysis in order to identify already existing areas of strength on which the organisation can build to meet external challenges or threats.
- The development of unique competencies within the organisation as promoted by Hamel and Prahalad.
- Focusing on innovation as a means of gaining competitive advantage as promoted in the Blue Ocean strategies.

These, and similar models, can help the organisation to decide where and when to compete, but the will to succeed still requires a commitment to the goals, strategies and plans in order to win. Commitment to the stated goals and perseverance with the implementation of the supporting plans can be achieved by ensuring that the plans are regularly monitored.

Become Mentally Prepared – Generic Steps to Consider for Fitness:

- Identify your existing or aspiring level of competence.

- Set and develop competitive ambition, goals and plans.

- Develop and nurture a supporting culture.

Obtain Relevant Support

The next step in a fitness programme is to ensure that the participant has access to the necessary equipment, supplies and support. From an individual's point of view, this includes the physical equipment and supplies, but also the necessary diet to encourage the development of the muscle units required for competition.

For organisations the support includes: equipment and supplies necessary for the service or product offering to the market; the recruitment of the right type of personnel; and the internal support of information, funding, workplace maintenance and protection to ensure effective working conditions.

These requirements affect the organisation's relationships with its suppliers; its commitments to capital investments in machinery, equipment and technology; and its internal support to its personnel. Without adequate supplies and support an organisation may struggle to survive, let alone compete to win in its market sector.

Obtain Relevant Support – Generic Steps to Consider for Fitness:

- Recruit the right people and procure the necessary resources.

- Ensure adequate and correct equipment and supplies.

- Support functional cooperation.

Become Physically Prepared

The most challenging and time consuming step in a fitness programme is the physical preparation and exercising of the participant. With the correct knowledge of the challenge and the expected strength of the competitors, it is possible to set goals and invest in the necessary equipment and supplies. This must, however, be supported by preparation and readiness programmes towards optimum competitiveness. In organisations these programmes should include the design and initiation of the product or service to be offered to the market, the effective training of relevant personnel and continuous monitoring against targets to ensure that the standards of performance can be achieved and maintained.

Similar to models and theories addressing the external environment and the setting of goals and plans for competition, various theories and models address the actual development and implementation of operating plans in order to win in a competitive market[4]. Organisations are encouraged to either adapt their products to the needs of the customer base, or to innovate in order to stay ahead of their competitors, suggestions which may be of relevance to manufacturing or technology organisations, but not necessarily applicable to a mining organisation.

From a physiological point of view, it is necessary to be aware of the different training programmes to develop different types of muscle units, and work accordingly. Similarly, operating units in different sectors are likely to require different sets of job related and knowledge-based training and development. In all instances success can only be achieved from a total commitment to the development programme and regular monitoring of the progress towards success.

Become Physically Prepared – Generic Steps to Consider for Fitness:

- Design and develop appropriate products and processes.

- Learn and practice.

- Monitor and control performance.

In Chapter Five, the different sectors in which organisations can be categorised from a physiological point of view did not strictly follow the known sector categories used in business and commerce today. It was considered more appropriate to link the categories to the ability of living beings to use their skeletal muscle units to participate, be mobile, agile and compete in their environments. Accordingly the different sectors were identified as: the endurance sector analogous to the dominant use of the skeletal slow muscle units in the legs and arms; the manufacturing or production sector analogous to the use of fingers for precision and dexterity together with tools; the service sector analogous to the direct application of fingers for manipulative and sensitive tasks; and the verbal sector analogous to the dominant use of facial muscle units for verbal and expressive communication to the external environment. By using this analogy, the generic fitness questions can be explored for each sector in order to determine the extent to which the sectors differ when it comes to fitness plans towards competitiveness[5].

Endurance Sector Fitness

Organisations in the endurance sector have been compared to individuals relying on the slow skeletal muscle units and bones in their limbs for movement or heavy activity such as walking, lifting and carrying. The use of skeletal muscle in humans relies on the composite functioning of bone, tendons and muscle in order to allow a smooth subconscious execution of movement. This cooperative functioning of muscle and bone necessitates protection against injuries during action. The units are also under subconscious control of the cerebellum in the brain for routine action, with the cognitive part of the brain only involved in issuing stimuli to commence or stop routine action.

- The endurance sector include organisations responsible for raw material, oil and mineral extractions; forestry; farming; heavy industry such as shipbuilding or major construction; and transport of goods and passengers[5].

Organisations in this sector: operate in relatively stable but cyclical markets; either offer their products on the commodities market or have specific customers to whom they are suppliers of the material, labour or service; may have limited competition due to a high entrance threshold imposed by extensive initial capital investment requirements. Cyclical market refers to the projects or time-period related activities in which they are involved or the cyclical demand for the product. Forestry, for instance, relies on the duration of growth of new forest plantations while construction work is project related. Transport could also be project related for the transport of specific goods, but may be scheduled, and the method of transport is important.

- Customers and competitors could be relatively limited; work is cyclical and project related and heavily reliant on major equipment resulting in high investment barriers to new entrants.

The focus of mental fitness strategies for competitive individuals in the field of sport, athletics or manual labour is predominantly on: the events or projects, whether in progress or in the future; what will be expected from the individual; and how to prepare for the event.

Building on the heavy industry sector characteristics, information required for strategic decisions are likely to be the potential impact of new technology, together with long term trends and forecasts of the need for raw material and project related work. More than any of the other sectors the endurance sector also can, and does, impact the environment, and the trends and changes in the general attitudes towards environmental and ecological ethics are likely to have a direct impact on their plans and operating procedures. Models like Porter's Five Forces or Hamel and Prahalad's core competency concepts[2] are unlikely to offer short term benefits, although some of these factors may contribute to the setting of long term goals and strategies.

- Strategies are likely to be set for a period of 10 to 15 years, not only for current activities, but in order to start preparing for new resources, capital investments and in obtaining potentially new projects at the end of the existing cycle.

Athletes and manual labourers are reliant on a diet rich in carbohydrates to generate energy, protein to build muscle, and minerals to ensure strong bone growth and maintenance. They also need to be aware of the danger of over-exertion or bone fractures as a result of accidents that can seriously affect competitiveness.

Similarly, the dominant interrelationships amongst functions in endurance sector organisations were found to be reliant on the right personnel; teamwork; effectively functioning equipment; and a strong emphasis on workplace and equipment maintenance activities to ensure safety and reliability[6]. Workplace conditions are often hazardous and difficult, thus the dependence on the team and equipment becomes imperative. This highlights the need to ensure that equipment breakdowns are investigated in order to prevent damaging incidents; and supplies are available to prevent delays.

- Necessary support would include the right staff for effective teamwork, reliable equipment and the integrated support of the survival functions, especially that of workplace maintenance, as well as protection, training and monitoring.

Learning and training for individuals competing with the slow muscle unit groups focus on repetitive learning and practice of routine tasks until they become a natural part of execution, demonstrated in the need to practice golf swings, weight lifting or long distance running. The involvement of the cognitive areas of the brain is to plan future and desirable moves, and to initiate action. The actual learning and control activities are within the subconscious cerebellum.

Development and training in endurance sector organisations follow a similar pattern. Operators are developed and trained as apprentices, or through job related training to an acceptable level of competency in the knowledge and execution of their tasks. This focused and dedicated training allow the operations to proceed within broad targets under local control during a project or allocated longer term task. Interference from senior management may only be required for malfunctioning or damaging incidents.

- The focus of competitive training programmes for endurance organisations should be to develop and train staff to a level of routine efficiency for safety and high quality teamwork.

Endurance Sector Competitive Characteristics:

Know the game:
- Few competitors.
- High barriers to entry.
- Close relationships with specific customers.

Mental preparation:
- Long term goals, strategies and supporting plans.
- Trend information of opportunities and wider environmental moves.
- Plans to meet long term goals.

Resource requirements:
- Teamwork with necessary tools and supplies.
- Reliable machinery and equipment, including regular maintenance.
- Awareness and preparedness against accidents or damaging incidents.

Physical preparation:
- Job related training to levels of routine competency.
- Local controls.

Manufacturing Sector Fitness

The physiological equivalent for the manufacturing and production sector is the functioning of the fast and nimble hand muscle units, especially when operating with tools, as demonstrated by craftsmen or artisans. Physiologically, the functioning of fingers in humans differs in various ways from functioning of the muscle units in the limbs. Both sets of muscle units are attached to bones and tendons, but in the fingers the bones are smaller with more joints to allow for flexibility in action and more in direct contact with the cognitive part of the brain through the sensitive touch sensors in the fingertips. Preparation for competitive participation of individuals using their hands and tools therefore focuses on skills to manipulate tools, design knowledge of the product, and knowledge of other competitive products that could influence the expectations of the buyers[6].

- Organisations in this sector include manufacturing, assembly and production. The main focus is on the products offered to a wide range of customers in a relatively strong competitive market.

The entrance threshold to the industry may be lower than in the endurance sector due to relatively lower capital investment requirements and the wider customer base for the products. However, this observation should not be generalised since companies could be producing parts for specific customers and manufacturing equipment may require significant investments, thus raising the barriers to entry.

Customers tend to be remote and it may be necessary to 'sell' the products to them either directly or through an intermediary. This is different from endurance organisations, who usually offer their services and raw material to selective customers in need of the service, labour, material or products for specific purposes. Stronger competition may encourage product innovation to stay ahead of rivals, as can be observed in the short lifespan of innovative digital products in the mobile and hand-held computer business.

- The sector is highly competitive, focusing on the product and with lower barriers to entry for potential competitors.

Strategy formulation and planning in the manufacturing sector are shorter and differ from that of organisations in the endurance sector. For these organisations the theoretical tools and models promoted for information gathering and strategy development are likely to be relevant. Porter's Five Forces model recommends information to be gathered on the competitive power of buyers, suppliers, new competitive entrants, substitute products and competitive rivalry, all of which are necessary in this highly competitive market. Trend information on competitor moves and changes in customer preferences and requirements are essential, and strategies should focus on the products which could appeal to customers. Whether Ansoff's SWOT tool is necessary to identify strengths, weaknesses, opportunities or threats to be addressed in the strategies; or Hamel and Prahalad's competency model to encourage innovation, depends on the types of product on offer[2].

- The strategy timeframe is likely to be relatively short – around two to five years, and the operational supporting plans may have to be flexible if market forces demand quick responses in product or service offers.

Organisations are strongly reliant on the support from market research into a potential need for products; awareness of competitive products; and the presentation of new or improved products to the market. However, due to strong competition, especially in a volatile market for innovative products, security of product research information is also essential.

Operating units are dependent on supporting logistic functions to ensure adequate, suitable and timely supplies for the production process. Breaks in the supply chain could seriously hamper or stop production runs to the detriment of the business. The reliance on, and therefore regular maintenance of equipment is still an integrated requirement for effective manufacturing tasks.

Manufactured products, however, need to be sold and close links to the sales and marketing departments in the organisation can ensure continued production, as well as a feedback of information – received from the customers – on the acceptability of the products.

- Closely interlinked functions in the manufacturing and production sector include research and development, information, logistics and internal verbal functions of sales and marketing.

This focus on the product, its manufacturing and offer to the market is in line with the preparation for competition of individuals interested in making a living from crafts. The product is important as is its quality and potential to sell.

Tactical plans should address the training of operating unit personnel to be innovative, flexible and able to adapt to changes in the design of quality products and services. The training of the design team includes knowledge about the product type, the industry and the customers in order to meet requirements, while the operators require the same job related training as those in the endurance sector organisations, although with the expectancy of greater flexibility in the execution of their tasks. For both teams it is important for the training to include the ability to adapt to flexible needs for product changes.

- Competitive preparation should focus on product knowledge, ability to adapt, innovation and product quality.

Manufacturing Sector Competitive Characteristics:

Know the game:
- Strong competition.
- Relatively low barriers to entry.
- Focus on product, usually sold to customers.

Mental preparation:
- Medium term goals, strategies and supporting plans.
- Innovative and flexible design team.
- Customer feedback on product performance and quality.
- Tactical plans to be flexible to meet changed needs.

Resource requirements:
- Operators supplied with necessary tools and equipment.
- Reliable machinery and equipment.
- Effective logistical support of parts and supplies.
- Reliance on sales and marketing teams to market the products.

Physical preparation:
- Product knowledge and innovative approaches.
- Job related training to levels of competency, but flexible to change.
- Potential tight targets and controls to ensure quality.

Service Sector Fitness

Similar to manufacturing organisations, the physiological equivalent for service sector organisations is the functioning of the fast hand muscle, this time in direct or close contact with the customers of the service. However, there is one analogous function in the fingers that is especially required in service organisations, namely the sensitivity which can be found in the fingertips as a result of the high number of touch sensors in this part of a body. This sensitivity allows individuals such as carers or hairdressers to be sensitive to customer response and be able to react accordingly. Individuals who are good at this level of service often find that they can increase their customer base through word-of-mouth references.

- Organisations in this sector include health and care services, retail, leisure and personal service organisations.

Competition may be high in certain areas such as retail, but because the level of demand depends on customers and their personal needs and preferences, it may not be as high as in the manufacturing sector where products have to be sold directly or through intermediaries to customers. Health, leisure and care services, for instance, rely more on customers with a need for, or interest in their services. Barriers to entry are, however, relatively low and this sector is often regarded as a good choice for entrepreneurs with the necessary interest and skills to deal directly with their customers.

- The market is predominantly customer-centred with relatively low barriers to entrance.

Strategy formulation and planning in the service sector focus on the customer and the services required by them. This customer focus has received strong support from various theorists and has, in particular, influenced the recommendations for identifying and setting soft values of empathy, compassion and integrity in organisations as part of the strategy to build customer loyalty. Promoters of customer focused models and tools include the strong customer focus in Kaplan and Norton's Balanced Scorecard, and the development of loyalty promoted by Reichheld[7]. The customer focus of the organisation requires the services to be continuously monitored and aligned with customer demands.

- The goal and strategy timeframe could be longer than for the manufacturing sector at around five to eight years, since the market tends to be less volatile. Supporting plans, however, have to be flexible to adapt to changing customer needs.

Most of the related and linked functions required for the effective functioning of the manufacturing sector can also be identified for the service sector. However, services that are in direct contact with customers require organisations to be more sensitive to their customers' needs, therefore including strong and effective customer service departments or skills.

In addition to functions involved in the collection of market and customer information, the operating team needs to stay up to date with relevant and new services on offer and be accountable through regular monitoring of performance and customer treatment by staff.

Support services should also be customer focused. Due to the direct customer contact, the workplace is often also the meeting place with the customer, for example in retail shops or health centres. Workplace maintenance functions must be able to display effective coverage and presentation of services and products to the customers, accompanied by an environment that is sensitive to their comfort, safety and security.

- Support from the logistics and distribution systems are important both in ensuring that necessary supplies are available, as well as in offering local or remote supply distribution to the customers as and when required. Locations of service also need to offer security, safety and comfort to both customers and employees.

Tactical plans address the training of staff in being knowledgeable and sensitive to customer needs and the services on offer, analogous to the preparation of skills required by caring individuals. The training and role of design teams are likely to be less innovative and more predictable. Customers are more likely to insist on consistency and quality of a service, rather than be willing to accept continuous changes. It is, however, important to gain knowledge and competency in the latest treatments or services on offer.

The training of the operating staff will require in-depth knowledge of the service and the ability to communicate and demonstrate this knowledge and their own competency to the customers in a manner that will build confidence and satisfaction. Progress monitoring is likely to include meeting of personal targets, and especially the outcome of customer surveys. A popular method used in retail, for instance, is mystery shopping by independent advisors in order to determine the level of service.

- Competitive preparation should address competency in tasks on offer and sensitivity towards customer needs as part of training.

Service Sector Competitive Characteristics:

Know the game:
- Strong competition.
- Relatively low barriers to entry, popular with entrepreneurs.
- Focus on customers.

Mental preparation:
- Medium term goals, strategies and supporting plans.
- Culture of empathy and soft values.
- Customer feedback on needs and service received.
- Tactical plans to be adaptable to meet customer needs.

Resource requirements:
- Customer facing operators with necessary tools and equipment.
- Effective logistical support of supplies.
- Reliance on safety and protection of operators and customers.

Physical preparation:
- Job related training to levels of competency, but sensitive to needs.
- Customer service controls to ensure trust and confidence.

Verbal Sector Fitness

From a physiological point of view it was necessary to identify an additional sector of operation in Chapter Five analogous to the use of facial and verbal muscle units in individuals, predominantly used by singers, educationalists or advisors. Physiologically, these muscle units operate in direct cooperation with the cognitive brain in order to transfer specific messages to audiences. While the messages are generated within the cognitive areas of the brain, the means of external transmissions can be various such as verbal transmission through speech or singing; by means of facial expression; or by means of 'body language'. Competitive individuals in this category will not only be familiar and schooled in the contents of messages to transfer to their segmented audiences, but be adaptable in using relevant means of transmission for the best effect.

- Organisations in this sector include education and training, media, the arts, as well as organisations involved in offering professional advice such as legal, accountancy and consultancy firms. Design and development services of, for example, games and software development would also be included.

The market tends to be segmented, with customers forming alliances with presenters of knowledge and messages which meet their personal value requirements and timeliness. Competition, therefore, also tends to be segmented but may be strong within each segment with relatively low barriers to entry. The major barrier is the investment in the development of professional knowledge and, if applicable, capital investments in the means to communicate.

While knowledge contents are of key importance, the method of presentation may vary within segments and change over time such as in print, television, online, digital, or direct verbal communications. This is in line with the use of the facial and vocal muscle units, directly influenced by messages from the cognitive brain, but flexible in their locale and method of presentation.

- Segmented market focused on the message and its targeted audience, but also on the means of transmission.

With respect to strategy and planning preparedness of organisations in the verbal sector, it is clear that the more popular tools and models on offer by management theorists are less applicable to the multi-dimensional segments of verbal organisations. Timeframes for strategies and plans are different, and so is the need for innovation and preparation to change[8].

With respect to the medium of transfer, information for strategic decisions will need to focus on trends and demand, especially with respect to available traditional versus the new technological options. Strategies in this area are likely to be longer term (5-8 years) in order to balance the effort to incorporate new means of message distribution, and still be able to compete with organisations already using the new technology.

On the other hand, strategies and action plans to change the contents and tone of the messages are likely to be short term, for example: which categories of immediate news items to cover; how to change some of the educational subjects to ensure correct and up-to-date coverage; or techniques to use in negotiations, consultancy, advice or development situations.

- Strategies of which medium to use for transmission tend to be longer term than the supporting plans for the actual presentation.

These plans tend to focus on the close cooperation between the preparation of the messages and the person/medium through which it will be transmitted.

Interrelated functions in the verbal sector organisations include information and knowledge about the contents of transmitted messages; physical support of the means of transmission; measurement of the impact of the messages on the target segment of customers or audience; as well as security and accuracy of the sources and contents.

In addition to the close link to management and the sources of information in enabling operating units to transmit the messages, additional support is required from various functions. The means to transmit messages could include well maintained print or digital equipment for message preparation as required by the media, or venues for presentation such as for educational institutions or arts and entertainment. These latter operational workplaces require safety and maintenance support, which are not only important for the presenters, but for the audience as well.

- Interrelated functional support should include support for the means of message transmission, but also adequate protection for both operator and audience, especially where required in the field of education or entertainment.

The physical preparation in the verbal sector must be multi-dimensional. Message presenters need to be fully knowledgeable and competent in the background knowledge as well as confident in its accuracy and timeliness.

The operating unit which provides the medium for message transmission needs to be able to adapt to the different types of available mechanical or electronic equipment, as well as to the various venues of presentation. Knowledge and effectiveness in the use of the medium is crucial for messages to be transmitted and accepted.

Individuals actually transmitting the messages have to be prepared in the subject matter and methods of transmission. Although the timescale of transmission is usually short, the preparation of background knowledge could be lengthy for professional competency, although shorter with respect to the method of transmission.

- Physical preparation focuses mainly on the professional competence of the operators with respect to the contents of the messages as well as their capability in the use of the preferred medium of transmission.

Verbal Sector Competitive Characteristics:

Know the game:
- Segmented market with relatively strong competition per segment.
- Barriers to entry are predominantly capital investment in knowledge.
- Focus on message and audience.

Mental preparation:
- Longer term goals and strategies for the method of transmission.
- Longer term strategies for professional knowledge development.
- Short term tactics for information collection and message transfer.
- Audience feedback on acceptance of messages.

Resource requirements:
- Presenters with necessary knowledge and expertise.
- Links to relevant and current sources of external information.
- Transmission medium equipment, technology with trained operators.
- Reliance on workplace maintenance and protection for audience.

Physical preparation:
- Knowledge and efficiency in the use of the transmission medium.
- Professional development of subject matter and contents.
- Audience acceptance of message to ensure quality and effectiveness.

Health to Support Fitness

As discussed in this chapter, a major difference between fitness for competition and health is that health checks consider the functioning of an organisation holistically, while competitive fitness mainly focuses on the operating units involved in the competition. By identifying the unique factors per sector as guided by the mental and physical fitness programmes applicable to the different human competitors, it was possible to develop a framework of analogous programmes for organisations in the various sectors as seen in Table 10.1.

This summary in Table 10.1 presents the major differences among the sectors with respect to their approaches to competitiveness by identifying:

their competitive environments; what they need to focus on to prepare for competition; what support is required in their competitive action; and the operating plans and training required to become a winner.

Endurance	Manufacturing	Services	Verbal
Know the Game			
Task or project oriented	Product focused	Customer focused	Message focused
Few competitors	Strong competition	Competitive	Segmented market
High entry barriers	Lower barriers	Lower barriers	Knowledge barriers
Become Mentally Prepared			
Trend information	Market information	Customer information	Knowledge information
Long term plans	Medium term plans	Medium term plans	Short term action
Local control	Targets and quality	Customer satisfaction	Audience acceptance
Obtain Relevant Support			
Right Equipment	Equipment	Customer service support	Information
Maintenance	Sales and marketing	Work and customer area maintenance	Transmission media support
Safety and protection	Logistics – supplies	Customer supplies	Safety and security
Become Physically Prepared			
Future projects or sources	Innovation	Empathy and customer focus	Knowledge development
Job related training	Product related training	Service training and competency	Media training
Local controls	Target and quality controls	Customer response	Audience response

Table 10.1   Main sector focus for competitive fitness

The competitive game focus is likely to be on projects or tasks for endurance; products for manufacturing; customers for service; and message presentation to audiences for verbal organisations.

Strategies and plans to prepare for competition were identified as: long term for endurance; medium term for manufacturing and service; and mixed for verbal organisations. While the plans about transmission media in the verbal sector are likely to be medium to longer term, the actual tactical plans for information gathering and delivery could be very short term.

Similarly, the supporting functions that will enable these units to operate effectively were identified as: plant and equipment maintenance and employee safety for endurance; design, logistics, sales and marketing for manufacturing; logistics and customer feedback for service; and the acceptability of the knowledge and links to external information for the verbal organisations.

However, certain functions may be overlooked or accepted as given in the attempt to be a winner. Supporting operating units may, for instance, include internal or external company transport, while sales and marketing are important functions in most organisations. In addition, the survival functions of finance and accounting, logistics, utilities and equipment maintenance are not only supporting operating units for current and new strategic projects, but all functions including back office staff and management. Internal communication is also important to build and maintain the desired culture and value set throughout the organisation.

By referring to the health diagnostics developed for the case study franchise retail shop, the impact of only focusing on competition as opposed to general health was demonstrated. The only function which operated at an acceptable healthy level was the operating unit of sales staff in the shop. However, due to other concerns in functions which did not get their necessary health check attention, even this function was found to be suffering in the long run. The incomplete focus of finance and accounting practices resulted in cash flow and financial problems. Logistics became unaffordable with the result that the work environment suffered both for the staff as well as the customers. Access control procedures were inadequately addressed and resulted in theft and therefore further financial concerns. The deterioration of the shop environment resulted in the more affluent customers moving away, but external information research was still focused on old market and external promotional information was therefore misplaced. Due to these difficult circumstances little attention was given to the internal culture and the need to change, resulting in management's misunderstanding of options. Focusing on competition alone was clearly inadequate.

Conclusion

Caring for the health of an organisation requires a holistic approach to organisational functioning. Health concerns are common to all types of organisations, although it is possible to detect a pattern between health issues and the development phase or age of the organisation.

Gaining fitness to compete in a market environment focuses mainly on the development of selective functions. Which functions, and how they interact and support each other, are dependent on the main sector in which the organisation is operating and competing.

There is, however, another important difference which has to be taken into account before moving towards a combined health and fitness regime. Health diagnostics are inward and backward looking, while competitive fitness programmes are outward and forward looking. Chapters Two and Nine discussed the importance of recording the history and trends of previous health diagnostic results and events before reaching a concluding prognosis. The notion of poor competitive performance being overlooked or regarded as a disability instead of a health issue could be problematic.

Similarly, competitive fitness tests and programmes are mainly concerned with information about the customer, the current and future competition, and the fitness of the selected operating and support functions. Limited attention is awarded to the potential impact of health issues in the functions not directly related to the competitiveness. This could also result in the danger of not learning from past events or issues.

Chapter Eleven addresses the differences and similarities and concludes that it could be possible, and also valuable, to combine both health and fitness to the overall benefit of an organisation.

Notes

1. Training programmes are widely available for all types of competitive activities or sport, both on the internet and in books, including: www.allthingsgym.com/programming-training-intensity-weightlifters; http://voices.yahoo.com/becoming-opera-singer-career-guide-1855300.html ; http://www.nhs.uk/CarersDirect/workandlearning/ Studying Craft: Trends in Craft Education and Training: Summary Report. Accessed on www.craftscouncil.org.uk in April 2014.
2. The importance of external information for strategy formulation was especially promoted by: Kotler, P. (1986) *Principles of Marketing*, Third Edition, Prentice Hall, Englewood Cliffs; Porter, M. (1980) *Competitive Strategy*, Free Press, New York; and Kaplan, R. and Norton, D, (1996) *The Balanced Scorecard*. Harvard Business School, Boston.
3. Classical theorists in the field of strategic management and offering models and tools, include: Ansoff, I. (1965) *Corporate Strategy*. McGraw Hill, New York; Hamel, G. and Prahalad, C.K. (1994), *Competing for the Future*, Harvard Business School Press, Boston. Also Kim, W.C. and Mauborgne, R.

(2005). *Blue Ocean Strategy: How to Create an Uncontested Market Space and Make the Competition Irrelevant.* Harvard Business School Press.

4. Models and tools for the development and monitoring of operating plans are widely on offer as project management guides or tools, for example: Newton, R. (2012). *Project Management Step by Step: How to Plan and Manage a Highly Successful Project.* Pearson Business; and software systems, such as Project on offer by Microsoft.

5. Unique interrelationships for the different operational sectors can be determined from research by Dean, C.M. (2012) *Physiology of Organisations: An Integrated Functional Perspective*, Cambridge Scholars Publishing, Newcastle upon Tyne, pp. 110-116.

6. Unique interrelationships for various industry and manufacturing organisations are covered in: Batty, J. (1969) *Industrial Administration and Management*, Second Edition, MacDonald and Evans Ltd. London.

7. Unique interrelationships for service sector organisations can be determined from books, including: Berman, B.R. and Evans, J.R. (2012). *Retail Management: A Strategic Approach*, 12th Edition. Pearson Education Ltd, Harlow UK; Walshe, K. and Smith, J. (2006). *Healthcare Management.* Open University Press, Maidenhead. Also Reichheld, F.F. (2001): *The Loyalty Effect: The Hidden Force behind Growth, Profits and Lasting Value.* Harvard Business School Press.

8. Unique interrelationships for verbal sector organisations can be identified in: Goel, S.L. and Goel, A. (2009) *Educational Administration and Management: An Integrated Approach.* Deep & Deep Publications; Fitzgerrald, T. and Gunter, H. (eds.) (2008) *Educational Administration and History*, Routledge Abington, Oxon.

CHAPTER ELEVEN

BE HEALTHY AND FIT FOR COMPETITION

Does a holistic approach to health and fitness really add value to organisational management, and how can it be practically implemented? By exploring the similarity between organisational functioning and the physiology of living organisms – specifically the human body – it is possible to learn from the methods used by medical practitioners to diagnose health issues, and from fitness advisers on how to develop competitive fitness programmes. A practical method to implement a combined holistic approach involves the following steps:

Obtain Information to Support Decisions

Diagnose Health and its Impact on Fitness

Plan for Competitive Fitness Supported by Health

Currently the main focus in business schools and by management consultants is on strategic management, finance, operations and marketing functions and how to ensure that they can and do function effectively within their markets. This chapter addresses a wider perspective of what is meant by health and fitness, separately and in combination. Findings from the process of diagnosing the health of an organisation using the SPOILS model are combined with the competitive planning process. This integration ensures that lessons from concerns and their impact on past performance can be taken into consideration to temper unrealistic competitive goals and strategies for future performance.

Obtain Information to Support Decisions

Figure 11.1 presents a timeline sequence for effective decision-making in organisations when combining health and fitness. A key factor in the decision-making process is the availability of information to support the decisions and the means of recording, retrieving and interpreting this information. Historical and diagnostic information obtained during the development of the case study in Chapters Three to Eight, for instance, used a simplified version of the dashboard method of information presentation[1]. The choice of an adequate information display system will differ by organisation but should ensure that all relevant information is available at the time of decision-making.

Managers have to make regular decisions on how to respond to current issues (backward looking) or to set and guide action plans towards the achievement of future goals and strategies (forward looking) as demonstrated in the top level blocks in Figure 11.1. While this is an acceptable norm, it could narrow the scope for decisions by only focusing on individual functional problems to improve healthy functioning, and on the external customer and market trends and expectations to guide decisions for the future. Lessons should be learnt from the impact of health on past performance in order to identify which of these health issues can also impact future performances.

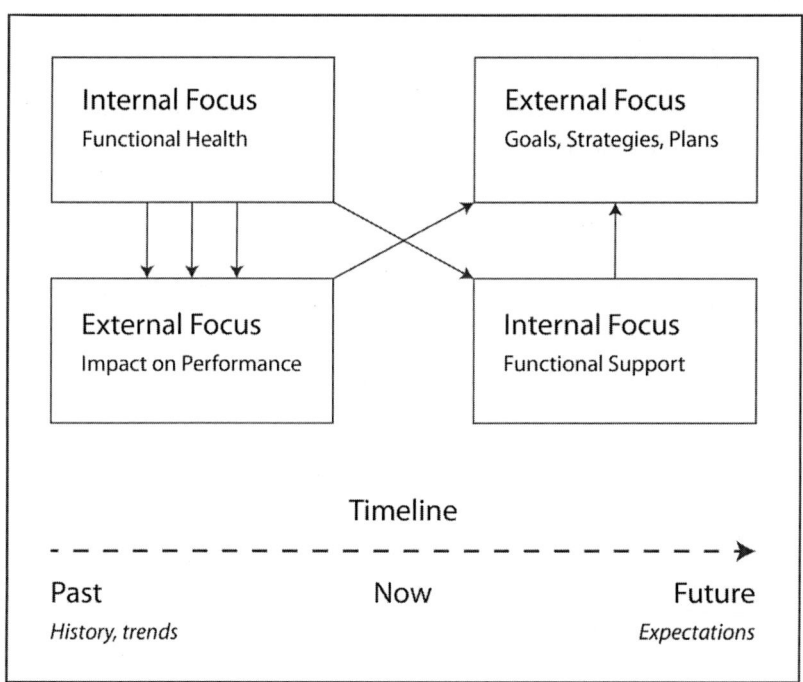

Figure 11.1 Combining health and fitness for effective decisions

During a health check, as presented on the left hand side of Figure 11.1, the focus is on the present, past and historical health concerns. By combining information obtained from these regular health checks with comparative historical market performance results, it is possible to create a holistic picture of organisational health concerns and the impact these concerns had on past performance.

- Regular health checks provide a historical timeline of issues or events impacting healthy functioning.
- When linked to a market performance timeline these issues and events offer visibility to their impact on past market performance.
- By comparing the issues and events in both the health check and the performance timelines, lessons can be learnt from previous serious issues to assist in damage limitation of future recurrences.

During the process of planning for future competitive participation, as indicated on the right hand side of Figure 11.1, the focus is on market opportunities and the setting of goals and plans to achieve them. Historical competitive performance data is sometimes used together with market expectations to formulate strategies, thus allowing past market performance to guide future goals and plans. A danger arising from this approach is that poor performance history can result in the setting of unrealistic and over-optimistic plans to improve, while previous good performances may result in plans for equal or better goals, whether these goals and plans are achievable or not. However, similar to the insight that can be gained by comparing past health concerns and their impact on historical performance, the inclusion of the health prognosis should influence forecasts, goals and plans.

- Future goals and strategies are usually based on external trends and performance expectation rather than on health.
- It is, however, important to include an evaluation of whether diagnosed weaknesses or past events may deter successful achievements of these goals and plans.

The importance of allowing historical lessons to impact goals and plans dates back to the emphasis on knowledge of military successes and failures in order to prevent a repetition of the failures. This can prevent the setting of over-ambitious targets without some degree of confidence that they can be met, or decisions based on subjective views of management[2].

A practical method to combine health and fitness in decision-making is therefore to analyse the past (health) as indicated in the left hand historical section of Figure 11.1 before reaching a 'now' prognosis and conclusion. After this analysis, it should be more meaningful to switch to the right hand future expectation side in Figure 11.1 in order to determine future expectations (fitness), while checking for potential health concerns which could deter or negatively affect the ability to achieve future goals. The following two sections address this link between health and fitness, including applicable references to the case study used in the book.

Diagnose Health and its Impact on Fitness

Before commencing with functional diagnosis of patients, medical practitioners gather as much general and historical knowledge about the patient to assist in the final prognosis and plans for treatment. Questions asked and areas to explore would include[3]:

- Current health concerns; when first observed; historical trends of previous diagnoses of current concerns and their impact on health; treatments prescribed and results.
- Past history of other related or independent events and symptoms impacting health; prescribed treatments and results.
- General personal, family and social history including lifestyle and interests.

The reference and use of historical concerns, events and trends focus on the past information collection section of the decision-support model in Figure 11.1. Health diagnostics, using the functional model of SPOILS can be used to identify concerns and treatment by functional category. The impact of the concerns, history, events and treatment for each functional category on competitive performance are briefly discussed below as well as how they can be interpreted for The Corner Shop case study.

Survival Functions

Survival functions, addressed in Chapter Three, have been compared to the internal survival functions of the respiratory, digestive, cardio vascular and renal systems in a human body, which are essential in ensuring that all cells are provided with oxygen, nutrients and a balanced environment.

In organisations, the focus is therefore on the individual functions and members to ensure that they all have the right and necessary people, funding, equipment, supplies and a suitable and functioning work environment that allows them to perform their allocated tasks towards the overall survival and success of the organisation.

Survival Functions	
Support to all functions and employees according to their needs.	
Functions	**Indication of Healthy and Integrated Functions**
Finance	Adequate income and funding is available to meet employee remuneration, operational expenses, creditor commitments and capital investments.
Logistics	All functions and members of the organisation are provided with suitable and timely supplies and resources to enable effective execution of their tasks.
Workplace	The work environment is conducive and supportive of the task requirements of each member of the organisation.

Financial results play a significant role in measuring the profitability and therefore competitiveness of the organisation. From a health point of view it is, however, important to consider: the continuity and consistency of the income stream; the appropriate distribution of available funds to all functions and members; the ability of the organisation to meet its debt commitments; and if applicable, suitable investment of excess funds during times of prosperity. The inability to meet financial commitments may result in liquidity problems which could have serious consequences. Trends in changes of the other factors, such as equitable remuneration, may result in morale concerns manifested in absenteeism or strikes and, unless addressed, could be just as debilitating.

Historical incidents or concerns regarding the provision of supplies, equipment and material may be as a result of isolated events such as a natural disaster affecting the normal supply flow process. In these cases, lessons should have been learnt on how to mitigate the effects or arrange for alternatives in case of recurrences. However, it could also point to internal blockages or an inability to obtain essential supplies, which is not only serious in the current situation, but can hinder the successful implementation of future plans and strategies.

The survival function receiving least attention, but which can have serious consequences, is the function of workplace maintenance. In order to operate effectively, members of the organisation must be able to rely on suitable work environments, whether in offices, factories or in the field. Without adequately maintained equipment, protective clothing or suitable protection or compensation in adverse environments, the morale as well as the health of the individuals can be compromised.

Specific events and concerns in survival functions which impacted the performance of The Corner Shop in the past include: the positive impact of obtaining stock on demand to affluent customers during the first two years of operations and which subsequently became a costly burden; and the acquisition of a butcher shop in year 03, financed by loans. The increased commitments damaged the ability to maintain stock levels and image in the store and customers moved away, resulting in reduced revenue and profit streams.

Protection Functions

Protection functions, as discussed in Chapter Four, have been compared to the skin or exoskeleton of living organisms to protect the internal organs and cells, while the immune system is responsible for fighting unwanted intrusion or action by foreign organisms already in the body. The white blood cells and platelets also have a responsibility to assist in the healing process of damaged tissue and cells.

Protection Functions	
Focus on protection and security of assets and resources, including health, safety and wellbeing of staff.	
Functions	**Indication of Healthy and Integrated Functions**
Protection	The organisational boundary is secure against unwanted intrusion, damage or theft of assets, resources and information.
Security	The organisation complies with regulatory requirements and protects internal secure areas and resources.
Health and Wellbeing	Members are provided with good health and welfare benefits and offered assistance during times of health or safety concerns.

In organisations the protection functions protect against unwanted external access or damage to the organisational assets, as well as against security risks, loss or damage caused by external parties or existing members within the organisation. It also concerns itself with damage limitation, the reparation of affected functions and assets, as well as the general wellbeing of individuals within the organisation. Therefore, the general focus is on damage prevention and subsequent cure.

A health concern in the protection functions will manifest itself in events when the function is not operating effectively, such as in incidents of natural disaster, theft, damage to property, accidents, unnecessary illness of staff, or lapses in security that result in a loss of sensitive information. Unless preventative processes are in place or a history of previous events is available, including lessons learnt and preventative measures implemented, the danger of an inability in the successful handling of similar situations can detrimentally impact future success.

Specific events and concerns in protection functions which impacted the performance of The Corner Shop in the past included two events of break-in and theft in years 04 and 05. This damaged staff morale and the customer trust of store safety, resulting in a reduction in revenue stream and profitability. The incidents were addressed individually with localised improvements.

Operations Functions

The operations functions, as discussed in Chapter Five, are being compared to skeletal muscle units which allow a living organism to be mobile and agile within its external environment.

Organisational functions, analogous to the different types of skeletal muscle units in the body, include: main revenue generating operating units; sales and marketing; customer service; and other supporting functions such as customer distribution services. The functions offer products or services to the market environment and liaise through sales and marketing or customer services. Similar to muscle units, their activities are usually initiated from executive-directed research, design and development departments, analogous to the relevant cortical areas in the brain, while the operators are trained to a level of competent task execution and regularly monitored for performance and efficiency.

Of all the functions in a living organism, it is the skeletal muscle units that react to cognitive responses to external impulses in order to act defensively, to attack, or to negotiate the organism's position within its environment. This also applies to the operations functions within organisations. Although organisations are likely to have units covering all the different analogous muscle types, the main operating units are sector related, such as endurance, manufacturing, service or verbal sectors.

Under current methods of measurement and control the concerns in the operating units can be linked to the organisation's market performance. A reduction in the quality of products and services usually result in a loss of customers, and if the sector is highly competitive, a lack of innovation may have similar negative results. It is, however, still advisable to ensure that the internal integration and support of the various functions are effective to ensure that the operating units are able to perform efficiently.

Operations Functions *Facilitate mobility and agility in the environment.*	
Functions	**Indication of Healthy and Integrated Functions**
Operating units	The revenue-generating operating units, including sales and customer service functions, are functioning effectively.
Learning and Control	Operating unit staff are suitably trained and monitored for the effective execution of their tasks and quality of products or services.
Design and Development	New or modified processes, products and services are well identified, researched and designed for implementation.

Specific events in the operations functions that impacted the performance of The Corner Shop in the past include the development of a special recipe for bread which was highly favoured by special customers, even though the production and delivery to their premises eventually became costly and unsustainable. However, the deterioration of the store image in years 04 and 05 resulted in loss of customers.

Information Functions

Information functions are discussed in Chapter Six. A living being cannot effectively respond to its external environment unless it can observe and interpret stimuli through its senses of sight, hearing, smell and touch. Stimuli are also perceived internally through the senses of pressure, pain and temperature.

Similarly, information functions in organisations need to collect, interpret, distribute and store accurate and timely information from sources both external and internal to the organisation. External information can be obtained as specific market related information, or from wider scanning to pick up trends and changes in the environmental, regulatory or ecological understanding. Internal information is about the general health of the functions and needs to be able to detect early signals of discontent or morale concerns. This functional category also includes the ability of the organisation to store and retrieve the collected and interpreted information for future use, analogous to the use of memory as part of experience and learning in living organisms.

Information Functions	
Observe and interpret external and internal warnings requiring action.	
Functions	**Indication of Healthy and Integrated Functions**
External Information	Relevant market and environmental information is collected, interpreted and made available to assist decision-making.
Internal Information	The morale and performance is in line with the organisational value set. Internal concerns are detected and addressed early.
Information Storage and Retrieval	Historical information on performance, events and trends are captured, retrieved and analysed for balanced decisions.

Less event driven than the protection functions, the health concerns in the information functions can be observed by analysing the availability of relevant information, the basis on which previous strategic decisions were made in the organisation and the consequences, whether favourable or not, of the decisions. A trend and history of poor decisions may continue in the future unless the identified health concerns have been addressed and corrected.

Inadequate decisions may be as a result of: the absence of the external and/or internal information; the misinterpretation of available information; or as a result of deliberately ignoring the information in favour of emotional decisions, all of which could have detrimental impacts on future performances.

The lack of background information on the status of the acquired butcher shop in year 03 had a negative financial impact due to undisclosed contractual obligations. This resulted in an increase in financial commitments which became an unsustainable burden on the owners. The lack of good sales and customer trend information furthermore suppressed early warnings about the loss of customers and resulted in ineffective stock control management.

Language and Communications Functions

Language and communications functions, as discussed in Chapter Seven, operate in response to information-based decisions and can also be either internal or external.

Internal language and communication functions, analogous to the hormonal or endocrine system of living organisms, are closely linked to development of, or changes to, organisational culture and values. Changes may be initiated and promoted as part of a motivational drive or in order to adapt to significant organisational changes, such as mergers.

External language and communications functions respond to market and environmental information through image building; brand development; marketing; negotiations; and other public relations activities. External communication messages are often directly initiated and controlled by executive management, whereas the internal communication can be in response to local concerns or in order to develop or change culture, policies or practices.

Language and Communication Functions	
Enable the organisation to communicate internally and externally.	
Functions	**Indication of Healthy and Integrated Functions**
Internal Language and Communications	The internal culture and values are well communicated and nurtured through staff development, support, motivational messages and actions.
External Language and Communications	The organisation presents and projects its image in line with its vision and this is supported by its public relations actions.

Health concerns in external language and communications functions, similar to the concerns in operating units, are closely linked to the market performance and image of the organisation. These concerns are therefore easier to detect, but the ability to address them effectively may still require a comprehensive understanding of all the functions and their state of health in order to determine the 'why' in addition to the 'what'.

Health concerns in internal language and communications functions, in other words, the development and maintenance of the culture, including motivational changes, may be more difficult to detect and to correct. It is necessary to understand organisational culture and to identify the factors which can influence and change culture. With this knowledge it is easier to diagnose a healthy internal communications process which can either assist or damage future plans and strategies.

Specific events and concerns, especially in external language and communications functions which impacted the performance of The Corner Shop in the past, include the initial promotion before the opening of the store in year 00 which resulted in high customer expectations and had a positive impact. However, the announcement of 'business as usual' in year 04 after the incidents of theft and the new butcher shop was not supported by store image improvements and rejected by the target customers.

Strategy and Guidance Functions

However, in order to understand the external stimuli and make a decision on how to respond to them, or how to operate in a pro-active instead of a reactive mode, living organisms require cognition, situated in the frontal lobe of the brain. This category of functions was discussed in Chapter Eight.

Strategy and Guidance Functions	
Focus on setting and achieving goals for future performance.	
Functions	**Indication of Healthy and Integrated Functions**
Knowledge and Understanding	Executive decisions are based on current and historical internal and external information, together with anticipated future forecasts.
Strategies and Plans	The organisation has a clear vision of its long-term goals and the strategies and tactical plans required to meet them.
Directing and Guidance	Strategies and plans are directly supported at senior level and adequately monitored for progress and success.

In organisations this can be compared to the executive responsibilities in determining the longer term goals, strategies and supporting plans to ensure organisational sustainability and persistency. The functions include the ability of the executive to interpret and use relevant internal and external information for decision-making and to set the goals and strategies for the organisation. It is also necessary to be able to develop or approve a set of plans towards achieving the goals and to be able to effectively monitor the progress of the plans or to modify them in the case of changing circumstances and information.

Major innovative strategies and plans are unlikely to succeed unless they receive the visible and active guidance, support and encouragement from the executive management. It is often accepted that the existence of goals, strategies and tactical plans are sufficient to prove the healthy functioning of the strategic management functions. The danger is that this misconception may lead to complacency, and that the organisational performance is allowed to drift, resulting in unacceptable results. Good historical diagnostics will include checks on progress against goals and plans at regular intervals, and the analysis of deviations.

Specific events and concerns in the strategy and guidance functions which impacted the performance of The Corner Shop in the past include the operational focus of the owners which detracted from their strategic responsibilities and resulted in a strategic drift and inability to collect and interpret information relevant to future plans. The decision to expand the business by acquiring the butcher shop in year 03 was impulsive, based on an inadequate cost justification exercise and negatively impacted the financial status of the business.

Case Study Historical Health Events and Issues – Impact on Performance:

- Initial customer demand focus – positive customer response, but eventually costly.

- Offer of special recipe bread as unique selling feature – positive performance, but with high production and delivery costs.

- Lack of visibility of profitable products and sales performance – poor stock control system, poor store image and loss of customers.

- Two events of break-in and theft – reduced trust in store safety and loss of customers.

- Attempts to regain customers through 'business as usual' promotions – not supported by an improved image and service, and ignored.

- The unsubstantiated decision to purchase a butcher shop, funded by loans – resulted in the current serious financial concerns.

In Chapter Two, the owners of The Corner Shop emphasised the financial problems as their main health concern. They admitted they made a mistake by purchasing the butcher shop and have to cut cost even if additional funds can be obtained to cover immediate financial commitments. However, since the grocery store was in a prime location, their future expectations were still to attempt to regain the original affluent customer base and recover to their previous standards of market performance and position.

Plan for Competitive Fitness Supported by Health

Planning for the future, as indicated on the right hand side of Figure 11.1, switches the information focus from internal functional health to external projected operational performance.

This change in focus is consistent with the fitness programmes for individuals and helps in their preparation to be mobile and agile in their selected field of participation. Unlike health diagnostics, common to all organisations, the fitness programmes, addressed in Chapter Ten, are directly sector-related. They are also the most covered area in management training programmes by business schools and theoretical advice offered to managers. Strategic management, marketing, operational performance and above all, finance and profitable operations are addressed in well-known competitive theories and models.

A balanced view of planning for the future should, however, take cognisance of the current external focus of future expectations, strategies and plans, but then also consider the potential positive or negative impact of already diagnosed health issues on future plans.

Plan for Competitive Fitness

Chapter Ten explored similarities and differences in forecasts and planning activities within different operational sectors, and concluded that – in particular – the links to and reliance on supporting functions differ per sector. Analogous to the development of training programmes for individuals participating in different types of competition, organisations should recognise the importance of the following steps:

- Know the game: obtain external information to gain knowledge about the selected sector market and expected competition.
- Mental preparation: set goals and develop strategies for competitive achievement.
- Obtain support: ensure effective support can be obtained from supporting functions such as finance, logistics, information and protection, in order to deliver the products or services to the selected market.
- Physical preparation: ensure that the operating teams are proficient in their tasks to offer quality products and services to the market.

While the functions of strategy, operations and language were found to be common to all sectors, the contents of what is important in each function were found to differ by sector.

Organisations in the endurance sector, such as mining or heavy industry, would develop long term strategies and plans due to the longer cycle of operations and the need for high capital investments in equipment as set-up or replacement costs. Operations tend to be process related to meet operating requirements in producing raw material, or to meet labour project-related services, for example major construction work. In addition, the culture tends to emphasise safety of the operating team and prevention of accidents. The analogy is for athletes preparing to compete for sporting events or for labourers ensuring employability in major project operations.

Manufacturing organisations, on the other hand, generally have shorter planning cycles. Products need to be actively sold to customers in the market and the competition is usually strong. Goals, strategies and plans are more flexible and may have to change to meet differing market demands and sometimes regulatory changes. Operations are submitted to strict performance and quality controls, but may also have to be flexible to adapt to changing production schedules and lines. Analogies refer to craftsmen working on products with tools for eventual selling, usually at a distance, to potential customers.

Organisations in the service sector operate in direct contact with their customers such as in retail, health and hospitality organisations. For these organisations it is customer satisfaction that is important. This includes training in customer needs and knowing how to meet their expectations. The analogy is for persons working in direct contact with others, such as carers, and who need to know their customers directly.

Verbal services include educational institutions, consultancy work, the media, advisory (for instance financial or legal) and technical services such as IT development. In this case the operating members of the organisation are in possession of professional knowledge which allows them to be in an advisory or informative position with respect to their customer market. While this knowledge is essential for competitive functioning, it is also important to include the method in which the knowledge or information has to be transmitted to the audience, i.e. verbal, paper or electronic, and the audience segment to which the service will appeal.

These sector differences are important, especially since the competitive tools offered to organisations are likely to be generic and may not be applicable to a specific sector or organisation. A typical example is the insistence of innovation as essential for winning. This is more applicable to manufacturing than the other sectors. Similarly, the message that the customer is 'always right' is valid for most organisations in the services industry, but may be of less relevance to other sectors where the customer is remote or a close relationship with a small number of customers is more applicable.

In the case study of The Corner Shop, the owners, in Chapter Two, acknowledged that if they manage to attract the necessary funding to survive in the short term, they still have to change their future plans. Being a retail business, the importance of the customer has been recognised by the owners, and revised plans were expected to focus on meeting their anticipated demands for at least an acceptable grocery store:

Case Study – Owner Proposed Strategy to Recover the Business:

- Save on cost by closing down the bakery and stop further developments in the butchery.

- Re-launch the business as the original core grocery business in order to recover the original customer base.

- Develop a new business plan to support the revised goals, strategies and plans.

These alternative plans would be in line with normal expectations from funding institutions. However, by including health events and issues which had an impact on past performance, they may not be the best plans.

Health Issues Affecting Competitive Fitness

Competitive planning focuses on the external environment and develops plans for the future. However, it may be dangerous to ignore the historic impact of the health issues on previous performance, including issues arising from the background functions, such as:

- The protection functions – often ignored in future plans.
- Internal information and communications embedded in the culture of the organisation.
- Morale issues arising from inadequate support to any part of the organisation, especially from the survival functions.

Of the functions identified as potential health risks leading to serious damage to the organisations, the one common to all are the protection functions. These functions are able to perform risk analyses and develop damage limitation plans against harmful external or internal events or incidents. The functions refer to the skin and immune system protection for individuals, and also to potential silent killers of cancer. Occurrences may not be widespread, but unless an organisation is at least in a position to know how to react in these instances, the consequences may be serious. It is important to incorporate this level of protection against incidental events or damaging activities in future strategies and plans.

Health issues affecting competitive performance could include: the availability of internal information on a culture unsupportive of the proposed goals and plans; executive decisions based on personal experience of what worked in the past instead of heeding changing trends in the environment or performance; complacency in operating procedures resulting in an internally focused or uncaring culture; or creeping inefficiencies as a result of the complacency or the inattention to supportive processes in the various functions. Although most of these health issues are usually not severe enough to lead to extensive financial or physical loss, continuous poor performance and complacency is likely to lead to ineffective competitiveness and overall poor performance.

A lack of consideration of the morale of staff in all parts of the organisation could be a sign of inadequate support to these areas from the survival functions of finance, logistics or workplace maintenance, and could lead to dissatisfaction, strikes or absenteeism, thus impacting on successful completion of strategies and plans.

Learning from the diagnosed health issues and their past impact on the performance of The Corner Shop, the suggestions for the future direction of the business by the owners would require further analysis. Key health concerns impacting the performance of the business included: the impact of excessive customer focus without adequate analysis of longer term cost implications; unavailability of analysed data and information; and inadequate protection cover. These concerns could be addressed individually with some local improvements.

However, by integrating the concerns, as well as previous successes, with the future plans, a different direction may become visible, analogous to including a change in diet and lifestyle for competitors. The realism of a potential change in the target market should be accepted but at the same time past successes of own brand products can also be explored and incorporated in future market developments. All other concerns should be addressed as part of the future strategies and not in isolation.

Case Study – Potential Adjustments to Future Goals, Strategies and Plans:

- Accept that it is easier to lose customers than to regain their support and revise the target market accordingly.

- Closing the bakery will remove the one unique selling point for retaining or recovering the affluent customers. It may be better to develop the bakery into a separate business unit as a possible future link to regain lost customers.

- Learn from the lessons after theft and do a full risk analysis to prevent future similar losses.

- Learn from the lessons of the impact of a poor store image on customers and ensure that the desired image can be maintained.

- Take heed of the other health concerns not identified by specific events, but inherent to the business, such as inadequate information on stock and management's inexperience to collect, read and interpret essential information.

The inclusion of above issues only highlights a few instances where the future plans can be improved by combining health and fitness to impact decisions, thus allowing a wider and more objective view for the future of the case study business.

Conclusion

Structures do not necessarily reflect the functions performed within an organisation, analogous to the fact that you cannot determine the functioning of organs in a living organism only from its anatomy. In small and start-up businesses, employees need to multi-task while in larger organisations a single function could be repeated in various locations or departments. Departments generally accepted as homogenous, such as information technology (IT) or human resource management (HR) are, for instance, responsible for the execution of multiple physiological functions. An IT department will need to: establish and maintain distribution channels for digital information transfer (logistics); maintain the IT equipment and systems for all staff (workplace maintenance); ensure adequate database storage, backup and retrieval facilities (information): and develop firewalls to guard against external hacking of data (protection). HR departments, similarly, have a responsibility for recruitment (logistics); staff welfare (protection); the general development of staff and culture (internal communications); and the monitoring and management of morale and values (internal information). However, while anatomy can be changed through surgery, the physiological functions in a living organism remain essential for its survival, mobility, agility and persistence in its environment regardless of by whom, or where, these functions are performed.

It is this concept of the functioning, or physiology, of living organisms that forms the basis of this book in which a clinical guide is offered to diagnose and address issues in the health of an organisation. The categories of survival, protection, operations, information, language and strategy functions (SPOILS) have been identified to present a holistic view of the functions required for an organisation to survive, persist and compete in its environment. By using a case study to demonstrate the applicability of the health check, it was possible to determine the value of using this holistic approach not only to identify issues, but to offer practical support to future competitive aspirations and plans.

Discussions around the combination of health and fitness explored the value of health, history and the impact of concerns or events on past performance as the starting point for improved development of future goals, strategies and plans. Furthermore, it demonstrated the value of heeding the health concerns as part of the future plans in order to ensure that competitiveness is fully supported by healthy functions.

Organisations should not choose between health or fitness but need to address both and (especially) health as the underlying prerequisite for fitness. Concerns identified in any of the SPOILS functions could negatively influence success during competition. Therefore, it is advisable to submit the organisational functioning to regular health checks guided by diagnostic questions as adapted for the specific organisation. This will help to pinpoint early signs of potential problem areas and address them before they become serious concerns and result in a belated appreciation that:

Poor health SPOILS *the competitive readiness of an organisation.*

Notes

1. The use of dashboard displays has been widely accepted by organisations to allow a drill-down facility to information. A practical reference is to Eckerson, W.W. (2011) *Performance Dashboards: Measuring, Monitoring and Managing your Business*. Second Edition, John Wiley & Sons, Hoboken NJ.

2. Research into poor executive decision either based on emotion or on anticipated numbers was conducted and presented by: Pfeffer, J. and Sutton, R.I. (2006). *Hard Facts, Dangerous Half-Truths, and Total Nonsense: Profiting from Evidence-Based Management*. Harvard Business School Press, Boston, Mass; and Locke, R. and Spender, J.-C. (1988) *Confronting Managerialism: How Business Elite and Their Schools Threw our Lives out of Balance*. Zed Books, London.

3. Various sources of diagnostic guidelines are available to general medical practitioners. The publication used as the source for this book is: Turner, R. and Blackwood, R. (1998). *Clinical Skills: Lecture Notes*. Third Edition. Blackwell Science Ltd, Oxford.

Appendix 1

Health Checklist

The summary checklist broadly compares organisational health checks as discussed in the book to similar checks used by medical and fitness practitioners. The three sections cover initial impressions, detailed functional diagnostics and a combined health and fitness checklist.

The focus of initial impressions is on gathering background and historical information from management and general records in order to position the organisation within a comparable environment based on age, stage of development and peers. Concerns will mostly be from the perspective of the owners or executive, analogous to listening to the concerns voiced by a patient.

Initial Impression and History (Chapter Two)	
Medical Steps	Organisational Steps
• Current medical concern	• Current concerns by management
• Past history of treatments	• Positional market perspective
• Other symptoms	• Other known concerns
• Personal, family and social history	• Culture, history and trends

Functional diagnostics, as the next phase, are based on detailed and where possible objective and measurable evidence of actual issues identified within the functional categories of survival, protection, operations, information, language and strategy (SPOILS) functions of the organisation. This is analogous to diagnostic tests by clinicians to establish the level of healthy functioning of various organs and systems in a body and together with the initial observations, should offer a balanced perspective of the state of health of an organisation.

Functional Diagnostics

Medical Steps	Organisational Steps
Respiratory function • Observe normal breathing patterns • Observe impact on extremities • Observe breathing after exercise • Identify obstructions, air quality	**Survival – Finance (Chapter Three)** • Accounting practices and procedures • Budgeting • Financial status • Funding, investments
Digestive & Circulatory systems • Appetite, nutrient content • Bodymass • Cardiac and circulation problems • Observe impact on extremities	**Survival – Logistics (Chapter Three)** • Recruitment and procurement • Inventory control • Internal/customer distribution • Blockages in supply
Kidneys, Urinary and Bowel • Chemical fluid balance • Bowel and urinary movements	**Survival – Workplace (Chapter Three)** • Workplace and equipment maintenance • Cleaning and waste management
Skin and Immune systems • Inspection of skin (lesions) • Lymph nodes • Inoculations or genetic concerns • Natural healing	**Protection (Chapter Four)** • Physical and access control • Security and safety • Damage limitation and prevention • Health and wellbeing
Skeletomuscular (motor) system • Normal movement, gait, balance • Coordination • Joint pains, movement concerns	**Operations (Chapter Five)** • Operating units – performance • Training and control • Initiation and support
Special and Somatosensory system • Special senses – peripheral awareness and acuity • Somatosensory perception • Interpretation and memory	**Information (Chapter Six)** • External environmental and market awareness • Internal awareness • Information storage and retrieval

Medical Steps	Organisational Steps
Hormonal, Emotions and Speech	**Language (Chapter Seven)**
• Emotional state, current and trend • Hormonal balance or deficiencies • Appearance, behaviour, speech	• Culture • Internal communications • External image and public relations
Cognitive mental state	**Strategy (Chapter Eight)**
• Understanding of situation • Clarity of reasoning and thinking • Concentration of action	• Knowledge and understanding • Strategy and planning • Directing and guiding

Once the current state of health is known, can organisations effectively decide, plan and prepare for readiness to compete in their selected sector of operation. Analogous to competitive fitness programmes for individuals, the focus moves from inward health issues, to outward competitive challenges, this time as a combined effort to ensure that health will not deter performance.

Planning for Health and Fitness (Chapters Ten and Eleven)	
• Know the game • Mental preparedness • Diet, equipment and support • Physical preparation • Regular health checks	• Know the sector • Set goals and supporting plans • Correct, adequate equipment, supplies • Training, performance monitoring • Address any organisational concerns

Health and fitness need not be an either/or decision, but should be combined for best results.

INDEX